Arthurian

BRITAIN

Arthurian BRITAIN

GEOFFREY ASHE

GOTHIC IMAGE PUBLICATIONS

First published 1980 in the Longman Travellers Series as
A Guidebook to Arthurian Britain
by the Longman Group Limited, London.
Second edition published 1983 by the Aquarian Press

This edition published 1997 by Gothic Image Publications,
7 High Street, Glastonbury, Somerset, BA8 9DP, England

ISBN 0 906362 38 5
A catalogue record for this book is available from the British Library

Cover photograph of the hermitage and St Nectan's Glen, near Tintagel,
by Simant Bostock, Glastonbury

Editorial service, maps and typesetting,
in 10-point Acorn Trinity, by
Abbey Press Glastonbury

Printed and bound in Great Britain by
Biddles Ltd, Guildford, Surrey

Contents

Acknowledgements

I am indebted to Mr E. G. H. Kempson for information on Merlin's Mount in Marlborough, and to the Custodian of the Meigle Museum for information on the supposed monument of Guinevere; also to Professor Leslie Alcock for advice on one or two other Scottish sites.

Picture credits

Aerofilms: 56, 66, 118, 218
Archbishop of Canterbury and Trustees of Lambeth Palace Library: 111
Janet and Colin Bord (Fortean Picture Library): 40, 49, 50, 59, 69, 79, 104, 107, 109, 114, 122, 123, 143, 156, 158, 170, 173, 184, 188, 191, 193, 195
Simant Bostock, Glastonbury: 43, 93, 135, 177, 199, 202, 209, 211, 215 and cover
Fortean Picture Library: 170
Justin, Arunet: 185
George Lisensky, Beloit University: 190
Ian Newsham: 182
Private collection: 178
Ralegh Radford: 73
Jim Nagel after Radford: 126
Radio Times Hulton Picture Library: 165
Roger Brown (Fortean Picture Library): 154, 160, 175, 187
Thames & Hudson: 74, 75
Reece Winston: 130

Introduction

The Arthurian Legend is unique. Nothing else is quite like it. During the Middle Ages, it was the favourite theme of imaginative writing throughout western Europe. In modern times it has re-surfaced to inspire novels, plays, films. Nor is it confined to such media. Britain, where it began, has well over 150 places that are associated with it. Arthur is more widespread in local lore than anyone else—except, it is said, the Devil.

Given this persistent spell, one naturally asks a plain question: Did Arthur exist? There is no plain answer. "Yes" implies that the monarch of the Legend, with his medieval splendour and magnificent court, was real. He was not. He is a literary creation. But the alternative "no" implies that Arthur is purely fictitious, with no factual basis at all, and that doesn't work either. Simply to say that no such person existed is not enough. More is involved than mere doubt or lack of evidence. His Legend does exist, copious and multiple, and has done for a very long time. Anyone who denies him can be fairly asked to account for it without him, to explain where the Legend came from if there was no Arthur of any kind. Few sceptics have seriously tried, and none has produced a theory that is any better than guesswork.

Since the question "Did Arthur exist?" can't be given a straight answer, the constructive course if we want to probe the mystery is to ask another question, starting from what does exist—the Legend itself. How did it originate, what facts is it rooted in? If we can trace it to its sources, we may find somebody lurking there. We must have no preconceptions as to who or what that somebody was. But, to be acceptable, he must account directly or indirectly for the items in this Guide.

Most of the Legend as we know it dates from the twelfth and thirteenth centuries. A series of authors built up the montage of characters and themes: the king himself, with his glorious and dangerous queen; Merlin, prophet and magician; the magic sword Excalibur; the Knights of the Round Table, dedicated to high ideals; the tragic love-stories of Lancelot and Guinevere, Tristan and Iseult; the Quest of the Grail; Arthur's downfall through treachery, his departure to Avalon, his cryptic death or more cryptic immortality. None of this is history as it stands. It is imaginative romance. King Arthur is an idealized medieval monarch, his Britain is a chivalric Utopia that never existed—certainly not in the far-off past when Arthur might be supposed to have reigned.

However, this lack of authenticity doesn't mean that there is no factual basis. Medieval romancers were not like modern novelists. Authenticity was not their concern. A novelist today, dealing with long-ago events, will try to portray people as they were, to re-create their ideas and beliefs, the houses they lived in, the food they ate, the clothes they wore. Writers in the Middle Ages had a different approach. When dealing with an ancient story they updated it, presenting it in terms of their own day and their readers' interests. Artists did much the same, as illustrated manuscripts show. The romancers who developed the story of Arthur were well aware that it belonged to a far-off time. What we would call their anachronism carries no implication that they didn't know what they were talking about. It was simply the custom of the age when they wrote.

Their romances, in fact, fitted loosely into a framework that *was* taken to be history. This was mainly due to one highly inventive author. He is known as Geoffrey of Monmouth, and he gave Arthur what amounted to an official biography. We must examine what he says. And we must ask where, if anywhere, he got it from. That is not an academic question. For a guidebook it is vital. Here are those numerous places with Arthurian connections: Tintagel, Glastonbury and many more. Should we treat all this as pure fantasy, concocted by Geoffrey and writers after him? Or are there underlying realities which their imagination fastened upon?

A "biography" and its setting

Monmouth, Geoffrey's presumed birthplace, is on the south-east fringe of Wales. His family background is unknown, but he was familiar with Welsh traditions, and interested in the Celtic Britons from whom the Welsh were descended. A cleric, and probably a teacher, he was at Oxford from 1129 to 1151. In the late 1130s he produced a Latin *History of the Kings of Britain* covering a stretch of time not far short of two thousand years. It makes out that wandering Trojans founded a monarchy in the island then called Albion and re-named it Britain. Geoffrey runs through a long series of British kings including Shakespeare's King Lear, nearly all of them fictitious. When he gets to the Roman conquest, and thus to recorded history, he has to be a little more factual. But he claims that it wasn't a true conquest, and British kings went on reigning as tributary rulers.

Britain, in his narrative, breaks away from the Roman Empire, and here he begins building up to an Arthurian climax. He tells us that a sinister British noble, Vortigern, made himself king, and two rightful princes went into exile. The usurper had trouble with the Picts in the north, and invited some Saxons, led by Hengist, to cross over from the Continent and settle in Britain as auxiliary troops. More Saxons flooded into the country and got out of control, seizing land for themselves and spreading chaos through Britain. Vortigern fled to Wales, where he encountered Merlin, who prophesied his doom and the advent of a deliverer. The princes returned, Vortigern was killed, and the Saxons were partially contained, though still turbulent and aggressive.

The elder prince, Aurelius Ambrosius, reigned for a short time. His brother Uther succeeded him. At a banquet in London Uther was seized with ungovernable desire for Ygerna, the wife of Gorlois, duke of Cornwall. Gorlois withdrew from the court taking her with him. Uther considered himself insulted and led an army into Cornwall to ravage the ducal lands. Gorlois left Ygerna for safety in a fortress out on the headland of Tintagel, accessible only along a narrow ridge, and marched off to oppose the king. He was outwitted. Merlin gave Uther a magic potion that turned him into an exact replica of Gorlois, and in that effective disguise he entered Tintagel past its guards and found his way to Ygerna, who, thinking him to be her husband, made no difficulties. She conceived Arthur. The real Gorlois had just fallen in battle, so Uther resumed his own shape and made Ygerna his queen.

Uther was poisoned by a Saxon, and Arthur became king while still in his teens. He soon showed gifts of leadership, and launched a series of campaigns, routing and dispersing the Saxons and subduing the Picts and Scots. He had a special sword called Caliburn, forged in the Isle of Avalon. He married Guinevere and made himself popular with his subjects. Next he conquered Ireland, and then Iceland (which would not have been difficult, because in those days Iceland was uninhabited). Twelve years of peace and prosperity ensued. Arthur founded an order of knighthood enrolling distinguished men from various lands. Britain was fast becoming pre-eminent in Europe. This was the time, or at least the beginning of the time, when the adventures related in romance were said to have happened.

The Roman Empire still had a shaky hold on Gaul, now France. Arthur had designs on the Empire himself. He won over many Gauls to his side, crossed the Channel with an army, and took possession. Around this part of the story we are beginning to get familiar names in the royal entourage —Gawain, Bedivere, Kay. Some years later Arthur was holding court at Caerleon in Wales when envoys arrived from Rome demanding that he restore his conquests and pay tribute, as earlier British kings had done. Judging attack to be the best defence, Arthur led another army to Gaul, leaving his nephew Modred at home as his deputy, in joint charge with Guinevere. While he was away Modred proclaimed himself king, conspired with the Saxons, and persuaded the queen to live in adultery with him. Arthur, who had got as far as Burgundian territory, was forced to return. He defeated and killed the traitor in a battle by the River Camel in Cornwall, but was seriously wounded himself and "carried off to the Isle of Avalon so that his wounds might be attended to", handing over the crown to a cousin. It is not stated that he died. Geoffrey knew of a folk-belief that he was still alive, and left the door open for it, but did not commit himself.

As to the time when all this is supposed to have happened, an important clue is that western Europe still has a Roman ruler. Since there were no emperors in the west after 476, Arthur's continental exploits must be before that. Allusions to a real emperor Leo, who ruled in the east from 457 to 474, narrow the range. This context for Arthur is in harmony with his family relationships. Unfortunately Geoffrey's readers are also given something rare in his *History*, an exact date, and it doesn't fit. Arthur's passing is assigned to the year 542. Its total incompatibility is one of several reasons for thinking it an error, and it can in fact be brought into line as an error of a known medieval kind, which we need not go into. If we dismiss it and take everything else together, we see a fairly coherent picture of a reign lasting twenty-five to thirty years, largely in the 450s and 460s.

So again, where did Geoffrey get this from? Did he get it from anywhere? Or was the entire Legend born in his imagination?

We need to understand how he works. In the previous part of his *History* dealing with the Roman period, where there is solid information, we can compare. First, he is not really writing history and he can never be trusted for facts. What he says about Julius Caesar and others is a travesty of the truth. Secondly, however, it is a travesty of a truth which is on record, and which he does to some extent know. He habitually *uses* history, or what he would like to think is history, to evolve his fiction. Except in the early chapters on mythical Britons in an impenetrable past, he doesn't contrive major episodes out of nothing at all. He draws his inspiration from real events or established stories or names or monuments; always from something. With his biography of Arthur, we can be sure that he has some basis for it ... or thinks he has.

As far as the hero's setting is concerned, he has. Post-Roman Britain is very poorly documented, but we can allow that his story shows knowledge of things that actually happened. Archaeology, while not supplying all the support we could wish, does supply some.

Most of Britain was under Roman rule for well over three hundred years. Its people were British Celts, ancestors of the Welsh, Cornish and Bretons; there were no English as yet. The upper classes received a veneer of imperial civilization and, in course of time, Christianity. As the Empire weakened in the west, under pressure from barbarians, the island on the fringe was exposed and hard to defend. Britain was beset by Irish, Picts and Saxons.

About 410, political upheavals cut if off from the centre and it broke away. The emperor authorized the Britons to look after themselves.

The administration carried on for a while, but regional chiefs were rising in importance, and one of them seems to have attained paramountcy over a good deal of the country. This was the Vortigern whom Geoffrey medievalizes as a crafty usurper. He played a leading part in a policy on imperial lines, providing a group of barbarians with land and supplies in return for keeping order and driving off other barbarians. Saxons, Angles and Jutes, ancestors of the English, were settled in Britain on this basis to contain the Picts. Here again, in the tale of Vortigern and Hengist, Geoffrey romanticizes facts. More settlers arrived without permission. Somewhere in the 440s the reinforced Saxons allied themselves with the Picts they were supposed to contain and began raiding far and wide, right across to the western sea. This phase of revolt probably dragged on into the 450s, a side-effect being a flight of Britons across the Channel, laying the foundations of Brittany.

At last the raiders withdrew into their authorized enclaves. The sequel was without parallel anywhere else. Alone among Roman ex-provincials, the Britons had become independent before the barbarians moved in. Now, alone among Roman ex-provincials, they cared enough to fight back. A noble, Ambrosius Aurelianus, organized counter-action. His name shows that his family was still Roman in its traditions and sympathies. To-and-fro warfare followed, and Saxon incursions at new points. Britain probably had long spells of partial and even general peace, but fighting in the 490s culminated in a British success at "Mount Badon", unidentified, though almost certainly in the south. For a while the situation was stabilized. A brief Celtic resurgence was marked by activity in the Church and swift growth of the colonies that were forming Brittany. Eventually the Anglo-Saxons took over most of the country and made it England—Angle-land—but the Britons' descendants held out in Wales and elsewhere, handing down songs and stories about the phase of independence.

Gildas, a monk writing in the 530s or thereabouts, testifies to the main post-Roman course of events. He is a sermonizer, not a historian. He makes terrible mistakes, and the only Briton whom he names between the break with Rome and his own time—a stretch of well over a century—is Ambrosius. Nevertheless he is an early witness for the Saxon disaster, the partial recovery, and the battle of Badon.

Geoffrey, in his corresponding chapters, is giving his own treatment to these happenings. He knows of Vortigern and he knows of Ambrosius Aurelianus, whom he turns into King Aurelius Ambrosius. Since he did have some awareness of this near-anonymous turmoil, we can reasonably ask whether he found a real Arthur in it—not, of course, the King Arthur of the Legend, but some Briton whom he built up into his towering monarch.

If we could trust his preface the answer would be "yes". He claims that he translated the *History* from "a certain very ancient book in the British language" given to him by Walter, Archdeacon of Oxford. The British language could be either Welsh or Breton. Geoffrey and Walter were acquainted. Moreover, Geoffrey makes one specific statement about the book's contents, that it gave him information on Arthur's downfall: hence, presumably, on his reign. What he says about the book is, alas, incredible. He is simply trying to make his inventions more respectable by alleging an older source for them. Other medieval authors do much the same. Still, the touch about Arthur's downfall is an extra. Geoffrey may have had some Welsh or Breton text, now lost, that told of him.

While "may have" is not an argument, an original Arthur would at least fit into the sequence of events, as a leader during the phase of British recovery. There is a curious piece of evidence for him. His name is a Welsh form of the Roman "Artorius". It suggests someone from a family like Ambrosius's, still not remote from the imperial world. It doesn't suggest a Celtic god or fairy-tale paladin. Such a being would hardly have had a Roman name. The name is actually on record in Roman Britain, proof that it was known. Lucius Artorius Castus took a legion across the Channel in 184 to suppress a rebellion. He is much too early to be the original, and the notion of his having descendants or name-sakes is a pure guess. But after a long gap with no other men so called, we begin to find several in the sixth century, up and down Britain, even in Scotland. It looks as if some saga had elevated a post-Roman Briton into a national hero.

We may be closing in on him. Failing the ancient book, what can we say Geoffrey of Monmouth knew that gave him inklings of such a person?

Arthur in Wales

Before his time, Welsh bards, story-tellers and clerics had generated a varied body of literature—much more, written and oral, than survives today. Arthur occurs in several connections. Poems extolled him as proverbial for prowess in war, and one said there was a mystery about his grave, though it stopped short of saying he was immortal and never had one. Other poems gave him a train of followers, some decidedly larger than life and credited with slaying monsters as well as enemies. Popular tales abounded. Most of them are lost, and we must infer their contents from tantalizing summaries grouped in threes, called triads. Early triads mention Arthur quite often, attesting his fame, but they are not much help as background for Geoffrey's narrative. From that point of view the only interesting ones are a few that refer to a sort of feud between Arthur and "Medrawd", and to a fatal battle at Camlan. There are hints here for Modred's turning against Arthur, though not for the circumstances, and for the final clash by the River Camel.

A single pre-Geoffrey tale has survived complete, composed in its present form late in the tenth century. *Culhwch and Olwen* ("Culhwch" is pronounced Kil-hooch, with the *ch* as in "loch") is colourful and extravagant and savage and comic. Arthur is the chief prince of Britain with a court assembling most of the men and women of note in Welsh tradition, as well as many mythical figures. Pre-Christian Celtic beliefs make their presence felt. One was that there are "Otherworld" regions—places not in our world yet somehow in contact with it—which are abodes of spirits and fairy-folk. An Otherworld ruler, Gwyn, is among the characters. Arthur and his company have fantastic adventures. They hunt a colossal boar, Twrch Trwyth, who is really a wicked king under a spell. This boar-hunt has left its mark on local lore. Apart from its literary merits, *Culhwch and Olwen* is a storehouse of information on Welsh legend. However, it is hard to trace any use of it by Geoffrey. He may have got the idea of Arthur's court from it, but the court he portrays is very different.

Finally, several Latin "Lives" of Welsh saints include anecdotes of Arthur. They are rather hostile, and inconsistent, making him sometimes king of Britain and sometimes a war-lord or "tyrant". A recurring motif is the saints' superiority, shown when their supernatural powers make him repent of his misdeeds.

From this Welsh matter, Geoffrey picked up some notions, and he picked up some characters—Merlin (originally Myrddin), Guinevere, Kay, Bedivere, Modred. However, none of it adds up to a real source for his Arthur story or any large part of it. Fabulous adventures, as in *Culhwch and Olwen*, don't disprove Arthur's reality. Fabulous adventures were ascribed to Alexander the Great and other real people. But we are certainly a long way from history.

Just two Welsh items—Latin items from Wales—are on a different footing. A tenth-century chronicle, the *Annales Cambriae* or Annals of Wales, has a couple of Arthur entries. It notes the victory of Badon, noted long before in Gildas's tract, and assigns Arthur a major role in it, saying he "carried the cross of Our Lord Jesus Christ"—probably meaning an emblem, or one of the reputed fragments of the True Cross that were treasured as relics. Arthur is a Christian champion here against the heathen Saxons, as he is not in the Saints' Lives. The Annals also note "the strife of Camlann in which Arthur and Medraut fell". While Medraut is Medrawd or Modred, the chronicler does not say that he was a traitor or even that the two were opposed. Attempts have been made to argue that the Camlann entry was posted from a more trustworthy chronicle nearer to Arthur's time, but there is no sound reason to think so.

Delving back farther, we come to a book written early in the ninth century, the *Historia Brittonum* or History of the Britons. It is attributed to a monk named Nennius, perhaps wrongly, but it is convenient to say "Nennius" to mean the author. The book is a medley of Welsh legend, just-possible history, and fantasy. It includes two local legends bringing in Arthur. If we stick to the parts that may have some relation to fact, we find an account of Vortigern, his opening the door to the Saxons, and the consequent catastrophe. There is also an account of his meeting a mysterious boy-prophet in Snowdonia, named Ambrose, with discouraging results for himself.

Nennius has a chapter on Arthur. Dropping out of the blue without much preamble, it consists of a rapid survey of twelve battles which he is said to have won against the Saxons. It may be based on an older Welsh poem in his praise, though no such poem exists now. Nennius is unclear as to his status. He makes him the British war-leader, *dux bellorum*, co-ordinating the efforts of Britain's "kings" or regional rulers. This chapter was used briefly before Geoffrey by two non-Welsh historians, William of Malmesbury and Henry of Huntingdon. William infers that Arthur was a great, charismatic warrior in Ambrosius's service, not a king himself; Henry, that he was "the leader of the soldiers and kings of Britain". Both might have been the case at different stages of his career. Arthur is a Christian champion here too, carrying a holy image.

Nennius mentions Mount Badon, credited to Arthur as in the Annals, and presented as the climactic twelfth battle. The others build up to it, identified by puzzling place-names. The most comprehensible are in different parts of Lincolnshire, in the "Forest of Celidon", and in "the City of the Legion". The Forest of Celidon was in southern Scotland. Another passage shows that for Nennius the City of the Legion was Chester. All these battles, seven out of the twelve, would fit best into a mid-fifth-century setting. The Lincolnshire battles would have been against Angles encroaching up the Wash and Humber. There were no Saxons in Scotland till long afterwards, but during the anarchic phase of revolt and cross-country raiding they had Pictish allies who might have provoked reprisals. Chester, too far west for relevant war later in the century, could be allotted to the same phase, as the target of a cross-country raid.

Geoffrey makes use of these two texts. He improves Nennius's account of Vortigern, the Saxons, and the young prophet, though he makes out that the prophet was the youthful Merlin, thus introducing his second most famous character. He adapts some of the battles. He turns Medraut into Arthur's nephew Modred, deputy-ruler and traitor. He has Arthur fall at Camlann, revised and interpreted as the Camel. So parts at least of his Arthur story draw on earlier matter and are not total fantasy. His habitual practice is confirmed. However, if we are looking for real history, and particularly if we are looking for a real Arthur, the earlier matter is not early enough. It is written closer to the events, if any, but still centuries after them. And it already has touches of legend that cast doubt on it. At Badon, Nennius assures us, Arthur killed 960 of the enemy himself in a single charge. Heroes' deeds get exaggerated over the years, but not to this extent in contemporary reports.

Because the Welsh present Arthur in such different guises—as a feuding chief, as a protagonist in impossible exploits, as a foil for the saints, as Britain's war-leader—sceptics have urged that he is too inconsistent to be true. Not so. The best parallel here is not Alexander but a more recent person, the American folk-hero Davy Crockett, given juvenile cult status by Disney during the 1950s. Born in Tennessee in 1786, he hunted in wild country and fought Indians, then went into politics, entering Congress in Washington as a picturesque backwoodsman. In 1836 he joined the Texan volunteers defending the Alamo against a Mexican army, and died there. In his political campaigning he had made his mark by telling tall tales from the frontier and encouraging supporters to embroider his own life-story in the same spirit. After 1836 legends clustered around him. Within a year or two he was alleged to have killed 85 Mexicans during the siege—not 960, admittedly, but the time for exaggeration was shorter. He was rumoured to be still alive. Yarn-spinners took up his tall-tale aspect in print, going beyond anything in *Culhwch and Olwen*. Their fictitious Davy rode on the lightning, climbed Niagara on the back of an alligator, greased the earth's axis to set it spinning again in a freeze-up. An American historian once complained that Crockett's biography could not be written because there were half a dozen of him. Yet he existed, and he shows that Arthur's inflation and diversification don't disprove his own existence.

To revert to Nennius, he need not be rejected as discredited. He may be giving us facts, and so may the Annals. Some at least of the battles may be authentic; Gildas's tract is a much older testimony to Badon. But if we do try to treat this matter as history, we face an immediate problem. It makes Arthur's life-span absurd. The most acceptable battles, before Badon, only make good sense in the middle of the fifth century. Badon itself occurred not far from the year 500, probably a little before. So we would deduce from what Gildas says ... but the Annals contradict him, putting Badon in 518. They put Camlann in 539. To cover all the data Arthur would have to be an active warrior when over a hundred years old.

If these texts gave a chronological fix—a statement calibrating him with known history—we might be able to pin him down somewhere in the time-range, and then find explanations for whatever won't fit. The Welsh matter never gives such a fix. It never says Arthur was born when X was emperor, or died when Y was pope. Historically he hangs in a void.

Outside Britain?

All is not lost, however. We have one more resource, Geoffrey's account of the Gallic warfare, and it is far from negligible. It takes up half his Arthur story. Assessed by allocation of space, his Arthur is more a continental campaigner than anything else. He thinks this part of the king's career is very important. Romancers after him do not go so far, but their Arthur often has a continental domain. Modern readers and novelists are not sympathetic. After all, contemporaries across the Channel don't seem to have noticed any major British invasions. Yet if we dismiss this part of the story as imaginary, we must assume that Geoffrey is fabricating half of Arthur's career out of nothing at all. It is not his style. There has to be something, and since Welsh tradition has no trace of it, it must be elsewhere.

Furthermore, in his Gallic chapters he supplies what the Welsh never do, a chronological fix—the only one Arthur ever gets. The Gallic campaigns happen in the reign of the aforesaid Leo, emperor in the east from 457 to 474. Clues from other names tie down the final campaign much more closely, to a couple of years, 469–70. Geoffrey's indications of date are not often so precise. When writing of the final campaign he is thinking of something relevant which happened about then.

Something did. We are touching bedrock at last. In 467 Leo appointed a colleague, Anthemius, to take charge in the west. Anthemius tried to retrieve the situation in Gaul, much of it overrun by an assortment of barbarians. He negotiated an alliance with a man described as "the King of the Britons", who crossed to Gaul with 12,000 troops. Historians have underrated him in the belief that he was only a chief of Bretons, but that opinion no longer holds. He did come over from Britain. One historian, James Campbell, suggests that he had authority on both sides of the Channel.

After a pause north of the Loire, when he may have aided British settlers against marauding Saxons, he marched into central Gaul to oppose the Visigoths who were advancing from Spain. But Arvandus, the imperial governor, had been acting treacherously, proposing to the Visigoths that they should crush the Britons and share out Gaul with the Burgundians, who held parts of the east and south. Though Arvandus was detected, the Visigoths pushed ahead to Bourges, which the "King of the Britons" had occupied. After fierce fighting he retreated into Burgundian territory, probably in 470. No more is said about him.

Here we have raw materials for Geoffrey's story. The "King of the Britons" was in Gaul with his sea-borne army at the right time. He advanced to the Burgundian neighbourhood. He was betrayed by a deputy-ruler who conspired with barbarians. When we last see him he is even moving in the direction of a real town called Avallon (still there). Geoffrey's Latin form of that place-name doesn't correspond to its Welsh original and may well have been influenced by the town in Gaul.

Several authors have noticed this king and wondered if he was Arthur. The drawback is that he is referred to, with slight variations, as Riothamus. The *h* is due to scribes copying manuscripts with notions of their own about spelling. The correct form would have been Riotamus. Anyhow Geoffrey almost certainly has him in mind when relating Arthur's continental adventures. He inflates wildly, he changes the politics, he invents British successes— things he does in other parts of the *History*. But here, at last, the trail leads back to someone living at the right time who could be the original. Riotamus is the only documented person who does anything Arthurian, and he really is documented. We even have a letter to him.

The natural objection is, "Yes, but Geoffrey just took a hint from what this man did and made out that Arthur did it, or an exaggerated version of it. That needn't mean he thought Riotamus was Arthur. After all, the name is wrong." That fails to settle the question. Other people did think Riotamus was Arthur. A Breton, probably before Geoffrey and certainly not copying him, introduces a legend of a saint with a preface reviewing events in the fifth century, and sketches the activities of "Arthur, King of the Britons" (the same title) in terms that fit Riotamus. Half a dozen chroniclers, later than Geoffrey but still not copying him, concur to give Arthur a reign running from about 454 to 470, the year when Riotamus drops out of the record. Apparently they see the two as the same, and very likely they draw on somebody earlier who took that view. One other chronicle has an intriguing touch. It calls Arthur's betrayer Morvandus, which looks like a mix-up of "Mordred", the more literary form of the traitor's name, with "Arvandus", the name of Riotamus's actual betrayer.

As it seems that these authors equated Arthur with Riotamus, Geoffrey is probably doing likewise. The identification means that there has to be a solution of the name difficulty. Otherwise it could never have happened. It could be that Riotamus simply had two names, as some Britons did, that the other name was Arthur or rather Artorius, and that he passed into tradition under that one. A less conjectural notion would follow from the meaning of "Riotamus". It is a Latin version of a term in the British language, *Rigotamos*, "supreme king" or "supremely royal". It may have been a sobriquet, even a title, bestowed on a man after he rose to prominence, and used in addressing him or referring to him. He could have been Arthur.

That is to assume that "Arthur" came first and "Riotamus" was additional. It might have been the other way round, with "Riotamus" as the king's original style: more likely perhaps, since it appears later in Welsh adaptations as a proper name. As noted, a previous Arthur, Lucius Artorius Castus, took an army across the Channel. A leader taking another army across the Channel might have been hailed by some knowledgeable poet as a "second Artorius". And there is a last possibility, which is odd yet worth mentioning. If "Riotamus" was the king's original name, "Artorius" could have been a sort of nickname derived from it. ARTORIUS is almost an anagram of RIOTAMUS, and could have been suggested by a reading of the letters on (say) a medallion. RIOTAMUS, plus an *r* for *rex*, king, can be arranged quite neatly to give that result.

RIOTAMUS reads clockwise, omitting the R, which is slightly nearer the centre. The reading counter-clockwise, starting from A and bringing the R in, spells ARTORIUS. The M is left out, but it doesn't break the sequence of letters. Frivolous? Maybe. Still it is interesting that this can be done at all.

Nothing is on record concerning Riotamus, as such, back in Britain before he went overseas. However, he was important enough for word of him to reach Rome through the tumult of western Europe, and cause an emperor to seek his alliance. "King of the Britons" looks like an excessive title, but he was king of some of them and probably a good many, since he could raise a substantial army and assemble a fleet to carry it. His cross-Channel contact suggests that he ruled in the West Country, Arthurian territory, and he could just about have initiated the biggest "Arthurian" project revealed by archaeology, the refortification of Cadbury Castle, reputedly Camelot. If he was involved in the anti-Saxon resistance, all of Nennius's locatable battles could find a place in his time-frame. By the date of his overseas expedition, Saxon pressure had presumably eased.

We have a provisional answer to the question "Did Arthur exist?" though not the impossible yes-or-no. Arthur is almost entirely legend, at one level or another, but he has a real original, and that original may well have been the King of the Britons who went to Gaul. There is no firm evidence for any rival "real Arthur". Yet when we study these beginnings, we face legend-making in Britain as far back as we can get, even apart from the slaughter of 960 Saxons. No single leader is likely to have done everything Arthur is supposed to have done, fighting all the battles and falling at Camlann, especially if the Annals are right in putting Camlann in the sixth century. The Riotamus candidacy works well in the early part of the time-range. It gives an answer, if any is needed, to a cavil sometimes heard—that Arthur's name doesn't appear in Gildas. If he lived that much earlier, beyond living memory, no reader who has struggled with Gildas will be surprised that it doesn't. However, the candidacy runs into trouble later. If we forget all the medieval growth, Arthur still has to be a composite figure. The same could be said of Merlin, who presents difficulties of much the same kind.

In Riotamus we may have an authentic glimpse, a

moment in continental limelight. But when he or some unknown became a British hero, under the great name, the saga absorbed the exploits of others, possibly others called Arthur. A Welsh poem indicates that a war-band known as "Arthur's Men" may have continued in being after his death, perhaps long after. If so, bardic praises of Arthur's Men, on dimly-recalled occasions, might have inspired legends of their founder's presence in person when he was long since dead. In discussing places associated with Arthur, we must sometimes content ourselves with meaning "the man who is said to have done such-and-such at this place", with no commitment as to identity. The mystery, in the end, abides.

Arthur transfigured

The Anglo-Normans who ruled England in Geoffrey's time were receptive to his *History*, partly, no doubt, because it put the "Saxons" whom they had conquered in a poor light. Their successors ruled a large part of France as well, and were glad to have their parvenu empire given proud antecedents. In 1155 a poet named Wace, from Jersey, produced a free paraphrase of the *History* in French verse that made it more accessible. It was giving shape and coherence to a process which Wace noticed, the spread of other Arthurian matter. The saga which had grown up in Wales, and in Cornwall and Brittany too by now, was being disseminated piecemeal. A book by a French priest had recently recalled a visit to England as early as 1113, when West Country locals pointed out Arthurian sites, and, in Bodmin, insisted that King Arthur was still alive. Bretons were saying the same. There were at least two versions of this belief, that he was on an enchanted island—Geoffrey's Avalon—or that he was asleep in a cave. Either way, his return was hoped for. Breton minstrels said many other things about him, and spread through French-speaking lands and farther. Arthurian characters were carved over a doorway in Modena Cathedral, in Italy.

Without Geoffrey and Wace, it is unlikely that the scattered traditions would have converged in a single body of literature. Because of them, however, the latter part of the twelfth century saw the beginnings of an outpouring of narrative poems and prose tales in several languages. The great name is Chrétien de Troyes. The romancers created the full-blown Legend. New characters took the stage, among them Lancelot, and the Lady of the Lake. Merlin, who, in the *History*, had virtually dropped out after master-minding Arthur's birth, became the wonder-working sponsor of the whole reign. Other themes from Geoffrey were taken up and improved upon. He had introduced the knighthood, but the actual Round Table, imported by Wace from Breton folklore, became a ritual piece of furniture with symbolic meanings. Geoffrey had made Arthur hold court at Caerleon, an already-existing Roman city. Now he was given a headquarters of his own, Camelot. His sword Caliburn became Excalibur. Sometimes drawing on Celtic sources, more often not, romancers developed themes that are now familiar: the sword-in-the-stone test proving Arthur's right to the crown; the loves of the principal women; the fall of Merlin through his own love for an enchantress, who trapped him in a magic imprisonment; the acts of the ambiguous Gawain, though his greatest adventure, with the Green Knight, was a later topic; and the Quest of the Grail.

The last of these themes raises issues beyond the scope of fiction. Underlying it are pre-Christian myths about magical cauldrons and other marvellous vessels, and possibly, also, idiosyncrasies in the practices and beliefs of Celtic Christians. At its literary début the Grail has a strange and rather disquieting ritual context. When fully Christianized it is explained as a cup or dish used by Christ at the Last Supper, with miraculous properties. It came to the "Vales of Avalon" in Somerset through the agency of Joseph of Arimathea, the rich disciple who provided Christ's tomb. He had caught drops of the Saviour's blood in it. Some time after its arrival in Britain it passed into the custody of a succession of guardians in an elusive castle. Many of Arthur's knights went in search of it. The romances are puzzling and contradictory. In the most important, the vision of the Grail is a spiritual initiation which only Galahad is worthy to achieve fully.

The key to the symbolism may have been lost. Ecclesiastics generally ignored the Grail and made no attempt to interpret it. From their point of view the stories, however Christian, were suspect. However, Joseph was named as the builder of the first church at Glastonbury, in the "Vales of Avalon". There, the monks of the Abbey had nothing to say about the Grail. Their chief chronicler made some use of the romances, but he told only of two small vessels called cruets which Joseph had brought to Britain, containing drops of the Lord's blood and sweat. These were holy relics with no mystical implications.

Glastonbury was also woven into the legendary fabric by the Abbey's assertion that Arthur was buried there and it was the real Avalon. Some accepted the claim, some did not, though no one seriously challenged it with a rival grave. In a famous version of his passing, when lying wounded after his last battle, he tells Bedivere to cast Excalibur into a lake. The knight demurs twice but finally complies, whereupon a hand rises out of the water, catches the sword, and draws it under. The king is then taken away to an Avalon that is not defined, perhaps to be healed and wait undying till the hour comes for his return. His golden age may not be lost for ever, it may be reborn.

Throughout much of the medieval period, the romances enjoyed a large public among the aristocracy and upper middle classes. One reason was that women were gaining ground socially, and their literary tastes carried weight. Unlike the martial epics of earlier days, Arthurian fiction had something for everybody. The love-stories—Lancelot and Guinevere, Tristan and Iseult—were a novelty, and while Guinevere was slow to mature as an interesting character, Iseult was always vivid and capable. Lords and ladies held "Round Table" entertainments at which the guests enacted Arthurian roles, feasted, and engaged in jousts and other suitable sports. Ironically, Arthur became a national hero of England, his role as enemy of the early English forgotten. Plantagenet sovereigns took him seriously. Edward I held five Round Table entertainments, and bolstered his claim to rule Scotland by saying Arthur had ruled Scotland. Edward III contemplated reviving the Arthurian knighthood, though, in the end, he founded the Order of the Garter instead.

The Arthurian wave gradually ebbed, but during the Wars of the Roses some of the best-known romances, most of them in French, were adapted by Sir Thomas Malory. More than an adapter, he made contributions of his own, one of them a great enhancement of Guinevere as a character. In 1485 Caxton edited and printed his writings, and Malory's version became the standard presentation of the cycle in English. It was the basis for many later works including Tennyson's *Idylls of the King* and the novels of T. H. White.

New perspectives, new departures

To sum up, the Arthurian Legend is a complex growth. Some of the stories belong to history, after a fashion. Some are myths and folk-tales that have been worked into the saga, and date from earlier ages as well as later. Some are barbaric, wild, timeless—products of bardic imagination. Some are due to the courtly romancers, and portray the king and those around him transformed into medieval figures. Stories appear on more than one level and in different forms. Even names vary widely and confusingly. "Drystan" and "Tristan" and "Tristram" all stand for the same person; so do "Medraut" and "Modred" and "Mordred"; so do "Gwenhwyfar" and "Guinevere" and "Ginevra"; so do "Essyllt" and "Iseult" and "Isolde".

Arthur can be pictured in quite a variety of ways. T. H. White, in *The Once and Future King,* was still sticking to Malory in the mid-twentieth century, though he superimposed modern ideas. But Arthurian authorship was already beginning to be affected by new research. Historians were re-examining sources, archaeologists were probing legendary sites.

An influential step had been taken in 1936 by R. G. Collingwood. Accepting Nennius's chapter on the battles, he suggested that Arthur was a Roman-style commander-in-chief who organized a cavalry corps and routed the pedestrian Saxons. The poet Charles Williams, and C. S. Lewis, adopted Collingwood's theory. Others thought the cavalry fanciful, but, for several decades, were prepared to endorse the military view, sometimes looking toward the early sixth century rather than the fifth for Arthur's main activities. At length more critical studies swung the pendulum back toward scepticism. However, the "historical Arthur" issue had been raised and could not be exorcized. Riotamus, who had been noticed as a possible original long before (long before Collingwood, as a matter of fact), was rediscovered in the 1980s.

Archaeology had results which many found more exciting. Though never a deliberate search for Arthur, it drew attention to three places outstandingly linked with him: Tintagel, the scene of his conception and presumably birth; Glastonbury, with its Grail associations and grave; and Cadbury Castle, a hill-fort reputed to have been the real Camelot. In all three cases, the connection does not appear in written records for many centuries. Yet in all three cases, excavation showed that the places were British-occupied and important in the appropriate period. While it revealed nothing about Arthur, it proved that the people who focused on these places knew something about them and located him credibly. A purely accidental three-out-of-three score would have been too much. Knowledge of Arthur's Britain clearly persisted through a vast stretch of time. The story-tellers, therefore, were entitled to a hearing on other counts also.

When researchers dug into the strata underlying romance, some critics complained that their work was either destructive or pointless. New creative writing inspired by it refuted them. Rosemary Sutcliff in *Sword at Sunset*, Mary Stewart in novels of Merlin, Persia Woolley and Bernard Cornwell and others, bypassed the medieval scene and tried to recapture the world of Arthur as it might have been in its post-Roman reality. Marion Zimmer Bradley, in *The Mists of Avalon*, invented a new myth of her own with a woman as narrator. John Arden and Margaretta D'Arcy in drama, John Heath-Stubbs in poetry, approached the subject by other paths again. Extension of knowledge has done no harm to the medieval cycle, which remains immortal literature. But it has enlarged and enriched the mythos itself with new insights into the enduring impression which Arthur and his companions have made.

It is because of this impression that "Arthurian Britain" is a meaningful term. Arthurian names, Arthurian lore, spread in a network over the land—a network of history and fantasy, poetry and romance, tradition and fable. Yet Arthurian Britain has an elusive quality. The map is unfamiliar. Oxford, Birmingham, Glasgow, do not appear on it. Zennor, Aberffraw, Drumelzier, do. Except at a few spectacular places like Tintagel, what often confronts the traveller is a kind of enigma: a landscape where a legend hovers; or some natural feature, an Arthur's Cave or Arthur's Hill; or a standing stone or fortification which is linked with his name or the name of someone in his circle. Why the legend, why the name? Even when a reason can be inferred, explanation may be in order.

Yet the quest is worth pursuing, the presence can be evoked. The tradition takes remarkable forms, clinging as it sometimes does to earthwork "castles" or hill-forts dating from the pre-Roman Iron Age, and to prehistoric structures older than that. With a few hill-forts such tales have a degree of substance, because they were re-occupied by Britons of Arthur's day. Sometimes, however, we get a name or a story only. We seldom know why the name was localized or when the story took shape. The process began more than a thousand years ago and has gone on into recent times.

It is striking that the Arthur of local legend appears as he does. He has very little fame in great cities and major historic settings. We are apt to find him in out-of-way places and on sites of immemorial age. Legend and folklore may belong to a half-barbaric fairyland, or carry echoes from unseen "Otherworld" realms of Celtic myth. Since the romantic image of King Arthur and the Knights of the Round Table has so long been the accepted one, it is strange how little impact it has had on place-lore. Moreover, most of the sites are in parts of Britain—the West Country, Wales, Cumbria, southern Scotland—where Celtic people, descendants of Arthurian Britons, kept their identity longest and in some cases keep it still. Even today, after all the literary development, Arthur's presence belongs mainly to regions where he could actually have flourished, not to the more English parts of England. As with the three archaeological sites, we glimpse a body of tradition that is rooted far back beyond the romances.

TERMS IN THIS BOOK

A few words about this Guide. It raises questions of terminology. In any given entry, what exactly does the name "Arthur" mean? When a place belongs to romance, folklore or legend, no problem arises. "Arthur" means Arthur as a character in romance, folklore or legend. When the place is a location of history or supposed history, as with the site of an Arthurian battle, the case is not so simple. It would be presumptuous to insist on bringing in Riotamus or any other specific person, as if we could be sure about him. "Arthur" has to mean something like "the reputed protagonist in what happened here", leaving the question of identity open. Occasionally a phrase like "the real Arthur" is hard to avoid, but it should not cause a serious difficulty.

What to do about places that have no claim to inclusion outside medieval fancy—in other words, purely literary sites? When plainly fictitious they can be dismissed. It would be futile trying to locate Corbenic, the castle where the Grail was kept. However, if a romance-place can be identified with a real one, or people have said it can, it seems right to give it a mention and explain where it is meant to be. That applies, for instance, to Joyous Gard, Lancelot's castle. On the other hand a literary site may be real and well-known, but not in a way that makes it seriously Arthurian. The author is simply inventing. So it sometimes is with Geoffrey of Monmouth. He describes Arthur issuing edicts at York. He has no known grounds for doing so, and there is nothing relevant to see on the spot. York, therefore, despite its beauty and historical stature, does not qualify for this particular Guide.

There are hybrid cases, where a motif that started with romancers has generated a local legend, perhaps not very long ago. Thus, the casting away of Excalibur has given an Arthurian aura to Dozmary Pool in Cornwall and other bodies of water where the event is said—now—to have happened. Still, even in the absence of genuine tradition, there is one sound reason for putting such places in: you can go and see them. That, in the end, is what a Guide is about.

How to use the Guide

The main body of this Guide is simply a gazetteer listing all the places in alphabetical order. After it, there are two aids to the reader: a "Key by characters and themes" and a set of maps.

Suppose you have a special interest in (for example) Merlin. Turn to the "Key by characters and themes", and look him up. Under his name you will find all the headings which are concerned with him, grouped together. You can then turn back to the gazetteer, pick them out, and discover what is said under each.

Or suppose you are planning a tour, and want to know all the Arthurian sites in (for example) North Wales. Turn to the maps and look up North Wales. All the headings from the book are pinpointed on the map, so, as before, you can pick these out in the gazetteer and read what is said. But on the scale which is feasible in a book, these maps can supply only a rough guidance. So, with most items, information is given in the text to fix their whereabouts.

First, the heading includes the county (where applicable), or in Scotland the region, as laid down in 1974 when local government was reorganized. Where the old county reference would have been different, that is given also, in brackets. Since many of the new geographic units were formed by combining old ones, the bracketed name often gives a more exact definition, showing which part of the new unit is concerned. This is obvious with "Hereford and Worcester (Herefordshire)". It may be less obvious with "Gwynedd (Anglesey)" or "Borders (Peebles)".

(Ongoing reconstructions of local government present a problem, especially in Wales and Scotland. The headings in the first edition have been retained here; these names are embodied in may reference books and maps. But owing to further reorganization in 1996, some of them, though time-honoured geographically and historically—such as Dyfed, Gwynedd, Strathclyde—have been deprived of official status or re-defined. The bracked names may, as ever, be more descriptive. Some have been revived.)

Secondly, most headings are accompanied by a National Grid reference, so that the place can be found on an Ordnance Survey map. The chief exceptions are the headings over articles that deal with the following, where a reference would be pointless or misleading:

• Entire counties (e.g. Cornwall)
• Large cities with several Arthurian associations, or stories which are only vaguely located (e.g. London, Manchester)
• Places which are named in Arthurian texts, and are probably real, but cannot be firmly identified (e.g. Camlann)
• Places belonging to legend and romance, where any relationship to the real map is debatable (e.g. Camelot).

Finally, an indication is usually given of the road leading to the spot or the best method of reaching it. I have not, however, been able to re-visit every single site to make sure roads have not been re-routed or re-numbered since the previous edition of the book—but the Ordnance Survey reference remains reliable.

When something is printed in **bold type**, this means that there is a separate article under that heading, where the item can be looked up.

Ordnance Survey maps

In Britain, the Ordnance Survey produces extremely detailed maps of all parts of the country, and these are widely available from bookshops and stationers. A grid reference such as ST 628252 for Cadbury Castle locates a site to within 100 metres: ST identifies a 100-kilometre square in the national grid. Measuring from its bottom left corner, the site is 62·8km east and 25·2km north.

Tours of Arthurian Britain

Geoffrey Ashe joins Frances Howard-Gordon and Jamie George of Gothic Image in hoping that all who travel with this book will enjoy whatever they experience through it, and in wishing them each a safe and happy journey.

Regular tours through many of the places described in this book, and further afield to the shrines and holy places of Ireland and Scotland, are organized each year, from May to October, by Gothic Image Tours.

Parties are small and friendly and are accompanied by expert guides—sometimes Geoffrey Ashe himself—who know the history, lore and spiritual tradition of the places visited. Special arrangements can be made for those who would like to travel with their own groups of friends or associates.

For further details and discussion, write, fax or call Jamie George at Gothic Image:

7 High Street, Glastonbury, Somerset, England, BA6 9DP
telephone +44 1458 83 1453; fax 83 1666
email *idea@isleofavalon.co.uk*

Helpful information for travellers can be obtained from:

Australia
British Tourist Authority
8th Floor, University Centre
Midland House
210 Clarence Street
Sydney, NSW 2000
Tel: 264 3300
Fax: 267 4442

Belgium
British Tourist Authority
306 Avenue Louise
1050 Brussels
Tel: 646 35 10
Fax: 646 39 86

Canada
British Tourist Authority
111 Avenue Road, Suite 450
Toronto, Ontario, M5R 3J8
Tel: (416) 925 6326
Fax: (416) 961 2175

Denmark
British Tourist Authority
Montergade 3
1116 Copenhagen K
Tel: 33 12 34 41
Fax: 33 14 01 36

France
British Tourist Authority
Maison de la Grande Bretagne
19 rue des Mathurins
75009 Paris
Tel: 44 51 56 22
Fax: 44 51 56 21

Germany
British Tourist Authority
Taunusstrasse 52 60
60329 Frankfurt
Tel: 238 0711
Fax: 238 0717

Hong Kong
British Tourist Authority
Room 1504, Eton Tower
8 Hysan Avenue
Causeway Bay
Hong Kong
Tel: 2882 8724
Fax: 2577 1443

India
British Tourist Authority
306 Commercial Plaza
DLF Qutab Enclave Phase 1
Gurgaon, India 122002
Tel: 350 828
Fax: 350 829

Ireland
British Tourist Authority
18–19 College Green
Dublin 2
Tel: 670 8100
Fax: 670 8244

Italy
British Tourist Authority
Corso Vittorio Emanuele 337
00186 Rome
Tel: 688 06102
Fax: 687 9095

British Tourist Authority
Corso Magenta 32
20123 Milano
Tel: 7201 0099
Fax: 7201 0086

Japan
British Tourist Authority
Tokyo Club Bldg
3 2 6 Kasumigaseki
Chiyoda-Ku, Tokyo 100
Tel: 3592 5791/2
Fax: 3581 5797

Korea
British Tourist Authority
#723 Baijai Bldg
55-4 Seosomun-dong
Chung-Ku, Seoul
Tel: 773 1509
Fax: 779 6066

Netherlands
British Tourist Authority
Aurora Gebouw (5e)
Stadhouderskade 2
1054 ES Amsterdam
Tel: 685 2351
Fax: 618 6868

New Zealand
British Tourist Authority
3rd Floor, Dilworth Building
Corner Queen & Customs Streets
Auckland 1
Tel: 303 1446
Fax: 377 6965

Norway
British Tourist Authority
Nedre Slotts Gt 21, 4 etasje
N-0117 Oslo
Postbox 1554 Vika
N-0117 Oslo
Tel: 42 47 45 (as soon as
you hear voice, press 201)
Fax: 42 48 74

Portugal
British Tourist Authority
Rua Luciano Cordeiro, 123
2° Dr°
1050 Lisbon
Tel: 312 9023
Fax: 312 9030

Singapore
British Tourist Authority
24 Raffles Place
#19 06 Clifford Centre
Singapore 0104
Tel: 534 4702
Fax: 534 4703

South Africa
British Tourist Authority
Lancaster Gate
Hyde Park Lane
Hyde Park
Sandton 2196
Tel: (011) 325 0342
Fax: (011) 325 0344

Spain
British Tourist Authority
Torre de Madrid 6/5
Pza. de España 18
28008 Madrid
Tel: 559 65 91
Fax: 542 81 49

Sweden
British Tourist Authority
Box 745
S 101 35 Stockholm
Tel: 21 83 64
Fax: 21 31 29

Switzerland
British Tourist Authority
Limmatquai 78
CH-8001 Zurich
Tel: 261 42 77
Fax: 251 44 56

Taiwan
British Tourist Authority
7th Floor, Fu Key Building
99 Jen Ai Road. Sec 2
Taipei 10625
Tel: 2 351 0991
Fax: 2 392 6653

USA—New York
British Tourist Authority
7th Floor
551 Fifth Avenue
New York, NY 10176-0799
Tel: (212) 986 2200
Fax: (212) 986 1188

USA—Chicago
British Tourist Authority
625 N Michigan Avenue
Suite 1510
Chicago, IL 60611
Tel: (312) 787 0464
Fax: (312) 787 9641

USA—Miami
British Tourist Authority
Columbus Center
1 Alhambra Plaza
Suite 1465
Coral Gables, FL 33134
Tel: (305) 529 9444
Fax: (305) 529 1812

USA—Los Angeles
British Tourist Authority
PO Box 711087
Los Angeles, CA 90071
Tel: (213) 628 5731
Fax: (213) 628 8681

Arthurian
BRITAIN

ARTHURIAN SITES
A–Z

Aberffraw
Gwynedd (Anglesey)   *SH 355690*

A village in south-west **Anglesey** beside the A4080, at the
head of the estuary running down to Aberffraw Bay. It was
the capital of **Gwynedd**, which was taking shape as a
kingdom in the fifth century. There was an early belief that
Arthur would have come here to hold court as a paramount ruler. Medieval writers, however, prefer to connect
his Welsh activities with places better known in the Middle
Ages, such as **St David's**.

  Excavation has shown that the royal residence was
probably a Roman fort within the boundaries of the present
village. Its rampart seems to have been rebuilt in the fifth
or sixth century.

Aberystwyth
Dyfed (Cardiganshire)   *SN 582817*

Some say the Holy Grail is here (or was), in a bank vault.
See **Nanteos**. A short distance inland up the A44 is **Llanbadarn Fawr**, the scene of one of the most unflattering
stories ever told of Arthur.

Agned

Nennius says Arthur's eleventh battle "took place on the
mountain which is called Agned". This name is unhelpful.
It does not even imply mountainous country, because the
word *mons* in Nennius's Latin need not mean more than a
hill. No one has yet put forward a convincing identification. But see **Edinburgh**.

  Some copies of Nennius give the site of the eleventh
battle as **Breguoin**.

Alclud or Alcluith
—see **Dumbarton**

Alderley Edge
Cheshire   *SJ 859779*

A few miles west and north-west of Macclesfield the
ground falls away to the Cheshire plain. Alderley Edge is

the north side of a ridge along which the B5087 passes before descending into a town of the same name. A sign beside the road points along a path to "the Edge", which is a National Trust property. The path goes down a flight of steps to another path that runs at right angles to it, through woods clinging to a very steep slope—here and there, almost a cliff.

Geologically the Edge is sandstone, and shows reddish in places. If, at the bottom of the steps, you turn left, the path goes under huge outcrops of mossy rock and presently comes to a spot where water drips from the rock into a small stone trough. This is the visible token of the Alderley Edge legend.

Once upon a time, the story goes, a farmer was on his way to Macclesfield market riding a white mare which he

Alderley Edge: The carved face in the rock above the wishing-well associated with Merlin.

hoped to sell. As he went along the ridge road he was stopped by a grey-bearded man who offered to buy her. The farmer thought his offer too low and rode on to Macclesfield. But although the mare was warmly admired, no purchaser came forward and at last he remounted to return home.

Again the man stopped him, saying he had a fresh offer to make. He led the farmer off the highway and through the woods on the Edge, to a rock on which he laid his hand. It moved aside revealing a pair of gates. The awestruck farmer dismounted, and led the mare into a cavern beyond.

"In here," said the stranger. "King Arthur and his knights lie asleep till their country needs them. Their horses are with them—all but one. They want another white horse. Will you sell yours?" He held out a purse of gold. The farmer snatched it and ran from the cave in terror. As soon as he was out of the gates they crashed shut behind him. The rock returned to its place and no one has ever identified it since.

The story may have been inspired or at least encouraged by actual caves farther down, and by traditions of Roman copper mines. Supposedly, the horse buyer was Merlin. The little trough with the water dripping into it counts as a wishing well. On the rock about eight feet above is an inscription in capitals:

> DRINK OF THIS AND TAKE THY FILL FOR THE
> WATER FALLS BY THE WIZARDS WILL

The letters are cut deep. They are not ancient in style. Above the word "DRINK", however, a face is carved in the rock, and this is much more heavily weathered, as if it were older.

Compare the **Melrose** legend.

Alnwick

Northumberland   *NU 188136*

When speaking of Lancelot's castle **Joyous Gard**, Malory offers two locations for it. "Some men say it was Alnwick and some men say it was Bamburgh." Alnwick Castle dates from the eleventh century. The area was settled by Angles 400–500 years before it was built. But, for the story of Lancelot to have any factual backtround, there would have had to be a British stronghold earlier still, and there is no sign of this. Malory's other candidate, **Bamburgh**, is more interesting.

Amesbury
Wiltshire   *SU 150419*

The Welsh triads speak of "Three Perpetual Choirs"— British religious communities of the early sixth century, where monks chanted the Divine Office in relays without a break, a practice known as *laus perennis*. In each of them, it is claimed with an improbable flourish, "there were 2,400 religious men, that is there were a hundred for every hour of the day and night in rotation." One wonders how the 2,300 not on duty would have managed to sleep. As to which monasteries did this, different triads say differently. They agree, however, that one of them was **Glastonbury**, famous for its Arthurian connections. Another with such connections, which gets a triadic mention if not in the best and earliest texts, is Amesbury.

To judge from the early form of its name, "Ambres-byrig", it had some sort of link with Ambrosius Aurelianus, the Romanized Briton who launched the anti-Saxon counter-attack with which Arthur is associated. Geoffrey of Monmouth transposes his name into "Aurelius Ambrosius" and says he was Uther's brother, and therefore Arthur's uncle. Amesbury may have got its name because he founded the monastery. More likely, however, he stationed troops there. In the anarchic twilight of Rome, armies were sometimes named after the emperors or pretenders who raised them. Ambrosius's men would have been the Ambrosiaci, and any base of theirs might have become the "camp" or "settlement" of the Ambrosiaci and eventually, for the Saxons who took over, Ambres-byrig.

Amesbury lies below the east rim of **Salisbury Plain**, in the valley of the Avon. The river makes an S-shaped bend, and the monastery (which did exist, though hardly with 2,400 monks) was in the northern loop of the S, on what is now wooded ground behind the church of Saints Mary and Melor. The main through road is the A303. As it leaves the town on the west it passes the church, crosses the Avon by the more southerly of two bridges, and swings right in a long transverse climb on to the Plain. After that, **Stone-henge** comes into view fairly soon.

Geoffrey of Monmouth knows of Amesbury as well as **Stonehenge**, but he is muddled about them both. He speaks of a Cloister of Ambrius on Mount Ambrius, and says it was here that Hengist and the Saxons met the British nobles for a peace conference and murdered them. The victims were buried in the monks' graveyard. Later Merlin set up **Stonehenge** around the burial-place as a monument, on the same Mount Ambrius as the monastery. Nothing will make these assertions fit the map. Probably Geoffrey was never at the place himself, and only had a confused memory of someone talking about "the hill at Amesbury where you see Stonehenge from the top", or words to that effect.

Malory believed that there was a women's community at Amesbury as well as the male one. He may have been right, though he was probably thinking of a house founded by the Saxon queen Elfrida long after Arthur's time. The base of one of its columns is in the church of Saints Mary and Melor. In Malory's story Guinevere retires to Amesbury after her husband's passing. When Lancelot arrives from France, too late to rescue the kingdom, he rides to see her in the convent. She tells him of her sorrow that Arthur and so many good men are dead because of their love, and says they must never meet again, refusing even a farewell kiss. Thereupon Lancelot himself retires to a hermitage near **Glastonbury**.

Anglesey
Gwynedd

An early Welsh poem says that Cai (the Sir Kay of romance) went to Anglesey and confronted a monster, Palug's Cat, which had eaten 180 warriors. The poem breaks off before making it clear which killed the other, though it seems to imply a win for Cai.

This giant Anglesey cat is mentioned in several writings and spoken of as speckled. It began as a kitten that swam ashore from the Menai Strait. Palug's sons rescued and raised it, finding too late that this was ill-advised. A "rational" explanation would be that the story grew round a leopard cub which escaped from a ship bearing exotic cargo to some rich chieftain. But in the background of the Welsh legend there may be Irish ones about huge "sea-cats". Some of these sound as if they were based on yarns told by sailors who had seen walruses. After all, a large species of seal is still called a sea-lion; the feline notion has lingered on. Whatever Palug's Cat was, it left a memory of terror. One twelfth-century French writer quotes a poem about Arthur himself fighting it, and actually being slain by it, but he assures us that this is a "proven lie".

In the verse romance *Sir Gawain and the Green Knight*, Gawain passes Anglesey on the far side of the strait, but the island plays no part in the story. It does, however, have several Arthurian locations. See **Abberfraw**, **Arthur's Quoit (1)**, **(2)**, **Arthur's Stone (5)**, **Ogof Arthur**, **Round Table (2)**.

Annwn

An Otherworld or Underworld of Welsh legend, one of many survivals from pagan Celtic mythology. Various hills and islands are points of access to it. The most important hill is the Tor at **Glastonbury**; the most important island is **Lundy**. Another island is Grassholm off the Pembroke coast.

Annwn's inhabitants have human form, but are not strictly human. They are immortals—fairy-folk or demons, according to one's point of view. Some are gods thinly disguised. Living humans can enter Annwn, and so can spirits of the dead, but it is neither a heaven nor a hell in the Christian sense. To a certain extent it resembles **Avalon**. The two places, in fact, are not wholly distinguishable. But **Avalon** has no underworld aspect, and Annwn tends to seem more extensive, eerie and dangerous.

In the Welsh tale *Culhwch and Olwen*, one of the heroes at Arthur's court is Gwyn son of Nudd. Gwyn has a mysterious power over the demons of Annwn, given him by God "lest this world be destroyed". The legendary "Life" of St Collen portrays Gwyn as Annwn's king—certainly, no mortal figure—and locates his palace at **Glastonbury** on, or in, the Tor. In folkore he is a leader of what is known as the Wild Hunt, careering through the sky with a pack of red-eared hounds of Annwn, summoning the souls of the dead. A ghostly Arthur sometimes accompanies him, with spectral attendants. In the Middle Ages these were said to drop to ground level and ride through the woods under the full moon, telling foresters they were of Arthur's household.

Gwyn's father Nudd was once the British god Nodons, who had a temple at Lydney in the Forest of Dean, excavated in modern times; and his Otherworld is the scene of the oldest known story foreshadowing the Quest of the Grail. This is a Welsh poem called *The Spoils of Annwn*. It tells in cryptic language how Arthur and his men sailed through perilous waters among island fortresses, in quest of the magic cauldron of Annwn, kept by nine maidens. Only seven of the adventurers returned. If the poet has real places in mind at all, he may be thinking of offshore islands of Wales, or of the Somerset hills which once rose above a sheet of water covering what are now the "Levels".

Archenfield
—see **Ercing**

Arfderydd
—see **Arthuret**

Arthurbank
—see **Arthur's Fold**

Arthuret
Cumbria (Cumberland)   *NY 404729*

A parish adjoining the Scottish border below the confluence of the Liddel and Esk. Its largest populated place is Longtown. Arthuret's role in Arthurian tradition is an oddity. For one thing, the name has nothing to do with Arthur. Its early form is "Arfderydd". Also, the important event here was a battle fought between opposed British armies in 573, long after Arthur's time. It is important because of the part it played in the legend of Merlin.

The battlefield was on the northern edge of the parish, near the stronghold of one of the chief warriors, Gwenddolau. This was called Caer Gwenddolau, Gwenddolau's Fort, a name later corrupted to "Carwhinelow" and then to "Carwinley". It still appears as such on the map. All that can be seen at Carwinley today is a quiet prospect of woods and low hills. However, nearer to Liddel Water, traces of early fortifications remain.

Two of Gwenddolau's kinsmen, Peredur and Gwrgi, are mentioned among his enemies, so the clash had the special tragedy of a civil war. A Welsh triad calls the affair one of the three "frivolous" or "futile" battles, because it was fought over a lark's nest. This is a bitter joke. The quarrel was concerned with Caerlaverock, the Fort of the Lark, on the north side of the Solway Firth near the mouth of the Nith. The carnage was fearful and several of the leaders were killed.

Geoffrey of Monmouth brings this battle into a *Life of Merlin* which he wrote some years after his *History*. He solves the difficulty over the late date by simply changing it, putting the battle much sooner after Arthur's passing. Merlin, he says, took part in it, and his horror at the slaughter drove him half-mad so that he wandered off into the northern forest of **Celidon**. There he lived wild and uttered prophecies.

Strangely, it is in this tale that Geoffrey comes closest to giving us a Merlin who can be pinned down as a real person. The man he is thinking of is the bard Myrddin. Scraps of poetry survive which are attributed to him. The story of his wild wanderings and prophetic inspiration is earlier than Geoffrey. Much the same story is told of another sixth-century character called Lailoken. But the Lailoken story is so like Myrddin's that they are probably the same man under two different names. Myrddin, or Lailoken, was built up into the famous prophet and wizard partly through a belief that he was born at **Carmarthen** and was the hero of earlier Welsh exploits as well as the northern ones.

Geoffrey put together his account of Merlin piecemeal and somewhat confusedly. In the *History* he introduced Myrddin, his name Latinized into Merlin, as a wonder-worker in fifth-century Wales. Having, perhaps, found out more about him, he wrote the story of the battle of Arthuret afterwards. Medieval critics noticed that the battle happened too late, and some suggested that there were two Merlins, one of them senior to Arthur and the other junior. Certainly the only way of fitting all the Merlin stories to one person would be to suppose that he lived to be well over 100 and still had the stamina to fight in a battle and roam outdoors in Scottish forests. (Perhaps, after his treacherous lady imprisoned him in a cave or tree, he went into suspended animation and escaped many years later rejuvenated?)

For other places that figured in the process of Merlin-making, see **Carmarthen**, **Dinas Emrys**, **Drumelzier**, **Stonehenge**.

Arthurhouse
Grampian (Kincardineshire)   *NO 748718*

This name has been given to a cairn on the hill of Garvock east of Laurencekirk. A track and path lead along the ridge from the B9120. The reason why this cairn should have been so called is obscure. However, the name gives it the distinction of being the most northerly Arthurian site.

Arthur Lee
Strathclyde (Renfrewshire)   *NS 505588*

In Neilston parish there used to be three villages called Arthur Lee, Low Arthur Lee, and West Arthur Lee. Barrhead, on the A736 out of Glasgow, has virtually swallowed them up, but the name survives in Arthurlie and West Arthurlie, which are parts of the town. West Arthurlie (NS 491585) is still distinguishable. Some legend of Arthur's wars in **Strathclyde**, against Hueil and others, may account for his being commemorated here.

Arthurlie
—see **Arthur Lee**

Arthur's Bed
Cornwall   *SX 240757*

A granite monolith lying on a ridge among rocky outcroppings on Bodmin Moor. Wind and rain have hollowed the upper surface into a coffin-like shape. Access is from the B3254 at Berriowbridge, by minor road, track and footpath running west past Hawk's Tor.

    See also Appendix.

Arthur's Bridge
Somerset   *ST 638359*

A bridge over the Alham on the road from Castle Cary to Shepton Mallet (A371). The name is probably a modern one suggested by the Somerset Arthur legends.

Arthur's Castle

—see **Dumbarton**

Arthur's Cave

Hereford and Worcester (Herefordshire)   *SO 545155*

Two or three miles north-east of Monmouth, above the
Wye on the fringes of the Forest of Dean, is Arthur's Cave
—or *King* Arthur's, the royal prefix being a more settled
part of the name here than it is with the various seats,
stones and so forth. The approach is by a small road
leaving the A40 at **Ganarew**, which has a relevant legend
of its own, centred on the hill-fort of Little Doward. The
cave is on the far side of that hill, in a beech wood near a
quarry. Whatever the justification for its name, one fact is
known about it—that it goes farther back into the human
past than any other Arthurian site. Hunting families lived
in it towards the end of the Old Stone Age, 10,000 years or
more ago, leaving bones and flint implements. There was a
second phase of occupation during the Middle Stone Age,
and perhaps a third in late Roman times.

*Arthur's Cave, Herefordshire: This is one of the few caves
connected with Arthur that can be found and visited. Most of
them are supposed to be magically concealed.*

The cave owes its name to the associations of Little Doward and **Ganarew**. Something of the same kind happened at **Cadbury Castle**. Yet the connection of this particular cave with Arthur is unusual. Caves seldom figure in his personal folklore except as locales of the "sleeping king" legend. At **Cadbury** and almost everywhere else, that legend depends on the cave being elusive; nobody ever actually finds it. Here it is real and can be explored, revealing no sleeper. The explanation may lie in some old belief about a deeper chamber with a blocked entry; or in folk-memories of the ancient inhabitants, made uncanny by lapse of time, as with the witch of Wookey Hole in Somerset. See further **Cave-legend, sites of**.

A "rational" explanation of Arthur's Cave is that he used it as a hiding-place for his soldiers. The legend of **Ogof Arthur** might be cited in support of that theory.

Arthur's Chair

(1)

A rock formation, which was pointed out in 1113 to some French priests travelling west from Exeter, as one of the party recorded. It cannot now be identified, but was on Dartmoor or Bodmin Moor, and doubtless within sight of the road they travelled by. See also **Arthur's Oven**, and, for the full story of the priests and their journey, **Bodmin**.

(2)
—see **Brecon Beacons**

(3)
—see **Sewingshields**

(4)
—see **Tintagel**

Arthur's Cups and Saucers
—see **Tintagel**

Arthur's Downs
—see **Arthur's Hall**

Arthur Seat

—see **Arthur's Seat (3)**

Arthur's Fold
Tayside (Perthshire)

Scottish writers refer to a farm of this name near Arthur-stone, up the A94 north-east of Coupar Angus. The hint would have come from the Perthshire legend of Arthur. See **Arthur's Stone (6)**, **Barry Hill**, **Meigle**. The farm no longer exists under this name, but there is an Arthurbank (NO 254427).

Arthur's Fountain
Strathclyde (Lanarkshire)

In a land grant by David de Lindesay dated 1339, a *Fons Arthuri* in the parish of Crawford is mentioned as a land-mark. Crawford (NS 956205) is beside the A74 where it briefly runs close to the upper Clyde. The "Fountain" would have been a spring or a well. As with some other sites, the most interesting thing is the date of the document, proving as it does that the spring—or well—was named after Arthur so long ago.

Arthur's Grave

As an early poem testifies, while many British warriors had traditional graves, Arthur's was a mystery and not to be spoken of. Whatever the reason for that silence, the burgeoning folk-belief that he was not dead at all helped to preserve it. "Graves" of Arthur are not as numerous as sites of the cave-legend affirming his immortality. In fact there is only one serious claimant which has been written about, discussed, and examined, the grave at **Glastonbury**. In a few other places his name is mentioned, but he has been brought in fancifully on ground that does not belong to him. Two instances will make the point.

(1)   The Giant's Grave, Warbstow
Cornwall   *SX 202908*

This is a long mound in the double-ramparted hill-fort of

Warbstow Bury, up a small road that leaves the A395 at Hallworthy. Warbstow is six or seven miles to the north-east of **Slaughter Bridge** on the Camel, the Cornish candidate for the scene of **Camlann** where Arthur fell. Hence the name "Arthur's Grave" sometimes given to the barrow. But the giant was the original occupant. He lived in the hill-fort and was killed by a tool thrown at him by the giant of Launceston Castle.

(2)   Bedd Arthur, Prescelly Mountains
Dyfed (Pembrokeshire)   *SN 130325*

"Arthur's Grave" in Welsh. A cairn on a hill-top. This, or a nearby natural outcrop, is sometimes called Carn Arthur. In this part of the country Arthur hunted the boar Twrch Trwyth, as told in *Culhwch and Olwen*. The monster killed several of his fellow-hunters at Foel-cwmcerwyn a couple of miles away. But as Arthur himself survived, even the legend gives no basis for the "grave".

See also **Arthur's Stone (2)**, **Slaughter Bridge** (for Arthur's "tomb"), and **Snowdonia** (for Carnedd Arthur).

Arthur's Hall
Cornwall   *SX 130777*

A stone enclosure on Bodmin Moor, where the upward slope east of St Breward rises towards Garrow Tor. It is a rectangle lined with granite slabs. John Norden, who saw it

Arthur's Hall, Bodmin Moor.

in the late sixteenth century, describes it as "a square plot about 60 foot long and about 35 foot broad situated in a plain mountain wrought some 3 foot in the ground". He adds that it is "set round about with flat stones" and holds water. It has, in fact, a stone bottom, and while it may be prehistoric, it may also be a reservoir of much later date. Its water-holding aspect has not deterred fancy from seeing it as the remains of a building and even specifying its purpose. It is one of the Cornish sites sometimes called **Arthur's Hunting Lodge**.

The place can be reached by track and footpath from St Breward. A rise just north of it is "Arthur's Downs". Some rocky basins round about are "Arthur's Troughs", because, according to local lore, he fed his dogs in them.

See further the Appendix.

Arthur's Hill
—see **Arthur's Seat (3)**, **Brecon Beacons**, **Moel Arthur**, and the Appendix

Arthur's Hilltop
—see **Brecon Beacons**

Arthur's Hunting Causeway
—see **Cadbury Castle**

Arthur's Hunting Lodge
or **Hunting Seat**

Arthur as huntsman has been located at two Cornish sites which are linked with him, if tenuously, in other ways. One is **Arthur's Hall**, the stone-lined enclosure near Garrow Tor. The other is the hill-fort **Castle-an-Dinas**. These are quite unlike. But in both cases the moorland setting suggests the aristocratic sport of hunting wild deer.

Beside **Cadbury Castle** is Arthur's Hunting Causeway. For places connected with his great legendary boar-hunt in *Culhwch and Olwen*, see **Arthur's Grave (2)**, **Buelt**, **Pen-Arthur**. For his posthumous role as a huntsman in the realm of shades, see **Annwn**.

Arthur's Lane

—see **Cadbury Castle**

Arthur's O'en or O'on

Central (Stirlingshire)   *NS 879827*

"O'en", that is, "oven". A Roman building which formerly stood near the site of the Carron Ironworks, just north of Falkirk on the Stenhousemuir side of the River Carron. It is mentioned as a landmark, the *Furnus Arthuri*, in a document dated 1293. An eighteenth-century engraving shows a dome-shaped structure about 12 feet high, with steps leading up to an arched doorway and a window at the top. The Industrial Revolution effaced it and there is no longer anything to see. The main point of interest is that it can be proved to have been given its Arthurian name so long ago. Possibly the nearby Roman town of **Camelon** was thought to be **Camlann**.

Arthur's Oven

Pointed out in 1113 to some French priests travelling west from Exeter. What they saw may have been **King's Oven** on Dartmoor. See also **Arthur's Chair (1)** and **Bodmin**.

For another "oven", see the previous item.

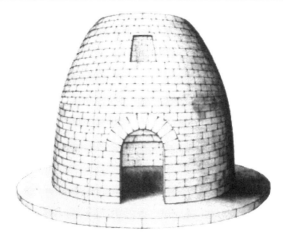

Arthur's O'en, which stood in Stenhousemuir.

Arthur's Palace
—see **Cadbury Castle**

Arthur's Pot
—see **Gwal y Filiast**

Arthur's Quoit

This is the commonest Arthurian name for a stone. Most of the Quoits are in Wales and generally known by the Welsh name Coetan Arthur.

(1)   near Llwydiarth Fawr
Gwynedd (Anglesey)   *SH 432855*

The "quoit" is a rocking stone, otherwise called Maen Chwyf. The closest road is the B5111, a mile north of Llanerchymedd.

(2)   near Moelfre
Gwynedd (Anglesey)   *SH 501860*

The capstone of the Lligwy dolmen or prehistoric burial-chamber.

(3)   south of Tudweilog
Gwynedd (Caernarvonshire)   *SH 230346*

Remains of a burial-chamber close to the B4417.

(4)   north of Criccieth
Gwynedd (Caernarvonshire)   *SH 499413*

The "quoit", as in several other places, is the capstone of a burial-chamber.

(5)   near Llanenddwyn
Gwynedd (Merionethshire)   *SH 588229*

Part of a chambered long cairn, also called Carreg Arthur, near the A496. When it was excavated a local man pro-

phesied that interference with the "old stones" would bring
bad weather, and bad weather duly followed. Treasure is
supposed to be hidden here.

(6)   on St David's Head
Dyfed (Pembrokeshire)   *SM 725281*

The capstone of a burial-chamber in a round barrow.

(7)   in Llanllawer parish
Dyfed (Pembrokeshire)   *SN 000360*

Two miles east of Fishguard on the A487 a minor road turns
south. Shortly before it reaches the B4313, another minor
road runs east from it and comes to a row of standing stones,
the only one in this part of Wales. Nearby are the remains
of a dolmen. The "quoit" was its capstone. The structure
was broken up in 1864 by a man who built the stones into a
house. He admitted that he had had bad luck thereafter.

(8)   near Newport
Dyfed (Pembrokeshire)   *SN 060394*

Remains of a burial-chamber. Perhaps through confusion,
the name has also been applied to the unusual and curiously spindly one at Pentre Ifan (SN 100370).

(9)   at Pontarllechau
Dyfed (Carmarthenshire)   *SN 729245*

This is on the A4069 three miles south of Llangadog. In
the bed of the River Sawdde are two rocks. One is the
"quoit". Arthur is said to have thrown it from the top of
Pen-Arthur, a mile away. The rock beside it was a pebble
in the shoe of a lady contemporary with him, who tossed it
into the river from the same hill.
     For other legends of this kind, with a "giant" motif, see
Arthur's Stone (1) and **Sewingshields**.

(10)
—see **Tintagel**

(11)
—see **Trethevy Quoit**

Arthur's Seat

(1)   in Edinburgh   *NT 275729*

Easily the best known of the natural features so called. A
hill to the east of the Scottish capital, 823 feet high, the
rocky remnant of an extinct volcano. With adjacent hills it
occupies most of Holyrood Park and overlooks the city.
The Palace of Holyroodhouse is at its foot. The "seat"
notion was suggested by the dip between two high points
(compare Arthur's Chair in the **Brecon Beacons**).

   The hill has traces of early defensive works. It is mentioned, and named, by the fifteenth-century Scots poet
Kennedy ("*Arthur Sate* or ony hicher hill"), and by William Camden in his *Britannia*, a survey of the British Isles
published in 1586. For the possible connection with Arthur,
see **Edinburgh**.

(2)   at Dumbarrow
Tayside (Angus)   *NO 552479*

"Arthur's Seat" is a name sometimes given to Dumbarrow
Hill. It lies to the south of the minor road running east from
Letham, and has remains of a small hill-fort. The "seat"
may have been suggested, as with (1), by the fact that the
hill has two tops with a slight dip between them. The
occurrence of Arthur's name so far afield must be ascribed
to his Perthshire legend (see **Barry Hill** and **Meigle**). At
some stage in story-telling Arthur probably took the place
of a Pictish hero. He is supposed to have fought a battle
with Modred near Dunnichen, on the other side of Letham.
But this was the battle of Nechtansmere, a Pictish affair in
685, long after Arthur.

(3)   east of Liddesdale
Cumbria (Cumberland)   *NY 495783*

This "Arthur's Seat" is also called Arthur Seat and Arthur's
Hill. No large town is anywhere near. The closest road is
the B6318. A lane runs north from the road through a
reafforested area with trees planted in rows. A few hundred
yards up the lane, the hill rises ahead. It is of very moderate size and wooded on top.

(4)   *Dumfries and Galloway (Dumfriesshire)*
NT 110126

A mountain in the Hart Fell area. This was in the ancient forest of Celidon, which has important associations with Merlin.

(5)
—see **Ben Arthur**

Arthur's Spear
—see **Ffon y Cawr**

Arthur's Stone

(1)   near Reynoldston
West Glamorgan   *SS 490905*

Outside Reynoldston on the road to Swansea is the ridge of Cefn Bryn Common. It is one of the highest parts of the Gower peninsula and centrally placed. Well up on the northern side is a megalithic burial-chamber known as Maen Cetti. As so often, whatever covering mound it once had has gone, leaving it bare. The stone uprights are small

Arthur's Stone (1), near Reynoldstone.

and squat. Four of them support a gigantic wedge-shaped capstone weighing about 25 tons. It is 14 feet long, 6½ feet across and 7 feet deep. It used to be even bigger, but pieces were broken off to be made into millstones, or simply for vandalism's own sake. There is a split in it, said to have been made by St David to destroy its aura of sacredness; or, perhaps, by Arthur. In any case the capstone is Arthur's Stone.

Legend has it that when Arthur was walking through Carmarthenshire on his way to **Camlann**, he felt a pebble in his shoe and tossed it away. It flew seven miles over Burry Inlet and landed in Gower, on top of the smaller stones of Maen Cetti, which were already there. Hence the capstone. This is one of the rare legends where Arthur is a giant himself and not simply a battler with giants. Compare the stories of **Arthur's Quoit (9)** and of King's Crags at **Sewingshields**. Another tale is that at full moon his ghost, clad in luminous armour, emerges from the dolmen and walks down towards the sea. The ghost is of normal size. At Midsummer Eve and All-Hallows Eve, the stones themselves go to the sea to drink or bathe.

Full moon used to witness a custom having nothing to do with Arthur. Girls climbed the hill at midnight and put honey-cakes dipped in milk on top of the great stone. Then they crawled round it three times—or seven times—on hands and knees and waited for their lovers, who, if sincere, were expected to come and join them.

Arthur's Stone (2), near Dorstone, Herefordshire.

(2)   near Dorstone
Hereford and Worcester (Herefordshire)
SO 318431

A lane leaving the B4348, just before it crosses the Dore into the village, runs transversely up a steep ridge towards the high point of Merbach Hill. The ridge overlooks the Golden Valley. Some distance up is Arthur's Stone, or the Stone of Arthur, a low exposed burial-chamber. It is 18 feet by 8. Its huge cracked capstone—"Arthur's Stone" proper —is shaped like a kite, with two smaller stones forming the tail. The entrance passage of the chamber goes in at the other end and makes a sharp turn.

Rival legends agree in claiming that this is a monument over someone's grave. Perhaps the person underneath is Arthur himself. Or it may be an aggressive king whom he killed. Or it may be a giant whom, likewise, he killed. On one stone are marks made by the giant's elbows when he fell dying. On another are marks made by Arthur's knees when he knelt in thanksgiving after the fight. But the real burials here were inside the chamber, not under it, at a time when it was enclosed in a mound, many centuries before Arthur.

(3)   near Llanafan
Dyfed (Cardiganshire)   *SN 726730*

Maen Arthur, Arthur's Stone, in Maen Arthur Wood.

(4)   near Mold
Clwyd (Flintshire)   *SJ 206626*

Two miles along the A494 to **Ruthin** is Colomendy School. Herabouts, nineteenth-century antiquaries speak of another stone called Maen Arthur, with a hollow in it said to be the impression of his horse's hoof. Its identity is uncertain.

(5)   near Llanfechell
Gwynedd (Anglesey)   *SH 368903*

Another Maen Arthur, to the south of the village.

(6)   near Coupar Angus
Tayside (Perthshire)   *NO 261430*

Between Coupar Angus and **Meigle** the A94 passes the large house of Arthurstone. There is, or was, an actual Arthur's

Stone or Stone of Arthur, but nothing is now visible to the public.

Arthur's Table
—see **Gwal y Filiast**, **Round Table (2)** and **(3)**, and Appendix

Arthur's Tomb
—see **Slaughter Bridge**

Arthurstone
—see **Arthur's Stone (6)**

Arthur's Troughs
—see **Arthur's Hall**

Arthur's Well

(1)   near Walltown
Northumberland   *NY 677667*

An Arthur's Well was once associated with "Waltoun-Crags", on the line of **Hadrian's Wall** near Greenhead. The same well had a legend about the baptism of converted Angles during Paulinus's mission to Northumbria, in 627. It cannot now be identified for certain, but may be Green-gate Well a mile to the north-west. Any Arthurian lore heareabouts could be an echo of the group of stories at **Sewingshields**.

(2)
—see **Cadbury Castle**

Arthur's Wood
—see **Coed Arthur**

Arthur's Yard
—see **Buarth Arthur**

Ascalot

An early form of a place-name found in Arthurian romance, better known as **Astolat**.

Astolat

In one of Tennyson's *Idylls of the King*, the poet introduces Elaine as "the lily maid of Astolat". She falls hopelessly in love with Sir Lancelot and dies of grief. The poem is based on Malory, who also calls the place Astolat. In older and less familiar versions it is "Ascalot" or "Escalot"—whence the odd-looking "Shalott" of Tennyson's other poem on the same theme.

When Elaine dies her body is floated downriver on a barge, to a place where Arthur's court is assembled nearby. Except in Malory, no clue emerges as to where Astolat could have been. He, however, speaks of the barge as coming to **Westminster**. We might expect Astolat to be up the Thames. Actually he says it was Guildford. Guildford is on the River Wey, which flows into the Thames well above **Westminster**, but it was not navigable in the Middle Ages, and Malory makes the dying Elaine ask her father and brother to take her body directly to the larger river, a distance of 10 or 12 miles.

The geography is so awkward that we might suspect a tradition of something Arthurian at Guildford, which Malory felt bound to respect. But the real reason is that his plot constrains him. When Arthur and the knights are on their way from **London** to **Camelot**, Astolat is their first halting-place. For Malory (at least in this part of his work) **Camelot** is more or less **Winchester**. Astolat, therefore has to be on the London-Winchester road, and not up the Thames. Hence Guildford.

In the upshot, Astolat seems to be imaginary. It is hard to see any logic in a modern theory making it out to be a misplaced Alclud: see **Dumbarton**.

Avalon

The most famous of the Otherworld places which passed into Arthurian legend from Celtic myth. It is an island, a realm of magic and of mysteries older than Christianity, though they have a role in the Christian order.

Geoffrey of Monmouth mentions it twice in his *History*. He says that Arthur's sword Caliburn was forged in the Isle of Avalon. He also says that when Arthur was mortally wounded in his last battle, he was "carried off to the Isle of Avalon so that his wounds might be attended to". Later, in his *Life of Merlin*, Geoffrey expands the second statement. He introduces the bard Taliesin telling Merlin about this island, which is called Fortunate because of its natural plenty. Its people live for 100 years or more. It is ruled by nine sisters, the chief of whom is Morgen. She is a healer and enchantress, able to fly and change her shape. Taliesin tells how he accompanied the wounded Arthur on that last voyage. Morgen received Arthur with honour, had him placed on a golden bed, and undertook to cure him if he remained on the island.

Geoffrey does not say where Avalon is in either of his books. In the second he seems to be picturing it somewhere over the western sea, but this is mainly because of bits of classical and Irish island-mythology he has worked in, which are false clues. Its name is supposed to be derived from a British word for an apple. Geoffrey, in fact, calls it "the Isle of Apples". Doubtless they would be magical or sacred apples, like those in the Garden of the Hesperides. In Welsh the island is Ynys Avallach or Afallach. This name confuses the issue, because, while it could mean a "place of apples" or orchard, we also find Avallach as the name of a person. Once probably a Celtic god, he is a former king of the island and father of Morgen. As for her, she is the Morgan le Fay of romance, certainly divine in her origins, whom the romancers turn into a sister of Arthur and often make a less attractive figure than she is in her Avalonian setting.

Some folklorists have claimed that Avalon was an abode of the dead. This is debatable. The whole point of Arthur's sojourn there, as the theme develops in legend after Geoffrey, is that he is not dead. He has become immortal, and will some day return to his kingdom. As with the cave-legend, which also makes him immortal, the belief has a Celtic myth in the background about a banished god asleep in a cave in a western island. The golden bed where Arthur lies may be a reminiscence of a "rock looking like gold" on which this god was said to be sleeping.

As an Otherworld, Avalon is like **Annwn**. Indeed, to judge from the group of nine women which appears in both, and from a common linkage with the Grail theme, it may be the same realm—Avalon being the visible part above ground, **Annwn** the vaguer part spreading out into unseen and subterraneous regions. The blurring and overlapping of Otherworlds has something to do with the idea that the real Avalon was **Glastonbury**, which, in folklore, had an entrance to **Annwn** through its Tor. In Arthur's time it was partly surrounded by water. According to the monks of its abbey he was taken there after his last battle, as he was to Avalon, though in their version he died of his wounds and was buried in the monastic graveyard.

In the earliest romance telling how the Grail came to Britain, written by Robert de Boron, it is brought to the "Vales of Avaron". The context makes it clear that this is a slip for "Avalon", and the phrase almost certainly refers to the central Somerset lowland. An "Isle" of Avalon might be purely mythical, but "vales" never had any other meaning than the geographical one.

Badbury

A place-name which has inspired several attempts to locate **Badon**, the scene of the British victory credited to Arthur as his twelfth and crowning battle. There are three villages so called, as well as a hill-fort in Dorset, and Badbury Hill at Great Coxwell near Faringdon in Oxfordshire (formerly Berkshire), which also has earthworks. The most important of the contenders suggested by this name are **Badbury Rings**, the Dorset hill-fort, and **Liddington Castle** near Swindon, which is above one of the villages and used to be called Badbury Castle itself.

Badbury Rings
Dorset   *ST 964030*

An Iron Age hill-fort believed by some to be **Badon**. It is beside the B3082 from Blandford to Wimborne, on a straight stretch where the road is converted into an avenue by lines of trees on both sides. The lane that leads off it to the Rings passes several tumuli, and is part of a Roman road which crossed another on the far side of the fort.

From the base of the triple ramparts the climb is easy, since the top is less than 100 feet higher. The chalky soil has been widely exposed and trampled. Patches of the hill

Badbury Rings.

are wooded, and the summit enclosure is entirely so. Hence, the highest point is hard to locate. Until recently Badbury Rings was one of the few English breeding-places of the raven, an Arthurian bird (see **London**, **Marazion**).

Its claim to be Badon depends, in essence, on the name. There are said to be traces of reoccupation at the right time, but the historical case is poor. Since Arthur's twelfth battle was a decisive triumph, which virtually halted Saxon progress for many years, it must have taken place in a part of Britain where the Saxons were strong—strong enough to fight a battle that was more than a skirmish, with defeat spelling disaster on a scale sufficient to check their whole invasion. This Dorset hinterland would have been a long way from their major early settlements, and not in the path of any plausible offensive.

Badon, Mount

In Latin, *Mons Badonicus*. The scene of Arthur's twelfth battle, the crushing victory over the Saxons which stopped their advance and secured Britain a spell of relative peace. Gildas, writing somewhere about the 530s, implies that it occurred within living memory. He calls it a siege, though he does not tell us who was besieging whom. Nor does he name the British commander. In the *Annales Cambriae* an entry records "the battle of Badon in which Arthur carried the cross of Our Lord Jesus Christ on his shoulders for three days and three nights and the Britons were victors". The "cross" may mean an emblem, or a relic of the supposed True Cross. It has been argued that this entry was inserted in the chronicle long afterwards and has no value as history, but there is a case for accepting it.

Finally, the list of the twelve battles in Nennius rises to this climax: "The twelfth battle was on Mount Badon, in which nine hundred and sixty men fell in one day from one charge of Arthur, and no one overthrew them except himself alone. And in all the battles he stood forth as victor." Again the statement has been challenged, this time on the ground that as no one could have killed 960 men single-handed, the whole passage is suspect. But rumour and heroic legend exaggerate, even when dealing with people much better documented than Arthur. Constantine the Great is said to have routed an army with twelve horsemen. That casts no doubt on Constantine.

Badon was a real battle. As to Arthur's role, tradition manifestly connected him with it, and the glory was never claimed for anyone else. Whether the Britons' commander was the original Arthur, or some associate or successor whose exploits came to be credited to him, is a question that raises issues of date. Gildas makes an obscure statement which is usually taken to mean that the battle happened in the year of his own birth, forty-four years before the time of writing. If so, Mount Badon was fought at a time not enormously remote from AD500. The *Annales* give what looks like a precise year for it, but unfortunately their scheme of numbering poses problems. Converted into our own terms, the year assisgned to Badon may be 518. One theory suggests that a scribe copying the chronicle made a slip, and it is really 499. That would fit in with the usual interpretation of Gildas's words. But the usual interpretation may not be right. "Late in the fifth century or early in the sixth" is the best we can do.

As to Badon's whereabouts, it must have been in the south of Britain. Not enough Angles or Saxons had settled anywhere else to mount a major campaign, nor would a defeat anywhere else have been serious enough to stop the invasion as a whole. Mount Badon may have been a hill-fort reoccupied as a British strongpoint. No one, however, actually says so. It may have been quite simply a hill. Geoffrey of Monmouth makes it out to have been one of those in the **Bath** area. Some modern attempts to identify it have fastened on places named **Badbury**, of which there are several.

Bamburgh
Northumberland   *NU 183351*

One of Malory's candidates for **Joyous Gard**, the castle of Sir Lancelot, where he gave hospitality to Tristan and Iseult. (Malory's alternative is **Alnwick**.) The present castle stands on a coastal hill by the North Sea, with a village alongside. It houses a museum. Behind it is low country stretching towards the Cheviots. The A1 is four miles away; the B1342 which connects it with Bamburgh turns off at Belford.

Bamburgh is far older than its castle, as, of course, any presence of Arthurian characters would require. From 547 it was the capital of the infant Northumbrian kingdom founded by Ida, the leader of the Angles who settled here. It has a number of legends which could help to account for its becoming a citadel of romance. Several connect it with St Aidan, the great Celtic bishop of Lindisfarne. It is said that the saint was so much impressed by the charitable deeds of King Oswald, Northumbria's first Christian ruler, that he prayed that Oswald's right hand should never wither. When Oswald died, the hand was cut off and kept in a silver casket in Bamburgh church, and did indeed remain uncorrupted. Another time, the village was set on fire by besieging pagans from Mercia. Aidan's prayers brought a shift in the wind which blew the flames back over the besiegers. Bamburgh also had its dragon, the Laidley Worm, a princess turned into reptilian form by her witch-stepmother. The king's son went to fight the mons-ter, but found out that it was his sister, whereupon the spell was broken, she resumed her proper shape, and the wicked stepmother was turned into a toad instead (she is still in a cave under the castle).

A place so rich in popular lore would surely be a good

place to put Sir Lancelot. But the suggestion that **Joyous Gard** was an earlier version of its castle has a slightly firmer basis than that. Bamburgh became King Ida's capital when he asserted his independence of the Britons around by fortifying the central area with a hedge or stockade. Yet he was not the first on the scene, and his stronghold was not even called "Bamburgh" till it was renamed for the wife of another king, several decades later. To judge from a note in Nennius, its previous name was Din Guayrdi. Seemingly, Ida seized and enlarged an already-existing British fort ("Din"), which had a name sounding like "Gard".

So Malory may have caught a faint echo from Arthurian times. Bamburgh is probably Joyous Gard so far as anything is. The reality of Sir Lancelot as the lord of Din Guayrdi is another matter.

Bann Arthur
—see **Brecon Beacons**

Bardsey
Gwynedd (Caernarvonshire)   *SH 122224*

Bardsey Island—Ynys Enlli in Welsh—lies off the tip of the Lleyn peninsula, across Bardsey Sound. It is about 1½

Bardsey Island.

miles long, with a high hill on its eastern side. Remains of medieval buildings mark the site of a Celtic monastery founded in the sixth century. For many years it was a place of pilgrimage. Legend inflates the size of the community: 20,000 monks are alleged to be buried here. When cowled ghosts wander on the shore they portend storms and shipwrecks.

The island has several Merlin stories. One of them refers, vaguely, to his grave. Another is a variant of the Arthurian cave-legend. It portrays Merlin sleeping in an underground chamber, not entrapped by any enchantress but immured by his own wish, and without companions— in this case Arthur and his knights are admitted to be elsewhere. Around the wizard are the Thirteen Treasures of Britain, ancient talismans and relics hidden from the Saxons and other conquerors. He also has the true throne of the British realm, where he will enthrone Arthur when the king returns and he awakens.

In still another version, Merlin's Bardsey retreat where he keeps the treasures is not a cave but an invisible house of glass. He has nine companions, and is not asserted so plainly to be asleep. Actually this may be the oldest story. His "house of glass" is a Celtic magical conception and is mentioned in medieval texts.

Barham Down
Kent   *TR 202518*

In Malory, after the rebellious Modred has failed to prevent Arthur's landing at **Dover**, he tries to stop his advance at Barham Down on the road to Canterbury. Arthur, however, wins again and Modred retreats.

No inter-British hostilities could have occurred here at this date, because the Jutes had long been in uncontested possession of Kent. But a group of Jutish barrows may have suggested the story of a battle followed by mass burials.

Barry Hill
Tayside (Perthshire)   *NO 263505*

From Blairgowrie the A926 runs eastwards. Off it to the left is Alyth, and above Alyth, overlooking the broad valley of Strathmore, are the Hill of Alyth and the Hill of Loyal.

Beside them, with the B954 passing through the gap between, is the lower Barry Hill. Brown and rocky, it has two lines of earthwork defences. Local legend claims it as Modred's fortress. Here, after worsting Arthur in battle at some stage in their quarrel before the final clash, he took the much-abducted Guinevere.

In this northern story the lady is not unwilling, and it has other features of its own (see **Meigle**). It may have begun as a Pictish tale about different characters entirely, with Modred and the rest being substituted later. This part of Scotland has several traces of it, perhaps because the battle of Nechtansmere, fought in the Forfar area in 685, came to be mis-dated and was supposed to have involved Arthur and Modred. Besides **Meigle**, see **Arthur's Fold**, **Arthur's Seat (2)**, **Arthur's Stone (6)**.

Bassas

According to Nennius, Arthur's sixth battle was fought "upon the river which is called Bassas". Its present name and whereabouts are unknown.

Bath

Avon (Somerset)   *ST 751647*

Fascinating on many levels, Bath has a place in British legend as well as history. Geoffrey of Monmouth mentions it several times, and claims in particular that it was **Badon**, the scene of Arthur's supreme victory. Because Gildas describes this clash as "the siege of Mount Badon", Geoffrey tells a rousing tale of a hotly contested British attack on a hill near the town where a Saxon host had entrenched itself. This is where we first hear of Arthur's wonderful sword, which Geoffrey calls Caliburn, saying it was forged in the Isle of **Avalon**.

Geoffrey may have picked on Bath merely because its name sounded like "Badon" and because he regarded it as one of the most important of British cities, a worthy place for Arthur's triumph. (Farther back in his *History* he tells how King Bladud founded it in the ninth century BC and built the baths.) But he may have heard an authentic tradition. Or his guess, if it was no more, may still have been right. In Roman times at least, Bath was a place with deep meaning for the Britons, as is shown by the religious sculpture among the Roman remains.

Some recent scholarship is disposed to agree with Geoffrey and accept Bath as **Badon**. The argument about the name—which, on the face of it, is English—depends on abstruse questions of spelling and potential misunder-standing. The argument from strategy is easier to follow. Bath might well have been a goal for a Saxon offensive. In 577, when the Saxons were advancing again, it was. As for the "mount", the city is surrounded by hills. Whether the Britons were besieging Saxons, or (as is perhaps more likely) the Saxons were besieging Britons, there are several choices. Bathampton Down, where the university is, has a hill-fort. So has Little Solsbury Hill north-east of the city, between Swainswick and Batheaston, which stands alone with defensible slopes on every side.

Bath figures in Arthurian romance also. In the verse tale *Lancelot* mainly written by Chrétien de Troyes, it appears as Bade, a principal town in the watery realm of Gorre. We are getting confused notions here about Somerset, **Glastonbury**, and the marshy lowlands around it.

Bedd Arthur
—see **Arthur's Grave (2)**

Ben Arthur
Strathclyde (Argyllshire)   *NN 259059*

A mountain to the west of the head of Loch Long. Its highest point is 2,891 feet above sea-level. Beside one of its peaks, called "The Cobbler", is an Arthur's Seat (compare the **Edinburgh** one, and see also **Brecon Beacons**.) The nearest road is the A83, which starts from Arrochar, rounds the end of Loch Long, and passes through Glen Croe.

This is the farthest into the Highlands that Arthur's geography stretches. It is interesting to find his name here, because of the tale of his visit to Loch **Lomond**, which is not far away; also, because of the theory that the "region **Linnuis**" where he fought four battles may have lain to the west of that loch and could even have included Ben Arthur itself.

Birdoswald
Cumbria (Cumberland)   *NY 615663*

The modern name of **Camboglanna**, a Roman fort which
has been proposed as **Camlann**, the scene of Arthur's last
battle.

Blackingstone Rock
Devon   *SX 786856*

As the road from Moretonhampstead to Exeter (the B3212)
twists upward among the hills before its descent into the
Teign valley, a smaller road leads off to the right climbing
higher still. At an altitude of over 1,000 feet, it bends
towards Heltor and drops sharply. On the right it passes
Blackingstone Rock. This is the locale of one of the few
stories of Arthur in Devon. He is said to have met the
Devil here. Trustworthy particulars, however, are lacking.

Blaengwaith Noe ab Arthur
—see Appendix

Bodmin
Cornwall   *SX 073670*

County town. The scene of an interesting quarrel recorded
by the chronicler Hermann of Tournai. In a history of the
shrine of Our Lady of Laon, written about 1146, he tells of
a journey through south-west England made by nine
canons from the city in 1113. Their cathedral had been
ruined by fire and they hoped to raise funds for its rebuild-
ing. With that aim they brought holy relics from the shrine,
and invited people to pray for miraculous cures.

On the way from Exeter to Bodmin the Frenchmen were
told that they were entering "the land of Arthur", and were
shown rock formations in open country called **Arthur's
Chair** and **Arthur's Oven**. (These are among the earliest
documented Arthurian sites.) When they arrived at Bodmin
and displayed their relics in the church, a man with a
withered arm came forward in hopes of being healed. He
told one of the French party that King Arthur still lived.
This caused merriment, but to the canons' surprise the
bystanders supported him, and a fight broke out which was
checked only with difficulty. The withered arm failed to

improve. Hermann compares the incident to disputes of the same kind between the French and Bretons, due to the same cause—that the Bretons maintained Arthur had never died, and would return some day to help them.

Bodmin's church where this fracas took place is in the oldest part of the town, in a deep cleft among hills. The French party would have approached from the north-east over the higher ground of Bodmin Moor. The Arthurian tradition they met with in 1113 survives at other sites in that area—for example **Arthur's Bed**, **Arthur's Hall**.

Bosherston
Dyfed (Pembrokeshire)   *SR 975946*

This long, sinuous lake south of Pembroke has an Excalibur legend. Here as in several other places, Arthur's sword was cast into the water after his last battle. It is not clear what prompted the idea. However, a little farther along the road is the reputed hermitage of Sir Gawain by **St Govan's Head**, and one Arthurian motif may have been enough to suggest others. A standing stone, usually known as Harold's Stone (SR 968958), may have helped.

See also **Dozmary Pool**, **Glastonbury** (Pomparles Bridge), **Llyn Llydaw**, **Llyn Ogwen**, and **Loe Pool**.

Brecon Beacons
Powys (Brecknockshire)   *SO 010214*

Among these mountains there is an early Arthurian presence in local lore, as there is nearby in the former districts of **Buelt** and **Ercing**. The twelfth-century author Giraldus (the same who records the digging up of Arthur at **Glastonbury**) says that two of the peaks, with the dip between, form Arthur's Chair.

The natural assumption is that he means the two highest, Corn Du and Pen y Fan, which are five miles south of the town of Brecon and slightly to the west. Support comes from John David Rhys, author of a Welsh grammar, writing in 1592. He tells us that he finished his work in a cottage at Cwm Llwch below the spurs of the Beacons. Farther up is a lake, Llyn Cwm Llwch. The height overlooking it, says Rhys, is sometimes called Moel Arthur or Bann Arthur, Arthur's Hill or Hill-top. And this is where the two highest peaks are, rising to about 2,900 feet above sea-level, so the placing of Arthur's Chair between them is almost certainly right.

A "chair" like this, taken literally, would evoke an image of Arthur as a giant—and so he is in a few other settings: see, for instance, **Arthur's Quoit (9)**, **Arthur's Stone (1)**, and **Sewingshields**. However, one Brecon legend tries to humanize him by explaining that he planted his throne here when he summoned an assembly to launch the Knighthood of the Round Table. Boulders strewn around the summit of Pen y Fan are claimed as pieces of the table itself.

Rhys's Llyn Cwm Llwch is still below, inaccessible by road. It has a story of fairy-folk, which is like some versions of Arthur's cave-legend. In the lake, the tale goes, there is an island. From the shore it is invisible, but the fairies' garden is there. Annually on May Day a door used to open in the rock near the lakeshore. You could enter a cave, pass under the lake, and come up in the island. But one visitor took a flower back with him, and the door never opened again. Later some men had the idea of draining the lake so as to find out the truth about it. They began cutting through the dam of glacial debris which holds the water in. Then a spectral form—a giant, or a man in a red coat, or an old woman, according to which version you prefer— rose above the surface and warned them to stop. If they cut through they would unleash enough water to drown Brecon. The same notion is found in other places in Wales: that if the waters were to be released at a key point, they would go on pouring up from below till the land was flooded.

Rhys in 1592 is aware of Llyn Cwm Llwch as uncanny. He says its depth is unknown, birds and animals avoid it, and the country people tell many wonders about it. However, he does not mention the rock doorway, and a real cave is geologically unlikely.

Breguoin

In several copies of Nennius this name (or something like it) is given to the hill which was the scene of Arthur's eleventh battle, either replacing **Agned** or in addition to it. One suggestion is that it is the same as "Brewyn", the Roman Bremenium, the fort of **High Rochester** below Cheviot. Another is that the right spelling is "Breguein", which could be derived from "Bravonium", the Roman name of **Leintwardine** in Herefordshire.

Brent Knoll

Somerset   *ST 341510*

An isolated hill 450 feet high, close to the Bristol Channel at Berrow. It rises steeply to a bare rounded top. Iron Age Celtic settlers dug into the hillside to make parts of it even steeper, and encircled the summit with a rampart and ditch.

Its Arthurian story concerns Ider, son of Nuth. When Arthur knighted him, he was assigned the task of challenging the three giants who lived on the Mount of Frogs, as Brent Knoll was then called. Arthur and other knights accompanied Ider to the hill, but he galloped ahead and slew all three single-handed. The effort was too much. His companions arrived and found him in a swoon, apparently dead. Arthur reproached himself and went to **Glastonbury**, where he asked the monks to pray for Ider's soul, and endowed the abbey with lands in the Brent Knoll area.

Legend apart, Brent Knoll is a link in the chain of hills comprised in an "Arthurian beacon" theory. When proofs

Brent Knoll.

of settlement about Arthur's time were found at **Cadbury Castle**, it was pointed out that similar proofs had been found on the Tor at **Glastonbury** and at **Dinas Powys** in Wales, and that these hills, with Brent Knoll, were visually linked in an approximate straight line. From **Cadbury**, the Tor can be easily seen in most weathers. From the Tor, Brent Knoll can be seen, and vice versa. Brent Knoll can also be seen from **Dinas Powys** across the Bristol Channel. We could picture a chain of beacon signal stations, enabling messages to pass rapidly back and forth between the lord of **Cadbury** and allies in Wales.

Brent Knoll's shape and singularity have inspired notions about its importance far earlier. The name "Brent" may be derived from the British root *brigant*. In some instances, such as the River Brent in Middlesex, it has been taken as pointing to worship of the mighty goddess Brigantia. However, the basic meaning of *brigant* is simply "high". Brigantia herself was the High One, and in the case of a hill, "Brent" might imply no more than outstanding height in constrast with the country round. More sensational than either the beacon theory or the Brigantia theory is a conjecture of the occult writer Dion Fortune, that Brent Knoll is a sacred mount artificially shaped by colonists from Atlantis. See her novel *The Sea Priestess*, where it appears, somewhat disguised, as Bell Knowle.

Brougham Castle

Cumbria (Westmorland)   *NY 537290*

Scene of an exploit of Sir Lancelot, near **Penrith**. The A6, leaving that town in a southerly direction, crosses the River Eamont by an old bridge into Westmorland. Just after passing the Mayburgh earthwork—see **Round Table (4)**—it goes over the Lowther, a tributary. Here the B6262 branches off to the castle, near the confluence of the Lowther with the Eamont. Lancelot slew a giant who occupied a cave close by. Some say that he was Isir, a cannibal, others that he was Tarquin (see also **Manchester**) and that he made the cave a prison for 64 captured knights.

His lair is fictitious. The oldest part of the castle, which is a well-preserved ruin, dates from about 1170. However, it was built near the site of the Roman fort of Brocavum, and this housed auxiliary troops with a large attached Celtic population. One can only guess at the lore which might have been handed down in the neighbourhood and been eventually given an Arthurian form.

Bryn Myrddin

—see **Carmarthen**

Buarth Arthur

Dyfed (Carmarthenshire)   *SN 142266*

"Arthur's Yard" or "Enclosure". Near the A478 north of Llandissilio. The remains of a stone circle, also called Meini Gwyr, a name of uncertain meaning.

Buelt

A south-central district of early Wales. The town of Builth Wells preserves the old name. In Buelt, Nennius places an Arthurian "marvel", one in a list of Wales's more mystifying features.

> There is another marvel in the district which is called Buelt. Here is a heap of stones, and on the top of the heap one stone bearing the footprint of a dog. When they hunted the boar Trwyth, Cabal which was the dog of Arthur the soldier, put his foot on that stone and marked it; and Arthur afterwards piled up a heap of stones and that stone on top, on which was the dog's footprint, and called it Carn Cabal. And men come and carry away the stone in their hands for a day and a night, and the next morning there it is back again on its heap.

The hunting of the monster boar, Twrch Trwyth, is described at length and with gusto in *Culhwch and Olwen*. This, too, gives Cabal as the name of Arthur's dog. But in other stories of footprints on stones it is Arthur's horse that makes the mark (see, for example, **Carn March Arthur**), and in Latin *caballus* means a horse. So the dog's name may be due to a misunderstanding.

Whether the animal (clearly no ordinary beast) was a horse or a dog, the name Carn Cabal, Cabal's Cairn, appears on the map today in the later form **Corngafallt**. This is given to a hill near Rhayader, which may or may not have been the place Nennius had in mind.

Nennius has another marvel in **Erging**.

Bwrdd Arthur
—see **Gwal y Filiast** and **Round Table (2)**, **(3)**

Cadbury Castle
Somerset   *ST 628252*

Best known and most interesting of the reputed sites of
Camelot. A hill-fort beside South Cadbury, down a small
road which leaves the A303 at Chapel Cross, 1½ miles east
of Sparkford.

The road passes through South Cadbury village and, a
short distance beyond the church, comes to the foot of the
only path up the hill. This is marked by a notice-board.
There is a small parking space, and a much larger one
farther on. The path climbs gently to a gate in a wall, and
then more steeply through woods, till it emerges in she
enclosure on top. After rain it is apt to be muddy and
slippery.

Cadbury is an isolated hill of limestone and sandstone.
The summit is about 500 feet above sea-level, with a wide
view of central Somerset, including the Tor at **Glastonbury** 12 miles away, and, in clear weather, **Brent Knoll**
beyond. It has four lines of bank-and-ditch defence. For
most of the way round they are densely wooded, and, in

Cadbury Castle.

spring, full of bluebells and primroses. Wherever the trees have grown, as they have in the place where the path goes up, the banks have crumbled and lost shape. But towards their south-east bend—reached by turning left when you enter the enclosure—they come out into the open, and you can look down and see them as they once were all round the hill, a formidable system. They surround a defended area of 18 acres, rising to a long, level central plateau. A break at the south-west above another village, Sutton Montis, is the original gateway.

The first known author to refer to Cadbury as **Camelot** is John Leland in 1542. He says: "At the very south end of the church of South-Cadbyri standeth Camallate, sometime a famous town or castle. ... The people can tell nothing there but that they have heard Arthur much resorted to Camalat." Sceptics have argued that there was no real local tradition, or perhaps a vague tradition of Arthur only, and that the evocative name is a guess of Leland's prompted by the villages of **Queen Camel** and West Camel not far away. Yet he speaks of **Camelot** without any discussion as a recognized fact, and his spelling with an *a* instead of *o* in the last syllable may echo a local pronunciation. This can be heard today; the *a* is sounded as in "father". It may have some bearing on the case that the first printed edition of a work by the classical geographer Ptolemy, which Leland could have read, notes a place called "Camudulanum" in this part of Britain.

Whatever the people of the neighbourhood were saying in 1542, they have certainly cherished Arthurian lore since then. Cadbury hill has its version of the cave-legend, which, in fact, can be documented earlier than any other, as far back as the sixteenth century. Arthur lies asleep in a cavern closed by iron gates, or maybe golden ones. Sometimes they open so that the fortunate wanderer can glimpse him inside. A party of Victorian archaeologists were asked by an old man if they meant to dig up the king. A well on the left of the path as you go up it is Arthur's Well, and the highest part of the hill is Arthur's Palace, a phrase on record as early as 1586. On Midsummer Eve, or Midsummer Night, or Christmas Eve (opinions differ, and some say it is only every seventh year), Arthur and his knights ride over the hilltop and down through the ancient gateway, and their horses drink at a spring beside Sutton Montis church. Whether or not they can be seen, their hoofbeats can be heard. Below the hill are traces of an old track running towards **Glastonbury**, called Arthur's Lane or Hunting Causeway, where a noise of spectral riders and hounds goes past on winter nights.

One theory about the name "Cadbury" is that this itself is a link with Arthur, because it means "Cadwy's Fort", and we find Arthur as the colleague—perhaps early in his career—of a prince named Cadwy at **Dunster**. He could have taken over Cadbury through some arrangement with its owner. But the derivation is dubious, and so is the argument, if only because there are other Cadburys.

The word "castle" suggests a medieval fortress with towers and battlements. The same warning applies here as at **Liddington** and elsewhere: Cadbury never had a castle like that. The fortified hill itself was the castle. Since nothing was ever here like the **Camelot** of romance (which, moreover, has no real geography), in what sense could Cadbury deserve the name? Solely in the sense of having been Arthur's headquarters and principal citadel, the far-off reality underlying the fiction. But that in itself is an impressive thing to be, and the nearby "Camel" place-names suggest how traditions of the Cadbury area might have helped to shape a name for the dream-city remotely recalling it.

Antiquarian writers from Leland on simply call Cadbury "Camelot" (variously spelled) without drawing such distinctions, and speak of Roman coins and fragments of buildings. No such fragments were left when the Rev. James Bennett, Rector of South Cadbury, carried out the first small excavation. In a paper published in 1890 he told how he had cut a trench through the top rampart, and judged that it was built up in layers over a long time. We now know that this was correct. On the plateau he dug down to a pit in the bedrock with scraps of pottery in it, and half a quern. The pit had a large flat stone at the bottom. A workman who was helping thought this covered a manhole leading down to the cave, but when they lifted it they found only another large flat stone. In 1913, H. St George Gray excavated again, chiefly near the south-west entrance, finding objects which showed that people were on the hill in the late Iron Age just before the Roman conquest.

The crucial step from an Arthurian point of view did not come till the middle 1950s. Part of the enclosure was ploughed, and a local archaeologist, Mrs Mary Harfield, picked up the flints and potsherds which appeared on the surface in the upturned soil. Among these Dr Ralegh Radford recognized pottery of the type he had found at **Tintagel**, which proved that somebody had lived here at about the time of Arthur, and most likely a "somebody" of wealth and standing who could import luxury goods. The interest thus aroused led to the formation of the Camelot Research Committee, which carried out large-scale excavations in 1966–70 under the direction of Leslie Alcock.

The results were copious. It became clear that British Celts of the Iron Age had not only built the earthwork defences, but reconstructed the top bank several times, as Bennett suspected. A village flourished on the plateau for hundreds of years. Then the Romans stormed Cadbury and evicted the survivors, resettling them at the foot of the hill so that they could not make it a strongpoint in any future rebellion. During most of the Roman period the enclosure was empty. However, a temple may have been built during a pagan revival which is known to have spread through Britain in the fourth century AD. After that comes a phase of total obscurity, and after that, the Arthurian period. For this the archaeological haul was richer than anyone had expected, or dared to predict.

In a central and commanding position, on the high part of the hill called Arthur's Palace, the foundations of a timber hall came to light. It was 63 feet by 34. Its walls were marked by post-holes cut in the bedrock. A trench running across it, closer to one end than the other, showed where a partition had divided it into large and small rooms. In outline it resembled the hall at **Castle Dore**, but there were grounds for inferring more skilful workmanship— quality rather than size. In this building the chief warriors would have assembled, feasted, listened to minstrels, planned campaigns. A smaller building close by could have been the kitchen, and others may also have belonged to an Arthurian complex, though it was only with the hall that dating was certain.

At the south-west entry were the remains of a gatehouse of the same period. A cobbled road ten feet wide climbed into the enclosure. It passed through double doors into a nearly square wooden tower, and out through similar doors the other side. All this, of course, has now been buried again and only the gap in the bank is visible, far shallower than it was.

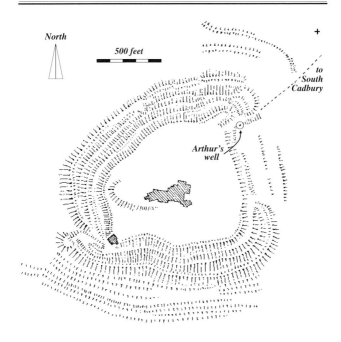

Cadbury Castle, showing excavation sites.

Most important of all was the discovery which was made in that bank, the three-quarter-mile perimeter of the hill. Cuts through it in several places—now refilled like the entrance—revealed a cross-section like a layer cake, with strata one above another showing how the rampart had been rebuilt at various times over the centuries. In Arthurian times it had been rebuilt grandiosely. On top of the earth at that level was a drystone bank or wall 16 feet thick. Gaps where ancient timber had rotted marked the places where massive posts had upheld a breastwork on the outside, protecting men who stood on the wall. Beams had run across, binding the structure together and supporting a platform, and perhaps, at intervals, wooden watchtowers.

This defensive system surrounding the hill made an impression in keeping with the period. The wall itself, with its timber bracing and superstructure, was very like what the British Celts were building before the Roman conquest. It incorporated fragments of Roman masonry, salvaged from derelict buildings, but it was strictly a national piece of work. On the other hand the gatehouse had Roman touches. When Arthurian Cadbury was formed, Britain's

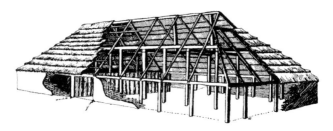

Cadbury Castle: artist's reconstruction of the Arthurian timber hall, with roof cut away to show the internal framework.

heritage of Roman architecture was seemingly almost forgotten, but not quite. By the later fifth century that might well have been the state of affairs.

Nothing was found with Arthur's name on it, and it would have been foolish to hope for that. What the project did prove was that Cadbury was reoccupied by the right sort of person, at approximately the right time. A leader with uncommon resources took possession of this vacant hill-fort and refortified it on a colossal scale. He was (as somebody phrased it during the excavations) an Arthur-type figure, if no more. At the centre he set up at least one fair-sized building and probably several smaller ones. He may have had others; even in 1970 after five seasons of digging, only a fraction of the site had been opened up. But quite possibly his soldiers used tents or huts leaving no lasting traces. When they were at Cadbury, their encampment held fully 1,000 men, plus ancillary staff, followers and families. During the campaign season the base may have been looked after by a garrison only. But it may have been a regional centre of government with a permanent civilian establishment.

The point about Cadbury–Camelot is not only that this hill-fort was converted into a vast citadel at the right time, but that there is no other known instance in ex-Roman Britain of such a thing having happened. A number of hill-forts were reoccupied, but simply as protected places of residence for a household. The areas resettled within their ramparts were much smaller; none became a base for substantial forces; and while, in a few, a little feeble wall-building was carried out, none acquired a new fortification remotely like the stone-and-timber rampart of Cadbury, with its gatehouse and implied use of the whole 18-acre enclosure. It is hard to believe that when Leland called this place "Camelot" he was merely guessing, rather than drawing on a valid tradition. A mere guess would have been most unlikely to pick on the one known place throughout Britain with the right characteristics. Even a modern archaeologist could not have made such a guess, simply by looking at the hill, with any confidence of being correct.

The Camelot Research Committee, of course, turned up material of value and interest covering a far longer stretch of time than the brief Arthurian period. Some of it still had an indirect bearing on the Arthurian Legend itself, or on stories related to it.

For instance, at the south-east bend of the uppermost rampart, a human skeleton was found. It was the skeleton of a young man rammed head-down into a pit, his knees drawn up to his chin. Fresh rampart-building had been done on top of him. The bones showed no physical defect, and the likeliest explanation is that this was a human sacrifice, performed for divine strengthening of the wall in

Cadbury Castle: artist's reconstruction of the gatehouse at the south-west entry in Arthur's time, with part of the rampart and timber breastwork which encircled the hill.

a pre-Roman phase of its reconstruction. That calls to mind the tale of Vortigern's stronghold and the Druids' advice about sprinkling its foundation with a boy's blood (see **Dinas Emrys**). Whoever first told that story knew something of pagan Celtic customs, and rituals which might have survived on the wild fringes of fifth-century Britain.

Again, one surprising outcome of the excavations was the discovery of evidence that the Iron Age village was not stormed by the Romans, its people were not deported, till a considerable time after this part of Britain was officially conquered. It was a centre for some last stand, some unchronicled resistance. Historians have nothing to say about this. But the Roman poet Juvenal speaks briefly of a British leader named Arviragus who would have been known or at least remembered in about AD 80–90 for causing trouble. Now in accounts of the Grail-bearer Joseph of Arimathea and his coming to **Glastonbury**, he and his companions are said to have been granted land there in AD 63 by a local king not subject to Rome. In some versions this king is named, and his name is Arviragus. Could that detail show a hazy awareness of traditions about a real person, a British Hereward the Wake who maintained a miniature kingdom in the hills and marshes of central Somerset, till the conquerors moved in on his strongest hill and dispersed its inhabitants?

While the archaeologists left the cave-legend alone, their project may have shed accidental light on it. There is no cave now. In such cases there seldom is. But a visitor who knew the hill well pointed out a place in the scarp on the south side of the central plateau, where a metal rod could be thrust horizontally far into the soil without hitting bedrock. Possibly a recess once existed there, and was filled in by crumbling, leaving a folk-memory which exaggerated its size and depth.

Lastly—though this was no part of the project—an amateur group which took an interest in it tested the "beacon" theory (see **Brent Knoll**) by building a large fire on the summit and posting observers on **Glastonbury** Tor, who reported that when the fire was lit after dark, they could easily see it across the low-lying country between.

For Cadbury in relation to the stories of Arthur's downfall, see **Cam**, **Camlann**.

Cader Idris
Gwynedd (Merionethshre)   *SH 711130*

A mountain ridge near Dolgellau. Its highest peak is Pen-y-Gader (2,927 feet). On the southern side is a natural amphitheatre enclosing the tarn of Llyn Cau. Legends of the battle of **Camlann** hover hereabouts, doubtless because of the little river-valley called Camlan seven miles eastward, beside the A458 to Welshpool. But some Welshmen maintain that any Arthurian stories were invented by the English.

"Cader Idris" means "Chair of Idris". Idris was a giant of Welsh legend. His actual chair is a stone formation on the highest part of the ridge. It is said that anybody who spends the night sitting in it will be found in the morning dead, or mad, or a poet.

Cadon Barrow
Cornwall   *SX 091872*

Supposed tomb of Cador or Cadwy (see **Dunster**). "Cadon", however, seems to be only a short form of the name of *Condolden* Barrow, 2½ miles north of **Camelford** on top of a 1,000-foot hill, the highest point in this part of the country. It would have been a place of distinction, but in pre-Christian rather than Arthurian times.

Caer Gai
Gwynedd (Merionethshire)   *SH 877315*

A hill-fort north of **Llanuwchllyn**, with a wide prospect of Llyn Tegid (Bala Lake), the source of the Dee. In Roman times it was the base of two cohorts of the Twentieth Legion, Valeria Victrix. Within the remains of the Roman walls is a fine Elizabethan farmhouse.

"Caer Gai" means the stronghold of Cai, the Sir Kay of romance. Medieval stories make him Arthur's seneschal, the chief officer of the household, and portray him unsympathetically. Malory brings him in also at an earlier stage, as the son of Sir Ector, to whose care Merlin entrusts the infant Arthur. In other words he is Arthur's foster-brother. As such he plays a discreditable part in the affair of the sword in the stone.

This is an instance of a once-popular hero being cut

down and supplanted by others, becuse, in the oldest Welsh matter, Cai or Cei is Arthur's principal lieutenant. The reason for his demotion by story-tellers may lie in an obscure tradition about a quarrel between them. He was quite possibly a real person, though his presence at Caer Gai may be fictitious. His name is the Roman Caius.

Caerleon

Gwent (Monmouthshire)   *ST 339906*

A small town beside the Usk north-east of Newport, on the A449. Beside it is the site of the Roman legionary fortress of Isca Silurum. In Geoffrey of Monmouth's *History*, Caerleon is where Arthur holds court after subduing all enemies in Britain and conquering an overseas empire. This is the first portrayal of him in literature as a mighty monarch. Geoffrey's Caerleon foreshadows **Camelot** as it is presented by later authors. He makes it a city and credits it with two famous churches and a college of 200 scholars, skilled in astrology and other arts. Arthur wears his crown in state and presides over a company of knights. They have distinctive liveries and coats of arms, which the ladies imitate in their dresses. Of the ladies, Geoffrey says: "They scorned to give their love to any man who had not proved himself three times in battle. In this way the womenfolk became chaste and for their love the knights were ever more daring."

Geoffrey's motive for locating the court at Caerleon was probably that it was the nearest place to his native Monmouth with impressive remains of ancient buildings, covering a wide area. Today the plan of the military base is exposed to view, and there is also an amphitheatre, the best in Britain. The town has a museum with many interesting items. But we know from the twelfth-century author Giraldus that in Geoffrey's time, far more was surviving on the site — remains of baths, vaults, central heating systems, and much else.

In bringing Arthur to Caerleon he made an attractive guess but not, probably, a right one. The only argument for a real connection is the meaning of the name, which makes this a candidate for the **City of the Legion** (Caer-leon) where Arthur fought his ninth battle. All the same Geoffrey's flight of imagination affected local lore. The amphitheatre, for instance, used to be pointed out as the true **Round Table**. After the Roman departure it had gradually vanished under a bank of earth, which rose to a height of 16 feet but preserved the shape, a hollow oval. The knights could have sat on the inside of the bank, facing the centre. It has now been excavated, so that the design can be seen more clearly.

Caerleon also has a cave-legend, which is like several others, especially the one told of **Craig-y-Ddinas**. Near the town a farmer met a man on horseback wearing a three-cornered hat, who offerd to show him a sight that no other living person had seen. In the middle of a wood the rider dismounted and gave a kick to a large stone by the road. It moved aside revealing a cave-mouth. They went in, and after walking for some distance came to the top of a flight of steps where two bells were hanging. The guide warned the farmer not to touch them. At the foot of the stairs was a great chamber with many fighting men lying asleep, their heads resting on guns. Despite the guns, the guide explained that these were 1,000 soldiers of Arthur waiting till Wales should need them. Returning up the steps, the farmer accidentally hit one of the bells. The soldiers woke

Caerleon: the Roman amphitheatre as it appears today.

shouting "Are the Cymry in need?" "Not yet," replied the man in the hat; "sleep on." Whereupon they lay down again. Outside the cave, he told the farmer never to speak of what he had seen for a year and a day. After that time had passed, the farmer searched for the stone, but without success.

Caerwent
Gwent (Monmouthshire)   *ST 469905*

Caxton, in his preface to Malory, speaks of the ruins of **Camelot** as still being visible in Wales. This is a puzzling statement, the more so as Malory himself usually places it at **Winchester**. One theory is that Caxton means Caerwent and that the Roman names of the two towns had caused a confusion. **Winchester** was Venta Belgarum, Caerwent was Venta Silurum. However arrived at, such a guess would be interesting. Caerwent was in fact the only Roman walled town in Wales, and furthermore it was one of the few British centres where an urbanized way of life did go on for a while after severance from the Empire.

It is on the A48, between Chepstow and Newport. Excavated remains are on view. The town included a church. Only one other church (at Silchester) has ever been identified in the ruins of Roman Britain. The Caerwent specimen was tiny, a room 21 feet by 17 with rough additions. Built in the late fourth century or early fifth, it incorporated a disused altar of the Celtic god Ocellus, the High One. Archaeology furnishes no proof that the church was still functioning in the time of Arthur, or, indeed, that Caerwent was still surviving at all by then. But while it may have died as a civic community, it had at least one notable inhabitant, an Irishman named Tatheus who ran a school. He taught St Cadoc, the founder of **Llancarfan**.

Cam, River
Somerset   *ST 610254*

A small tributary of the Yeo, which the A303 crosses just east of Sparkford on the way to Wincanton. It is a candidate for **Camlann**, the scene of Arthur's last battle— mainly because of its nearness both to **Cadbury Castle**, his reputed stronghold, and to **Glastonbury**, his reputed burial-place. The Cadbury hill rises in view within easy walking distance. The action leading to the battle could have been a sortie from it against an army approaching from the river. The only direct evidence, however, is a farmer's report many years ago of digging up skeletons huddled together near the west side of the hill, suggesting a mass grave.

Camboglanna
Cumbria (Cumberland)   *NY 615663*

A Roman fort on **Hadrian's Wall**, which has been claimed as **Camlann**. Otherwise know as Birdoswald, it stands beside a small road branching off from the B6318 near Gilsland. The ruined but massive walls enclose a spacious rectangle, with remains of a gateway and several rooms. Beyond, wooded ground drops steeply away to the River Irthing where it winds through a valley, supplying the element of "crookedness" which the name "Camlann" implies.

The motive for choosing this as Arthur's last battlefield is that a name which was "Camboglanna" in the British language would have become "Camlann" in Welsh. According to philologists the case is not actually so clearcut, because it would have passed through an intermediate form "Camglann" and been spelled thus in the Old Welsh of the sixth century. Of course the scribes of a later day might have modernized it in copying it out. Sound or not, the argument from the name is at present the only one. If Arthur's warriors were here, their stay was brief, leaving no trustworthy archaeological traces.

Camboglanna is a credible scene for an Arthurian clash of Britons with Britons. It then lay well within British territory and far from any Angles, Saxons or Picts. However, as a venue for this particular clash, it is unsatisfying. The entry in the *Annales Cambriae* about the "strife of Camlann in which Arthur and Medraut perished" has been cited as a firm Arthurian testimony. Hence Medraut, or Modred, has to be involved in the battle as the historians and romancers agree he was. But the early Welsh version of his conflict with Arthur locates at least the preliminaries in **Cornwall** (see **Kelliwic**); while the accounts of their final war, from Geoffrey of Monmouth onwards, trace the campaign across what is now England by different routes, yet never hint at any tradition of a march to the north.

Camelford

Cornwall   *SX 105837*

On the River Camel, which is crossed here by the A39.
Both **Camelot** and **Camlann** have been looked for at
Camelford or near it.

Some commentators think Shakespeare has it in mind in
King Lear, Act II, scene 2, where Kent says:

> Goose, if I had you upon Sarum Plain,
> I'd drive ye cackling home to Camelot.

The argument is that he is speaking to the Duke of Cornwall, and there is no reason why Camelot should be called
the Duke's home unless it is in his duchy. But while Kent
has indeed been speaking to the Duke a moment before,
these lines seem to be addressed to somebody else, namely
Oswald, with whom he was quarrelling before Cornwall's
entry. So it remains uncertain what Shakespeare meant.

If he did mean Camelford he was not following the
romancers. In so far as they locate **Camelot** at all, they
never picture it so far west, in the country of the sinister
Mark. Neither has Camelford any traces of a real Arthurian
stronghold, as at **Cadbury Castle**.

The belief that the battle of **Camlann** was fought
hereabouts appears first in Geoffrey of Monmouth's
History. He says that the rebellious Modred, twice defeated
by Arthur, withdrew westwards. Arthur caught up with him
at the "River Camblam" and their armies met in the final
clash. Modred was killed. Arthur received the wounds
which forced his enigmatic retirement to **Avalon**. By
"Camblam", his version of "Camlann", Geoffrey means
the Camel. He does not specify which part of the river.
Local legend has adopted his story and placed the battle at
Slaughter Bridge, a mile or so upstream from the town.

Camelon

Central (Stirlingshire)   *NS 867810*

A Roman settlement on the northern "Antonine" Wall,
which was built about AD 143 as a forward defence line,
but given up after a few decades. The site is between
Falkirk and the River Carron, and gives its name to a
suburb of the town. A notion that this is **Camlann** seems to

be pure speculation. Still, for whatever reason, a Roman building not far away was known by an Arthurian name as early as 1293. See **Arthur's O'en**.

Camelot

Arthur's splendid chief city in medieval romance. The earlier authors do not mention it. In Geoffrey of Monmouth, when Arthur has vanquished all his enemies, he holds court at **Caerleon**. Camelot makes its début in Chrétien de Troyes's *Lancelot*, composed during the 1170s. The name may be adapted from "Camulodunum", the Roman name of Colchester, but it is most unlikely that Colchester is the place intended. Generally speaking, the romancers neither know nor care where Camelot was. Sometimes it could be **London**. Malory, as a rule, more or less equates it with **Winchester**—perhaps because of that city's past greatness as the capital of Wessex, a place where several kings were crowned. But in an early text of his work, when some Roman envoys come to Arthur's capital to convey a message, it seems to be at **Carlisle**. So it may be doubted whether Malory cares either.

Yet we find hints that a few people in the Middle Ages did have some idea of Camelot's whereabouts, and its final fate. More than one author speaks of it as desolate and derelict. In a tale called *Palamedes*, written about 1240, the evil Mark of Cornwall is said to have laid it waste after Arthur's passing. That statement places it within Mark's reach, and might possibly point to **Cadbury Castle** in Somerset, with its conspicuous remnants of immense ramparts. The Cadbury–Camelot identification has been well known for many years and can be traced back to 1542. A fourteenth-century Italian poet, Fazio degli Uberti, claims to have seen "wasted, ruined Camelotto" with his own eyes—it is not clear where. Caxton, who edited and printed Malory's works, says (in defiance of Malory himself) that the ruins are in Wales. He may have in mind the Roman town of **Caerwent**. Another proposed site is **Camelford**, which, however, has no ruins to offer.

The truth is that guesswork like this must always be misguided, because the Camelot of romance is a medieval dream-city which never existed anywhere. The vagueness of the romancers would be proof enough, even apart from the anachronism of such a city at such an early date. It is proper to speak of a "real Camelot", but only in the sense of a very different reality at the root of the legend—the headquarters of the real Arthur, his main base, the centre from which he wielded whatever power he had. Assessed thus, all the Camelots fail but one, **Cadbury Castle**, which archaeology has revealed to be a strong candidate. It was for this reason that in the film version of the musical *Camelot*, a map which King Arthur briefly displayed showed Camelot in Somerset, and the identification has been accepted by several historical novelists. Another point in Cadbury's favour is that if any traditions were handed down about it, two nearby place-names with "Camel" in them could help to account for the spelling of the dream-city which grew from it in medieval imagination.

Camlann or Camlan

Arthur's last battle, where he fell fighting the rebel and traitor Modred, and where most of the knighthood was destroyed. It is noted in the *Annales Cambriae* as "the strife of Camlann in which Arthur and Medraut perished", and this entry, if reliable, would prove not only that it happened but that Arthur and "Medraut" existed, though the date does not harmonize well with other clues—it can be interpreted as about 520 or about 539, in keeping with different theories. The Welsh triads also mention Camlann, calling it one of the Three Futile Battles—an understatement—and saying that only three of the combatants survived. Other traditions put the number of survivors at seven.

"Camlann" is a Welsh name derived from a British one which may have been "Camboglanna" meaning "crooked bank", or "Cambolanda" meaning "crooked enclosure". The usual opinion is that the battle was fought by a winding river. There is one called Afon Camlan west of the road that runs northward from Dolgellau, which crosses it at Ganllwyd. Another possibility would be a narrow valley with a bend in it. In Merioneth there is a valley of Camlan with a small river (SH 816168), beside the A458 east of Dolgellau. In Cumbria there is the Roman fort of **Camboglanna**. All are promisingly named; none is very plausibly placed.

Geoffrey of Monmouth dates the battle in 542 (though there are grounds for suspecting an error here), and identi-

fies Camlann with the Cornish river Camel, which he calls
Camblam. Local legend point to the fields near **Slaughter
Bridge**. Malory, following a thirteenth-century romancer,
transfers the battle to **Salisbury Plain** and does not
mention the name "Camlann" at all, or attempt to account
for it. The Merioneth Camlan may have helped to inspire
stories of Arthur's last fight around **Cader Idris**, seven
miles off. The Cumbrian fort is favoured by several
scholars, but on philological grounds only, with no support
from early writers or archaeology. A tale of Arthur's death
in **Snowdonia** may be due to a belief that Camlann was
Cwmllan, a valley among the mountains. **Camelon** in
Scotland has also been mentioned, as has the Somerset
river **Cam**, its name being construed as a shortened form.

Some of these notions are clearly fanciful, and only the
last has any archaeological backing—partly from the
discovery (not, however, properly recorded or followed up)
of a mass grave, partly from the Arthurian presence at
nearby **Cadbury Castle**. Also the **Cam** would fit in with
Arthur's burial at **Glastonbury**. If his grave in the Abbey
was genuine, it would be logical to look for the fatal battle
not far away; and if it was faked, a tradition of such a
battle could have helped to put the idea in the monks'
heads, and to confirm their announcement about the grave
when they professed to have found it.

Carduel
—see **Carlisle**

Carhampton
Somerset   *ST 009427*

A village near the coastal resort of Blue Anchor, between
Minehead and Watchet. Land which once belonged to its
church is said to have been granted by Arthur to a Welsh
monk, St Carannog.

The legend is early. It is in a "Life" of the saint written
at **Llancarfan**, like several other saints' lives mentioning
Arthur, and is not the only one giving a rather hostile
picture of him, as a war-lord who treated the monks with
less than total respect.

Carannog was a grandson of a northern chief named
Cunedda, whom the last Roman rulers of Britain, or their

immediate successors, transferred to Wales with a commission to pacify and reorganize it. The saint had a portable altar with strange properties. For instance, it floated. He launched it from the south Welsh coast, vowing to preach wherever it might land. It drifted over the Bristol Channel and went ashore near Dindraithov, now **Dunster**. Here Arthur ruled, as junior colleague of a prince named Cato or Cadwy. The story belongs to an early phase of his career.

Presently Carannog arrived. He learned that a huge serpent was ravaging the district, with Arthur in vain pursuit. Carannog gave Arthur a blessing and asked him about the altar. He replied that he knew where it was, and would tell Carannog, if the holy man could prove his worth by bringing the serpent under control. Carannog prayed, the monster slithered submissively to his feet, and he ordered it to leave. Arthur then produced the altar, which he had commandeered himself. He was not sorry to give it up. He had tried to convert it into a table, but it threw off everything he put on it. Besides returning the altar he gave Carannog an estate. That is how the land came to be church property, and that is why the place—orginally Carrum—took its name from a shortened form of the saint's.

Carlisle

Cumbria (Cumberland)   *NY 400510*

The Roman Luguvallium, known as Caer Luel to the Britons, Carlisle is at the confluence of the Petteril and Caldew rivers with the Eden. It was a principal Roman station behind the western end of **Hadrian's Wall**, and it has a long record of strategic importance. Because of the heroic traditions of the British kingdom in **Cumbria**, the kingdom called Rheged, Carlisle recurs in legends of Arthur.

Several French poems and romances speak of Carduel or Kardoil, and sometimes at least this is identified with Carlisle and depicted as one of Arthur's chief towns. It appears also in English stories having Sir Gawain as their hero. *The Carl of Carlisle* tells how Gawain released a giant from a spell and arranged his admission to the Round Table. *The Wedding of Sir Gawain and Dame Ragnell* is a version of the "Loathly Lady" fairy-story best known through Chaucer's *Wife of Bath's Tale*. It takes the form of a ballad, one of the few pieces of popular verse on an Arthurian theme.

South-east of Carlisle, in the Inglewood forest, there used to be a lake called Tarn Wadling. It was near High Hesket (NY 475445) but no longer exists. Here, the story goes, Arthur was captured by a certain Sir Gromersomer, who set him free on condition that he would come back within a year with the right answer to the question: "What is it that women most desire?" Arthur returned to Carlisle and questioned the court ladies with no useful result. However, on the road to his trysting-place with Gromersomer, he met a hideous woman who told him the answer —that women most desire to have their own way—and asked as her reward that she should be given Gawain as her husband. The knight loyally consented. After the wedding his bride explained that she was under a spell cast by her stepmother. She could be ugly by day and beautiful by night, or the other way round. The chivalrous Gawain, recognizing that she would wish to be beautiful by day when she had to appear among the ladies at court, allowed her to decide for herself and kissed her. Thereupon she became beautiful and remained so all the time. In the words of the ballad version:

> King Arthur beheld that lady faire
>   That was so faire and bright,
> And thanked Christ in Trinity
>   For Sir Gawain, that gentle knight.

In an early text of Malory, Carlisle seems to be the capital city where Arthur receives a Roman delegation—a piece of geography which either ignores **Camelot** or identifies it with Carlisle itself, contradicting what Malory says elsewhere. It is also at Carlisle that Guinevere is condemned to be burnt at the stake for her adultery with Lancelot, who, however, saves her and carries her off to **Joyous Gard**.

Carmarthen
Dyfed (Carmarthenshire)   *SN 417205*

Merlin's birthplace in Geoffrey of Monmouth, who is probably drawing on an older tradition. In Welsh the name is Caerfyrddin. "Caer" means a defended place, and hence, sometimes, a city. The *f* corresponds (in keeping with Welsh rules) to an *m* in the original word. So this is

Myrddin City; and there was a real Myrddin, the bard and prophet who wandered in northern forests and gave Geoffrey the first hint for his composite magician. (See **Arthuret**, **Drumelzier**.)

Actually "Myrddin" is a Welsh form of Carmarthen's Roman name, Moridunum, the sea-fortress. The city cannot have been named after the man. But perhaps the man could have been named after the city, especially if it was his birthplace. A surname such as Lincoln goes back to "So-and-so of Lincoln". Geoffrey himself was "of Monmouth". It appears that the bard-prophet was earlier known as Lailoken. He may have got his more famous name through being called "Lailoken of Myrddin" and thence, eventually, Myrddin alone.

Geoffrey presented him as "Merlin" because, when he built him up as a character in his own Latin writings, he struck a problem in tact. Simply Latinized, the name would have become "Merdinus". But at that time the language of literate conversation was French, and "Merdinus" would have suggested *merde*, a rude word. So he changed a letter, Latinizing as Merlinus or plain Merlin.

Whether or not the original was really born at Carmarthen, it has been securely his birthplace ever since Geoffrey wrote. A rhyme links its fortunes with Merlin's Tree, or Priory Oak, in the centre of the city. The couplet retains the Welsh form of his name:

> When Myrddin's Tree shall tumble down,
> Then shall fall Carmarthen Town.

The civic authorities long since took care to prevent such a disaster, bracing the tree with iron supports and later removing it.

Two and a half miles east, up the valley of the Tywi or Towy, is Bryn Myrddin, Merlin's Hill. It is a rather abrupt rise on the north side of the A40. A wood below it is Merlin's Grove. On the other side of the road is Carreg Fyrddin or Merlin's Stone (SN 459211), which once fell on a treasure seeker and crushed him, fulfilling a reputed prophecy by the wizard himself that a raven would drink a man's blood off the stone. A team of five horses was needed to set it up again.

There is also a legend of Merlin's Cave, a secret chamber in the lower part of the hill. It is said to be the one where he was immured by Vivien or Nimuë, whom he loved, and foolishly taught magical spells which she employed to imprison him. The old local tale was that he was still there, alive, and that if you could find the right place you could hear his subterranean groans.

Edmund Spenser, in *The Faery Queene*, gives a different account of this cave. He puts it farther up the Tywi, in the grounds of Dynevor Castle (SN 615224), and explains that Merlin used to retire to it to commune with spirits.

> There the wise Merlin whilom wont (they say)
> To make his wonne [dwelling] low underneath the ground,
> In a deep delve, far from the view of day,
> That of no living wight he might be found,
> When so he counselled with his sprites encompassed round.

Spenser goes on to give a piece of guidebook advice, though he spoils it slightly by getting the name of the river wrong.

> And if thou ever happen that same way
> To travel, go to see that dreadful place:
> It is an hideous hollow cave (they say)
> Under a rock that lies a little space
> From the swift Barry, tumbling down apace,
> Amongst the woody hills of Dynevowre;
> But dare thou not, I charge, in any case,
> To enter into that same baleful bower,
> For fear the cruel fiends should thee unwares devour.

In the next stanza he says that if you listen from the outside, you can hear strange noises from under the rock.

Still another product of the Carmarthen tradition is Myrddin's Quoit (SN 380160), a megalith three miles south-west of the town, near the B4312.

Geoffrey of Monmouth's development of Myrddin into the great enchanter was the result of a long-standing interest in him, yet a curiously ill-informed one. His own first work was a cryptic series of prophecies which Merlin, or Myrddin, was supposed to have uttered. Next he wrote his *History* and worked these prophecies into it, making Merlin appear before Vortigern and reveal a pool with dragons in it which was undermining his walls (see **Dinas Emrys**). In Nennius's earlier version of the same tale, the seer is a boy called Ambrose. Transformed by

Geoffrey into Merlin, he is a lad born under mysterious circumstances at Carmarthen. (Or rather at the place afterwards called so: Geoffrey would like to think that the town *was* named after him.) He reels off his prophecies after the pool episode. Later on in the *History* Geoffrey portrays him in adulthood, performing engineering feats by his magic arts, and contriving the conception of Arthur at **Tintagel**.

So far, so good. But Geoffrey seems to have done all this without grasping that the real Myrddin was not born till long after Vortigern's time and must have been junior, not senior, to Arthur himself. In a better-informed third book, the verse *Life of Merlin*, he changed dates and details in an effort to make his creation fit together. The final character is really a fusion of two, and may be even more complex than that, considering the implications of his role in the building of **Stonehenge**. One conjecture is that Myrddin was originally a god or spirit, that prophets inspired by him were Myrddin-men or simply Myrddins, and that Geoffrey combined two or three having that sobriquet under the impression that they were the same person.

Besides the Merlin associations, Carmarthen has a memorial stone in its museum which brings us quite close to the Arthurian period. It was discovered in 1895 at Castell Dwyran on the border between Carmarthenshire and Pembrokeshire. The stone is nearly seven feet high and is marked with a Celtic ring cross, and, below it, the words MEMORIA VOTEPORIGIS PROTICTORIS—the monument of Voteporix the protector. On the edge the same man's name is scratched in the old Irish Ogam script. He can be identified. He is one of the regional kings of the post-Arthur generation denounced by Gildas, who calls him Vortiporius, and accuses him of incest with his own daughter ... though she may have been only his stepdaughter. Voteporix seems to have been descended from an Irish chief, who was set in authority over Dyfed as a Roman vassal, perhaps by the Emperor Maximus in the 380s. The title "protector" applied to officer-cadets in the emperor's bodyguard. Possibly the chief's son was given such a post, and it was then treated as hereditary in the family.

A Welsh genealogy lists Voteporix's father as Aircol and his grandfather as Triphun. These are Roman-derived names, Agricola and Tribune, showing the imperial linkage. Since Voteporix was in late middle age when Gildas attacked him, his father Agricola—whom Gildas approves of—may well have been among the "kings of the Britons" who fought in battles which Nennius associates with the name of Arthur.

Carn Arthur
—see **Arthur's Grave (2)**

Carn Cabal
—see **Buelt**

Carnedd Arthur
—see **Snowdonia**

Carn March Arthur
Gwynedd (Merionethshire)   *SN 651982*

On a hill above the road on the north side of the Dovey estuary, the A493, is a rock supposedly indented with a hoofprint of Arthur's horse—*march Arthur*. Lanes and paths lead up to this high ground from Aberdovey and Abertafol. Arthur came here to kill a monster that lived in Llyn Barfog, the "Bearded Lake", a lonely tarn in a hollow among the hills on the far side.

What kind of monster? The folklorist who published the story in the mid-nineteenth century used the word *afanc*, and explained that this meant a crocodile. A more eminent folklorist, putting the story in a book of his own, dismissed the crocodile and said that an *afanc* was "a creature that would cast at every comer a poisoned spear from behind a pillar at the mouth of the cave inhabited by it".

Whatever the *afanc* was, Llyn Barfog is one of a number of Welsh lakes with otherworldly qualities. Green-clad fairy-folk, it is said, used to be seen near it with white cattle and dogs. A farmer at nearby Dysyrnant captured one of the cows, which bore noble calves and brought him good luck in other ways. Then he was foolish enough to hand it over to a butcher for slaughter. But the knife fell from the butcher's hand. A green-clad woman appeared on a crag above Llyn Barfog and, in a terrible voice, called the cow home. It ran to her with all its descendants in the farmer's herd, and they vanished with the woman into the lake. Needless to add, the farmer's luck deserted him. Wales has several similar legends. In the marvellous "fairy cattle" there may be folk-memories of the aurochs, the prehistoric wild species.

Carn Marth
Cornwall   *SW 715408*

"Mark's Cairn"—the name becomes "Marth" in Cornish. A tumulus on a hill south-east of Redruth, one of the highest points in this part of the county (772 feet). It has been proposed as the burial-place of Iseult's husband. Early excavators found "earthen vessels containing burned bones". While no rival grave exists, it is a long way from **Castle Dore**, Mark's reputed home.

Carreg Arthur
—see **Arthur's Quoit (5)**

Carreg Fyrddin
—see **Carmarthen**

Carrum
—see **Carhampton**

Castell Dinas Bran
—see **Llangollen**

Castellmarch
Gwynedd (Caernarvonshire)   *SH 315297*

"Mark's Castle", a seventeenth-century mansion off the A499, beside St Tudwal's Bay north of Abersoch. It was so called because of a belief that it stood on the site of a resi-dence of Iseult's husband, his name in Welsh being "March".

   The fact suggested a word-play and a legend, because, in Welsh, *march* means a horse. The original lord of Castell-march is alleged to have had horse's ears. He kept them covered and killed anyone who got a glimpse, a practice lethal to barbers who shaved him. The bodies were buried in a place where reeds grew. At last a musician cut one of the reeds to make a pipe. When he played it, the sound that came out was "March has horse's ears". "March" was about to put the player to death, but found, first, that the pipe made the same sound when he blew into it himself, and second, that the reed had grown where the corpses of his victims were hidden. After that, he made no further attempt to conceal his ears.

This is an echo of the Greek story of Midas, who had the ears of a donkey. It was told elsewhere in northern Wales, sometimes in a form even closer to the Midas legend. There was a Cornish version too. It could attach itself to Mark because he was an unsympathetic figure—not only in the Tristan triangle, but in other tales—and hence was fair game. See further **Castle Dore**.

Castle-an-Dinas
Cornwall   *SW 945624*

One of the finest Cornish hill-forts, strategically placed (perhaps to command trade routes) with wide views of the moors. A medieval author names it as the stronghold where Duke Gorlois was killed fighting Uther's army, an episode in the story of the birth of Arthur. See, however, **Dimilioc** and **St Dennis**. The fort is one of the two Cornish sites known as **Arthur's Hunting Lodge**. Arthur is said to have ridden out from it to hunt on Tregoss Moor to the south-east.

Castle-an-Dinas has three massive earthwork ramparts

Castle-an-Dinas.

of different dates, implying use over a long period, and there are traces of a fourth outside. The total diameter is 850 feet. A spring within it supplied the occupants with water. It is two or three miles east of **St Columb Major**, and most easily reached by the small road that crosses the moorland to the A30 on the way to Victoria. From Providence, a track leads through the ruins of a wolfram mine to the top of the hill, a steep half-mile ascent.

While Castle-an-Dinas is an Iron Age fort, it may be one of those that actually were used again in Arthur's time. Solid evidence, however, is lacking.

Castle Dore

Cornwall   *SX 103548*

One of the oldest trackways in Britain used to cross the Cornish peninsula by way of **Bodmin**. Part of it survives today as a modern road, the B3269. By the east side of this road, where it runs along a ridge two or three miles inland from **Fowey**, a notice draws attention to Castle Dore as a residence of King Mark, Iseult's husband in the Tristan romance. All that can be seen at this point is a bank covered with gorse. But a short distance to the south are buildings, from which a way leads back to the site, through a gate and across a large field.

As in other cases where such a stronghold has survived,

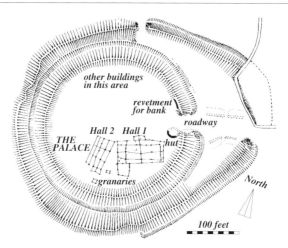

Castle Dore: post-Roman structures as reconstructed by Radford.

this is not a medieval castle, even a ruined one. The word "castle" is employed in its earthwork sense. Castle Dore has two concentric banks six or seven feet high, each with an outer ditch. Where they adjoin the road they are close together. To the east, on the far side of the enclosure, the outer one draws away from the inner so as to make a fair-sized space between, which could have been used as a market-place or a yard for animals. On that side is the break which forms the entrance, much widened over the centuries.

Excavations in 1935–36 showed that the fortification was built in the Iron Age, 200–300 BC. For a long time a prosperous community lived within it. During the Roman era it was empty. Then, from the fifth to the seventh century AD, it was occupied again.* Work was done on a part of the defences. A cobbled road was built leading in through the entrance, with a hut on an oval platform beside it, perhaps a guardhouse. In the enclosure, 220 feet across, digging revealed the foundations of two large timber buildings, marked out by stone-lined holes sunk in the bedrock to receive supporting posts. One building was 90 feet by 40, with a central line of posts indicating a roof-ridge along the middle. It had a porch and a hearth, and could properly be described as a hall. The other building was 65 feet by 35. In both, the floors had been destroyed by ploughing, but traces of a third building included a little of the floor, made of stones laid close together.

These buildings could be firmly dated to the Arthur period or thereabouts. In the light of other clues, it is reasonably certain that Castle Dore housed the court of Cynvawr or Cynfawr, who ruled over Dumnonia (the British kingdom of which **Cornwall** was part) during the first half of the sixth century. The Latin form of his name was Cunomorus, and he had a son named Drustanus ... i.e. Tristan. It was believed at an early date—well before the advent of medieval romancers—that "Mark" was another name of the same king. The place-name Kilmarth, Mark's Retreat, occurs 1½ miles away near Par Sands (SX 089525).

The sinister Mark certainly seems to have been real. His

---

* The interpretation of the site that is given here has been accepted and well known for so long that it has been retained. Its omission would puzzle many readers. However, it has been seriously challenged. See *The Arthur of the Welsh* in the Bibliography. In this book Castle Dore's "Arthurian" phase is rejected.

name is the Roman Marcus, and he was the son of Marcianus, probably a governor or magistrate named after a fifth-century Roman emperor. But was he actually the same person as Cynvawr? If he was, his full style in Latin was Marcus Cunomorus. The difficulty is that stories of Mark, and places seemingly called after him, are scattered widely (see **Carn Marth**, **Castellmarch**, **Mote of Mark**, **Penmark**). One theory is that Mark's real kingdom was in Wales. Story-tellers identified him with Cynvawr of Castle Dore because they thought Cynvawr's son Tristan had been the Tristan who loved Mark's wife, so Mark had to be equated with somebody in the neighbourhood, and the obvious choice was Cynvawr himself—though that led to an awkwardness over the relation between them. While there can be no firm answers at present, it is worth pointing out that the Cornish Tristan is more solidly proved, by his memorial stone at **Fowey**, than any other.

In August 1644 Castle Dore was occupied by Roundheads. A Royalist force then attacked and captured it.

Castle of Maidens

This intriguingly named establishment appears in several of the romances. Morgan le Fay, Arthur's equivocal sister or half-sister, sometimes figures as the lady in charge. The nature of the castle varies. It may be a sort of commune of seductive girls who tempt visiting knights. Or it may be a prison, as it is in one of the Galahad stories, where the girls have been kidnapped and Galahad frees them by driving away the kidnappers. Sometimes it is simply one of the castles where the nobility gather, and its female quality remains in the background. Thus it is the scene of a tournament at which Sir Tristan is mocked by the poet Dinadan.

Geoffrey of Monmouth speaks of "the Maidens' Castle" before any of the romancers do, and he may have supplied the hint for all of them. He identifies it with the castle of Mount **Agned**, and places it in **Edinburgh**, perhaps because of a tradition about a Pictish king sending his daughters there for safety in time of war. However, in some stories it is at or near Gloucester.

A real Maiden Castle exists in Dorset. It is a huge Iron Age earthwork, with traces of occupation in late Roman times, perhaps even after that. But the legendary one has no connection with it.

Catraeth

—see **Catterick**

Catterick

North Yorkshire   *SE 220990*

"Catraeth" in Old Welsh, the scene of a battle between
Britons and Angles commemorated in a poem by the bard
Aneirin. It was fought in or about 598, and he composed
the poem soon afterwards. One couplet is often quoted as
being the earliest reference to Arthur which has come
down in writing. This is by no means certain, because the
couplet may be an interpolation, though there is no cogent
reason to think so.

At any rate, what it says is simply that a British warrior
named Gwawrddur "glutted black ravens on the wall of the
fort, though he was not Arthur". Poetically, "feeding the
ravens" meant killing enemies. The point may be that even
though Gwawrddur wasn't actually Arthur, he was equally
good at raven-feeding; or perhaps that he was a great fighter
though admittedly he was no Arthur. Either way, the words
imply that by the date of the poem Arthur was proverbial
for martial prowess. They imply nothing more — nothing, for
instance, about his home territory, because although Aneirin's
theme is a northern campaign, he mentions warriors from
several parts of Britain, including the West Country.

His poem is intensely interesting on other counts. It is
really a series of elegies for men who fell in the battle. The
title is *Gododdin*, a form of the name of Manau Guotodin,
the kingdom around **Edinburgh** which was the mustering-
place of the British army. Three hundred and sixty horsemen (the extent of infantry and auxiliary support is not
clear) rode from there to attack the Angles at the former
Roman station of Cataractonium, the original Catterick,
near the strategic road junction now called Scotch Corner.
Hopelessly outnumbered, they fought heroically for days—
"seven times as many English they slew"—but in the end
they were all killed except a handful. One of the survivors
was Aneirin himself, who rode with the expedition and
escaped, in his own opinion, because of his "fine songs".

Many verses were added to *Gododdin* in the seventh
century and later, but Aneirin's basic poem is still there. It
tells us a good deal about the British nobles, their way of
life, and their methods of warfare. We get glimpses of them

hunting and fishing, drinking mead, listening to minstrels, taking baths, going to church. They feast round an open fire in a hall lit by rush candles and pinewood torches. They drink from vessels of horn, glass, silver and gold. In peacetime they wear silks and colourful plaids, with chaplets and brooches and amber beads. In war they put on leather cuirasses and probably a kind of chain mail. They carry swords, white shields, and throwing-spears. They ride to battle, and, so far as can be made out, they fight on horseback, though in the absence of stirrups (which did not reach Western Europe till later) they are not to be pictured fighting with the forcefulness and control of a medieval knight. This is probably not far from being a fair description of the warriors in the Arthurian period.

Cataractonium, the Roman fort, was on the south side of the Swale at Catterick Bridge. A settlement grew up round it. Remaining traces indicate that the wall on which Gwawrddur glutted the ravens was stone-built, 7½ feet thick. The country round about is level with no outstanding features, but the hill of **Richmond** with its story of Arthur himself is not far away.

Cave-legend, sites of

The classic Arthur cave-legend was a product of two main factors: first, a pre-Christian Celtic myth about a god who had ruled over a golden age, and was banished to a western island where he lay sleeping in a cave; and second, a belief among Celts that Arthur had never died and would return to lead his people. As the Arthurian saga grew more wonderful, the hero came to resemble the departed god. In literature his retreat was the island of **Avalon**. Popular lore preferred the notion of a cave where he slept in enchanted immortality. Some day he would awaken, and his glory would revive. Such tales have been told of other heroes, in Britain and elsewhere, but may well be copyings from Arthur's.

Often the king is not alone. He has his knights with him, or his treasure, or both. Sometimes, on the other hand, a cave is said to house only knights or only treasure, Arthur himself being in a different place.

Two real caves bear his name, **Arthur's Cave** in Herefordshire, and **Ogof Arthur** in **Anglesey**. With both of these it is highly doubtful whether the "sleeper" legend was the original motif. Where that is at work, the cave cannot usually be identified or marked on a map. It is hidden by magic so that only a handful of mortals ever see it. Hence, all that can be localized is the legend. Travellers cannot go to the spot and explore an actual cave. Or if they can (as is possible in one or two cases), they may be assured in advance that it is not the right one, or that even if it is, they will miss the important part of it.

Simple versions of the legend are found at **Cadbury Castle** and **Caerleon**, and in **Snowdonia**, embedded in matter of wider scope. Two places where we get the cave-legend by itself, with a few particulars, are **Marchlyn Mawr** and **Ogo'r Dinas**. More elaborate forms of it occur at **Alderley Edge**, **Craig-y-Ddinas**, **Melrose**, **Richmond**, and **Sewingshields**; while **Bardsey** has a variant where the sleeper is Merlin. All these are given separate treatment. Stories of the same type have been reported from the following places:

(1)   Llantrisant
Mid-Glamorgan

Perhaps because of a hill-fort a mile to the east.

(2)   Pumsaint
Dyfed (Carmarthenshire)

(3)   Gwynedd

In the part of **Gwynedd** which was formerly the county of Merioneth—nothing more exact as to location. The cave is called "Ogof Arthur" like the real one in **Anglesey**, and the story is like that of **Craig-y-Ddinas**. It begins with a man meeting a wizard, in this case at a fair at Bala.

(4)   Threlkeld
Cumbria (Cumberland)
See **Cumbria**.

(5)   Sneep
Northumberland

Though the Cornish had a belief in Arthur's immortality, there seems to be no Cornish instance of the cave-legend. Folklore offered an alternative, his survival in the form of a raven or other bird. See **Bodmin**, **Marazion**.

Caverswall
Staffordshire   *SJ 951429*

Caverswall Castle, three miles east of Longton, was built
in the thirteenth century. According to legend, nevertheless, Arthur held court here. A debate once arose as to
which of the ladies was the most virtuous. When they
danced, each wore a garland of leaves. The garland of the
Lady of Caverswall did not wither and she was judged to
have won. Arthur afterwards saved her from some unspeci-
fied peril. One version adds that this lady was Guinevere
herself and their marriage ensued, in which case it would
have become politic to avoid trying the garland test again.

Celidon

In Nennius's list of Arthur's twelve battles, the seventh is
in the Forest of Celidon. "Celidon" is the same as
"Caledonia", the old name of Scotland. The forest which
was called so by Welshmen like Nennius lay north of the
Border, but it is hard to be more precise about it. Probably
the area implied in the battle-list covered most of the
counties of Dumfries and Selkirk, and extended over high
country around the headwaters of the Clyde and the Tweed.
In Arthur's time the Anglo-Saxon invasion had not pene-
trated so far. He may have been fighting resurgent Picts, or
hostile Britons from the Clyde region. Support for the
second theory comes from the story of Hueil, Gildas's fiery
elder brother. See **Strathclyde**.

   Another person whose adventures bring him to Celidon
is Myrddin, the northern bard who is the part-original of
Merlin. Legend tells how he was driven almost out of his
mind by the slaughter at the battle of **Arthuret**, and
wandered away into the Forest of Celidon, uttering prophecies. Many folktales in different countries introduce
figures like this—"wild men of the woods" who are
outcast, ragged, crazy, yet free and somehow wiser than
those who are sane. Among the Celts at least two others
occur, the Irishman Suibhne Geilt (Mad Sweeney), and the
Briton Lailoken. Lailoken, however, roams in the same
territory as Myrddin at about the same time, and is thought
to be Myrddin under another name. In any case the tradition of the wild prophet is behind a belief that the
enchanter Merlin—into whom Geoffrey of Monmouth

built him up—is buried at **Drumelzier** on the upper Tweed.

Celliwig
—see **Kelliwic**

Cerrig Arthur
Gwynedd (Merionethshire)   *SH 632189*

"Arthur's Stones." Standing stones in the hills north of Barmouth. A small road goes most of the way.

Cerrig Meibion Arthur
Dyfed (Pembrokeshire)   *SN 118310*

"Stones of the sons of Arthur." Two standing stones in a valley among the Prescelly Mountains.

Chester
Cheshire   *SJ 405663*

Formerly a Roman city called after the River Dee, Deva. Its army base downstream was Devana Castra, the Deeside Camp, housing the Twentieth Legion. Afterwards only the legionary presence lingered in memory, and the city became simply Chester, "The Camp". In the *Annales Cambriae* its military style is given another form, Cair Legion. This makes it a candidate for the venue of Arthur's ninth battle in Nennius's list, "waged in the **City of the Legion**".

It is a stronger candidate than its rival **Caerleon**. In Arthur's time, admittedly, it was a long way from the Angles' east-coast settlements. For that reason critics of Nennius have argued that Arthur cannot have fought here, and that a real battle which took place at Chester about 614 has been fictitiously added to the list. But there are well-attested cases of long marches in the wars of the sixth and seventh centuries. Raids going clear across the country would have been feasible, and Gildas's story of the first Anglo-Saxon outbreak says they occurred.

Another explanation of the ninth battle would be that Chester was raided by hostile Britons. See **Ruthin**, **Strathclyde**.

City of the Legion

Scene of Arthur's ninth battle according to Nennius. It was
"waged in the City of the Legion". Early Welsh writings
show that this name was used for two places remembered
by Welshmen as bases of the Roman army. One was
Caerleon, where Geoffrey of Monmouth portrays Arthur
holding court. The other was **Chester**.

Coed Arthur
South Glamorgan   *ST 040715*

"Arthur's Wood", near **Llancarfan**.

Coetan Arthur
—see **Arthur's Quoit**

Corngafallt
Powys (Brecknockshire)   *SN 943644*

A forested ridge rising to a height of 1,530 feet, with cairns
near the crest. Its name indicates a long-standing belief that
one of these is Carn Cabal, Cabal's Cairn, once topped by
the stone which Arthur's dog Cabal marked by setting his
foot on it (see **Buelt**).

The nearest town is Rhayader, on the Wye. From here
the B4518 runs south-west and enters the valley of a
tributary, the Elan. At Elan village a lane turns off, climbing through woods and bracken to more open ground near
the top of the ridge. Some visitors have insisted that a
stone on one of the cairns actually has a hollow in it like a
dog's paw-print. The stone is described as about 2 feet by 1,
and the hollow is 4 inches long, 3 wide, and 2 deep. Others
find the claim unconvincing, pointing out that while it may
not be too hard to find stones with depressions in them,
nobody has yet produced one with any traces of toes or
claws.

Geologically a stone here would be a conglomerate, and
any hollow might be the gap left by an embedded pebble
coming out. In any case this may not be the right place at
all. Cabal is said to have marked the stone during the
hunting of the boar Twrch Trwyth, and it is doubtful
whetehr the account of the hunt in *Culhwch and Olwen*

brings Arthur and his men this way. There may of course have been different versions of the hunt, adapted for story-tellers in different parts of Wales.

Cornwall

Britain's extreme south-western land is often claimed as "Arthur's Country" in a pre-eminent sense. The main reason is the fame of **Tintagel**, his reputed birthplace, with its scenic grandeur and tourist traffic. But that is only the beginning. Cornwall has more relevant sites than any other county. Arthur seems always to have had Cornish associa-tions which were too strong for the wishful thinking of non-Cornishmen to dismiss. Even Geoffrey of Monmouth, ever willing to improve history for the glory of Wales, tells the story of his **Tintagel** origin and calls him "the Boar of Cornwall". In early Welsh tradition his fortress is not in Wales but at **Kelliwic**.

However, this is still hardly enough to explain the long list of sites and local legends, and the Cornish claim to events which almost certainly happened elsewhere, such as the battle of **Camlann**. The reason lies in Cornwall's prolonged independence after the rest of southern Britain had succumbed to the Saxons. It was once part of the British kingdom of Dumnonia, which extended through Devon into Somerset and perhaps farther. The West Saxons conquered Somerset in the seventh century and Devon early in the eighth. But the remnant of Dumnonia beyond the Tamar held out alone for more than 100 years longer, and was never fully assimilated. Even after Cornwall became a county of England it kept a quality of its own, and its Celtic language was still spoken as late as the eighteenth century. So its Arthurian story-tellers could not only improve on their heritage but annex legends and characters from other places, with little competition. Some of the results were becoming known to a wider public at least as early as 1113. See **Bodmin**.

It was from this area that many of the migrant Britons sailed who turned Armorica, on the other side of the Channel, into Brittany. Much of the continental Arthur tradition, which started there and was spread by Breton minstrels, had a far-off Cornish ancestry.

Craig Arthur
—see **Llangollen**

Craig-y-Ddinas (or **Dinas**)
Mid-Glamorgan   *SN 916081*

"Rock of the Fortress." A steep, bare crag at the head of the
Vale of Neath (Glynnedd), just above the confluence of two
rivers which flow together to form the Neath. The nearest
major road is the A465. Craig-y-Ddinas is the locale of the
most elaborate Welsh version of the cave-legend.

As the story goes, a Welshman was crossing London
Bridge. He had a hazel staff in his hand. An Englishman
asked him where he came from.

"I am from my own country," the Welshman replied.

"Don't be offended," said the stranger. "If you follow
my advice you can be rich. That stick grew at a place
where treasure is hidden. Take me there and I'll show
you."

The Welshman guessed that the stranger was a magician,
and hesitated, but finally took him to Craig-y-Ddinas and
pointed out the stump. They dug it up and uncovered a flat
stone, which they lifted, revealing the entrance to a pas-

Craig-y-Ddinas.

sage. As they went down it, the Welshman saw a bell hanging from the roof.

Soon the passage opened out into a large cavern where many warriors lay asleep in a circle, their heads pointing outwards. One, clearly the chief, had a gold crown beside him. All wore brightly polished armour, and weapons lay ready to hand. Within the circle were a heap of gold and a heap of silver. The wizard told the Welshman that he could take whatever he could carry from one heap or the other, but not from both. On no account must he touch the bell as he went out. If he did, one of the knights would wake and ask if it was day. In that case the only thing to do was to reply: "No, sleep on."

The Welshman loaded himself with so much gold that he moved clumsily and failed to avoid the bell. It rang, the knight woke and asked the question, he gave the answer, and they got safely out and replaced the stone and stump. The wizard told him that the chief of the warriors was Arthur, and that he and his men were waiting for the day when they should wake up and restore justice and peace throughout Britain. With a warning not to squander the gold, he left.

Despite the warning the Welshman did squander it, and wanted more. He returned alone to the cave, again over-loaded himself, and again hit the bell. Again a warrior asked him if it was day. This time he was out of breath and confused, and forgot the answer. Several more of the sleepers rose and took back the gold. They gave him a beating and threw him out, drawing the stone back over the cave-mouth. For the rest of his life he was infirm from the beating and very poor. He searched for the cave again but could never find it.

This tale has variations. One of them is more local. The victim is a drover and meets the wizard nearer the spot. Also he manages a second successful raid, only failing on the third. In another variant he is a shepherd and is shown the cave by fairies: Craig-y-Ddinas is said to be one of the last places in Wales where fairy-folk survived. Nor is the chief always Arthur. He may be Owen Lawgoch, a more purely Welsh hero.

There are parallels with the cave-legend as it is told at **Alderley Edge**, **Caerleon**, **Melrose**, **Richmond**, and **Sewingshields**. But the moral is different. The other stories have nothing about avarice in them.

Crochan Arthur
—see **Gwal y Filiast**

Cumbria

During the later sixth century Cumbria contained the heartland of the kingdom of Rheged, the only British state that won victories over the Anglo-Saxons in the decades after Arthur. Its greatest king was Urbgen or Urien, who reigned in the 570s and 580s. Rheged's frontiers are doubtful. It included the Eden valley, **Carlisle**, and the country around the Solway Firth as far as Annan, and it may have extended much farther along the Galloway coast. Urbgen also ruled part of Yorkshire, and it is possible that "Roch" in Rochdale, Lancashire, is derived from "Rheged".

With aid from Rhydderch, king of **Strathclyde**, Urbgen swept an army of Angles back to the sea and besieged them on Lindisfarne. Near here he was assassinated. His son Owein, who had played a part in his victories, carried on the war but lost ground to the Northumbrian king Aethelfrith. Owein was probably killed himself before 600.

Britain's northern rulers were patrons of a school of bards, authors of the oldest known poetry in Welsh. Nennius names five—Talhaern, Bluchbard, Cian, Aneirin, and Taliesin. Compositions by the last two survive, and have been claimed as the earliest poetry in a still-living European language, apart from Greek. Taliesin is the most famous. He was probably born in Wales, but his verses show his attachment to the royal house of Rheged. They praise Urbgen and Owein for their hospitality and prowess in war. Taliesin lived to compose Owein's elegy. For Aneirin, see **Catterick**. Another northern bard of the same period was Myrddin, the part-original of Merlin, who was involved in the tragic battle of **Arthuret**. Yet another northerner to whom some early verse is ascribed is Llywarch Hen, a cousin of Urbgen. In one of the Llywarch poems he imagines himself carrying the king's head, which was cut off and taken away after the murder, perhaps to save it from defacement by Angles.

> A head I hold up which once sustained me ...
> My arm is numb, my body trembles,
> My heart breaks;
> This head I cherish, formerly cherished me.

The flowering of poetry in and around Rheged is one reason why much Arthurian legend has to do with characters and events that belong in the north, or have northern affiliations. The traditions of this part of Britain were more fully and memorably preserved. Urbgen and Owein themselves appear in stories of Arthur (variously spelled: Owein has a French guise as Yvain). Romancers might be vague about dates, but they always knew that these men were heroes whose proper place was at the noblest court in the world.

See also **Penrith**.

Deganwy
Gwynedd (Caernarvonshire)   *SH 781794*

Castell Deganwy is on the east side of the River Conwy where it flows out through sands into Conwy Bay. Its main natural feature is a pair of small craggy hilltops set close together. Up here, according to tradition, was a citadel of the famous and formidable Maelgwn, king of **Gwynedd** in the sixth-century aftermath of the Arthur period.

A castle built by Henry III formerly covered both the hillocks. On the higher one, however, which has a fairly level top measuring 230 feet by 160, excavations in 1961–66 revealed traces of occupation much earlier. A drystone wall on the east side dated, perhaps, from the

Castell Deganwy, with River Conwy in the foreground.

second century AD, and coins of the third and fourth centuries hinted at a Roman strongpoint, doubtless for defence against Irish raiders. The site may have gone on being used without a break in the fifth century, with Britons taking over from Romans. Whether or not this was the case, imported **Tintagel** pottery showed the presence of a wealthy and powerful household about Maelgwn's time, and there is every reason to accept it as his. The lower ground between the hilltops may have been, so to speak, the servants' quarters.

Local legend has its say about Maelgwn's end. When an epidemic spread through Britain about 547, he shut himself in the nearby church of Rhos, with guards posted to prevent anyone entering. After some days he peeped out through a chink in the door. Presently his guards ceased to hear movement inside the building. They thought he was asleep, and perhaps, at first, he was. But when the silence had lasted for many hours they went in and found him dead. The plague had claimed him. This is the explanation of an old Welsh phrase referring to coma or death, "the long sleep of Maelgwn in the church of Rhos".

Llanrhos is on the small road behind the hills, linking the A496 and B3115. However, the church where Maelgwn slept his long sleep is supposed to have been down by the seashore.

Dimilioc

In Geoffrey of Monmouth's *History* this is the scene of the death of Gorlois, duke of Cornwall, whose wife Ygerna became the mother of Arthur by King Uther Pendragon. Uther's illicit passion for her had caused a quarrel between the king and the duke. Uther led an army against Gorlois, who left his wife at **Tintagel** and marched to "a fortified camp called Dimilioc". There Uther besieged him. After a week Uther slipped away to **Tintagel**, where, by Merlin's magic, he entered the castle disguised as Gorlois and spent the night with Ygerna. Just before, the real Gorlois led a sortie from Dimilioc and was killed. So when matters were sorted out, there was no query as to who, on that fateful night, had begotten Arthur.

It is sometimes said that the place Geoffrey has in mind is the prehistoric camp of **Tregeare Rounds**. This is fairly close to **Tintagel**, and appears on some maps as Castle

Dameliock. Almost certainly, however, it was not known by that name in Geoffrey's time. He is probably thinking of **St Dennis**, where William the Conqueror's Domesday survey lists a manor called "Dimelihoc".

Dinas Bran
—see **Llangollen**

Dinas Emrys
Gwynedd (Caernarvonshire)   *SH 606492*

A hill-fort in **Snowdonia**, in the valley of Nant Gwynant, one mile north-east of Beddgelert. The road along the valley is the A498. The fort is on a craggy height, isolated from neighbouring hills. Its ramparts defend a broad, fairly level summit, about 500 feet by 300. The original entrance was on the west, and it is possible to climb up to it through three lines of fortification. However, the access to a later entrance, on the east side, is easier.

   The name means "Fort of Ambrose" or Ambrosius, i.e. Ambrosius Aurelianus, who launched the fifth-century British rally against the Saxons associated also with Arthur. But legend does not make him the first possessor. In Geoffrey of Monmouth's *History*, Dinas Emrys is the place

Dinas Emrys: the hill-fort.

where Merlin comes on the scene, confronting King Vortigern.

In substance the tale is older than Geoffrey. Nennius gives a version of it. At Dinas Emrys, we are told, Vortigern tried to build a stronghold after his policy of settling Saxons in Britain had led to disaster. Even as a builder he failed. The walls kept collapsing. According to the pre-Geoffrey version he consulted his "wise men" or Druids, and was advised that his only resource was human sacrifice. He must find a boy born without a father, put him to death, and sprinkle his blood on the ground. (For archaeological confirmation of such a custom, see **Cadbury Castle**.)

A boy was found whose mother denied having had intercourse with any man. When brought to the spot, he asked Vortigern's advisers what was hidden under a certain stone. They could not tell him. He replied that there was a pool. This, it seems, was undermining the foundations. He added that it contained a folded tent and two vases. They were duly discovered. He then predicted that two serpents, a red and a white, would be found hidden in the tent. It was unfolded and the serpents emerged. They fought, the white got the advantage, but suddenly the red one recovered and drove the white from the tent. The boy explained that the tent symbolized Britain. The red serpent stood for the Britons, the white for the Saxons. Eventually the Britons, or their descendants, would reconquer their lost lands. But Vortigern himself, who had brought all these troubles on them, was doomed. He must give up the citadel, and the boy himself would take it over. The boy disclosed that he was Prince Ambrose. It is implied—though with some difficulty over dating—that he grew up to be the heroic Ambrosius of history.

When Geoffrey retells the story, the boy becomes Merlin and prophesies at much greater length. The serpents are dragons; hence, at least in part, the Red Dragon of Wales. Ambrosius is a separate character, in essence the historical British leader. Nothing is said about his taking over Dinas Emrys, but Welsh tradition and the name itself testify to a belief that he did.

The place has two further legends. One declares that Merlin lingered in Dinas Emrys for a while after Vortigern's departure. When he left, he filled a golden cauldron with treasure, and stowed it in a cave somewhere among

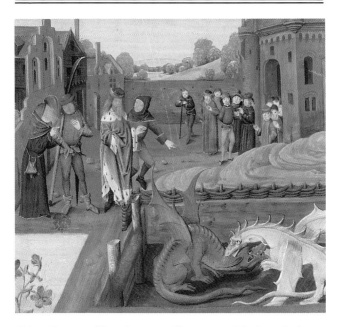

Dinas Emrys: a fifteenth-century illustration of the legend of the dragons revealed by Merlin to King Vortigern, under the foundations of a projected building. Merlin here is in his teens, Vortigern is old.

the rocks, blocking the entrance with a great stone and a pile of earth. The treasure can be recovered only by the person whom he intended to have it. This will be a youth with yellow hair and blue eyes. When he is near, a bell will ring. The barrier in the cave-mouth will fall the moment he sets his foot on it. Over the centuries, treasure-seekers have looked for the cave, but have always been scared away by thunderstorms and other portents.

(**Marchlyn Mawr**, on the other side of Snowdon, also has a treasure story.)

Besides the Vortigern–Ambrosius–Merlin legend, Dinas Emrys has a curious tale about a warrior named Owen. He is supposed to have been a son of Maximus, the emperor who was proclaimed in Britain in 383 and came to be viewed as an honorary Briton. Between Dinas Emrys and the lake of Llyn Dinas, Owen fought a giant. They used missiles—either arrows, or balls made of steel—and stood for cover in hollows in the ground. Neither of them survived the combat. If this tale has any link with the more famous legend, it may lie in some lost dynastic saga. A son of Maximus would have been Vortigern's brother-in-law. See **Llangollen**.

Archaeology shows that some of this has a basis, despite the marvels. Dinas Emrys is a rich site with a long history. Though founded in the pre-Roman Iron Age, it went on being occupied afterwards. Close to the stone foundation of a Roman building is a real pool—an artificial one, dug during the first century AD. Moreover, the fortress actually was in use about the time of Ambrosius. On a platform of ground in a swampy hollow, someone lived during the second half of the fifth century. Objects discovered, including fragments of imported **Tintagel** pottery, suggest Christianity and a certain comfort and wealth. Round about, there are traces of inhabitants at other times, including a twelfth-century tower.

Dinas Powys or Powis
South Glamorgan   *ST 155723*

A small hill-top stronghold near the A4055 south of Cardiff, on the wooded tip of a ridge of limestone. Its main earthwork fortifications are medieval, but excavation in 1958 revealed traces of simpler ones belonging to the fifth century. They defended what was apparently a chieftain's home. A fair-sized hall and at least one other building were occupied for 100 years or more. The site was archaeologically rich, with evidences of smelting, metal-working, and the making of jewellery, and much else to show how the household lived—on the whole, in a mixture of luxury and squalor which now seems odd.

Though the hill was inhabited round about the time of Arthur, no story connects him with it. However, since it commands a wide view across the Bristol Channel to **Brent Knoll** in Somerset, it is one of the proposed signal-stations in the "Arthurian beacon" theory.

Dindraithov, Dindraethou
—see **Dunster**

Dolorous Gard
—see **Joyous Gard**

Dolorous Mountain

Geoffrey of Monmouth gives this as an alternative name for the hill which he also calls **Agned**, and identifies as the site of the **Castle of Maidens**. He probably means Castle Rock in **Edinburgh**. However, the twelfth-century French poet Chrétien de Troyes locates the Dolorous Mountain near **Melrose**.

Dover

Kent   *TR 326418*

Dover Castle stands on a hill overlooking the town and harbour. A human skull formerly kept in it was alleged to be Sir Gawain's. Caxton mentions this relic in his preface to Malory, printed in 1485. Malory himself tells how it came to be there.

When Guinevere was about to be put to death in **Carlisle** for her adultery with Lancelot, he came with an armed following to rescue her. He succeeded, but in the struggle he killed Gawain's two brothers. The uproar over the queen's love-affair caused a split among the knights, with Gawain, understandably, as Lancelot's bitterest opponent. Lancelot withdrew to his lands in France, and Arthur followed with an army. Gawain challenged Lancelot to single combat. They fought hand to hand with swords for a long time. Owing to an enchantment, Gawain's strength grew as the sun climbed towards noon, but after that it decreased, and Lancelot was able to wound him. Then the revolt of Modred forced Arthur to return to Britain. He landed at Dover and fought his way ashore. Gawain took part in the battle and the wound Lancelot had given him reopened, fatally. He died at noon and Arthur had him buried in the chapel of Dover Castle.

The tale of Gawain's death at Dover is earlier than Malory. It occurs in a thirteenth-century French romance which he adapted for his own work (though in that, the body is taken to **Camelot** for burial). Gawain—despite his mythical-sounding "solar" quality—is more likely to have been a real person than most of the other knights. He appears in early texts as Gwalchmei. But he is not likely to have died at Dover. Its Roman lighthouse tower is part of the castle to this day, and the harbour below may still have been in use in the fifth century. However, the Jutish branch of the Saxon invasion overwhelmed Kent fairly rapidly, and no counter-attack ever brought British warriors back to the Straits. A Welsh tradition, prior to the medieval romances, has Gawain buried on the Pembrokeshire coast. See **St Govan's Head**.

Dozmary Pool
Cornwall   *SX 195745*

A tarn in the middle of Bodmin Moor, about 900 feet above sea-level, surrounded by open grassland and bleak hills rising slightly higher. It is reached by a minor road which leaves the A30 at Jamaica Inn, well known through Daphne du Maurier's novel. The road runs south-east and swings to the right. Shortly afterwards a footpath leads to the pool. This is one of the places where Sir Bedivere is said to have thrown away Excalibur, obeying Arthur's command after twice demurring. Probably the notion is only a modern romantic fancy. Dozmary Pool is not close to any reputed site of the battle of **Camlann** where Arthur fell, nor is there any reason why, mortally wounded, he should have been brought here.

Cornish lore of a more rooted kind regards the pool as sinister, naming not Arthur but the arch-villain Jan Tregeagle (pronounced Tregayle). He was a cruel and corrupt

Dozmary Pool.

magistrate guilty of many evil deeds around Wadebridge. After his death he was preserved from damnation for the sake of a single good action. As penance, however, his ghost was set impossible tasks, one of them being to empty Dozmary Pool with a leaking limpet shell. The impossibility is underlined by another folk belief—that the pool is bottomless. Actually it is fairly shallow, and in 1859 it dried up, since when the legend of its unfathomed depth has been heard less often.

All the same it is an atmospheric lake. In winter the mists can easily hide the farther shore. A little way to the south are the Brown Gelly Downs, with many traces of prehistoric inhabitants.

For other places where Excalibur was cast away, see **Bosherston**, **Glastonbury** (Pomparles Bridge), **Llyn Llydaw**, **Llyn Ogwen**, **Loe Pool**.

Drumelzier

Borders (Peebles)   *NT 135343*

Here in Tweeddale, between the B712 and the river, Merlin is said to be buried. Drumelzier is among high hills, but this part of the valley opens out and the hills draw back somewhat. Merlin's grave is beside a burn (the Pausayl or Powsail, i.e. Willow) near where it joins the Tweed.

Drumelzier itself is very small. The burn runs swiftly through it and passes under a canopy of trees. On the left is a steep bank going up to a bluff where the little church stands among its gravestones, with sparser trees round about. The burn emerges into the open, turns left around the base of the bluff, and flows on to the Tweed a short distance away across the meadows.

A nineteenth-century visitor was told that the grave was by a thorn-tree, near the foot of the bluff below the church. That seems the favoured site. However, a rival is mentioned—the corner of a field by the Tweed, where there was once a cairn. This second location is not beside the burn in its present course. But allegedly it flowed that way during a spate in 1603 when James VI of Scotland became James I of England. Thus a prophecy was fulfilled and, by the same event, the identity of the cairn was confirmed:

When Tweed and Pausayl meet at Merlin's grave,
Scotland and England shall one monarch have.

This couplet is ascribed to Thomas the Rhymer (see
Melrose). In the absence of any cairn today, the second
story seems to end with a query, but the valley floor is so
flat that the burn might have changed course.

Merlin's name is preserved in Merlindale, across the
bridge on the other side of the Tweed. According to the
Drumelzier legend his doom came upon him because he
stirred up a revolt of heathen tribesmen against the Britons
of **Strathclyde**. The rebels were defeated and slaughtered.
Guilt for their death being on the enchanter's head, he was
condemned to wander until he died himself. When he met
wayfarers who would listen to him, he prophesied how his
death would happen. To some he said he would fall from a
cliff, to others he said he would be hanged, to others he
said he would be drowned. His forecasts, therefore, were
not taken very seriously. Yet they all came true. Running
away from some shepherds who were menacing him, he
jumped off a cliff above the Tweed. Below were stakes
supporting salmon nets in the river. His feet were caught
and he hung head-down in the water till he drowned. He
was taken to Drumelzier for burial.

This tale cannot be fitted to the Merlin of romance, who
is shut in a cave or tree by bewitchment and never dies at
all. The battle motif shows that we are in touch with the
older tradition of the northern bard Myrddin, one of the
two or three men who are combined in the character of the
magician (see **Arthuret**, **Carmarthen**). Located as it is on
the upper Tweed, Drumelzier is within the vast, vague
Forest of **Celidon** which was the scene of Myrddin's
wanderings. The theme of a threefold death occurs in
Geoffrey of Monmouth's *Life of Merlin*, which is based on
legends of this northerner. There, he foretells it for
someone else. But a version in which a prophet applies it
to himself, and suffers it at Drumelzier and is buried there,
is told of the similar wanderer called Lailoken. Lailoken
has been supposed, probably rightly, to be Myrddin under
another name. So when Myrddin was built up into Merlin,
he trailed traditions of Lailoken behind him, including the
grave at Drumelzier.

Marlborough has another grave of Merlin.

Dubglas

In Nennius's account of Arthur's twelve battles, four of

them—the second, third, fourth, and fifth—are said to have taken place by a "river which is called Dubglas and is in the region Linnuis". Sceptics have urged that the statement cannot be trusted because it speaks of four battles, whereas the rest of the list assigns only a single battle to each place. The suggestion is that Nennius (or a previous writer copied by him) knew a tradition of Arthur's having fought twelve battles, but knew the names of only nine, and brought the list up to the proper number by simply inventing three more battles of Dubglas. It may be so. However, it may also be that Arthur fought four battles along the same river line because the area was important and involved him in a long campaign.

Unfortunately "Dubglas" defies pinning down. It means "blue-black". When every river still had its British name, this epithet might have been applied to many. It turns up on the modern map, with variants meaning "black stream", in such forms as "Douglas", "Dawlish", "Divelish". The river name "Blackwater" in Ireland is doubtless an English rendering of an Irish equivalent. Nennius may have realized that "Dubglas" was an imprecise clue, and added "in the region Linnuis" to define which of the black rivers he meant—as we speak now of "the Hampshire Avon" or "the Warwickshire Avon". Geoffrey of Monmouth calls the river "Douglas" and locates it near York, but it is unlikely that he does this out of any real knowledge.

In the search for this battle site, the other name, **Linnuis**, is probably the more helpful.

Dumbarton
Strathclyde (Dunbartonshire)   *NS 400745*

"Dumbarton" is from the Gaelic *Dun Breatann*, Fort of the Britons. The fort was on the rocky headland jutting into the Clyde from the modern town. Its former British possessors called the place "Alclud" or "Alcluith", the "Rock of Clyde". Bede, the historian, speaks of Alcluith in 731 as "a town or city of the Britons, strongly defended up to the present day". It had been so for several centuries, in the time of Arthur and earlier.

The headland is 240 feet high, a bare volcanic mass of basalt. A legend of St Patrick purports to account for it. The saint is said to have lived near Glasgow before his Irish mission. The Devil scented a major potential enemy,

and summoned a horde of witches who chased Patrick
down the Clyde. He found a boat on the shore and pushed
off for Ireland. Since witches cannot cross running water,
his pursuers went to a nearby hill, tore off a large part of it
and flung it after him. However, it fell short and is now the
rock.

In Arthur's time the fort was the capital of a British
kingdom extending southwards. Its name seems to have
been applied to the whole territory ruled from it, the
domain of Alclud. This kingdom was created by sons and
grandsons of British nobles who held the area, under
Roman sponsorship, during the last years of imperial rule.
It is better known by the still-surviving name probably
given to it somewhat later, **Strathclyde**.

Geoffrey of Monmouth asserts that Alclud proper—the
citadel on the Rock—was founded about 1000 BC by King
Ebraucus, who also founded **Edinburgh**. Geoffrey may
simply have made this up. Or he may have known some
tradition of a much older stronghold on the site. Excavations by Leslie Alcock have tended to confirm that it at

Dumbarton Rock, dominating the River Clyde.

least rose to importance in the fifth century AD, mainly as a centre of sovereignty. Geoffrey says further that when Arthur was campaigning against the Saxons, a British force in Alclud was besieged by the Picts and Scots. After finishing his Saxon war he had to march north to raise the siege. This was the occasion of his visit to Loch **Lomond**. A document of 1367 actually calls Dumbarton *Castrum Arthuri*, Arthur's Castle, and a Scottish legend makes it the birthplace of Modred.

There seems to be no basis for the notion that Alclud was **Astolat**, except that they both begin with "A".

Dunster

Somerset   *SS 992435*

Dunster Castle is three miles south-east of Minehead, on a hillside at the approaches of Exmoor. The building is of various dates, with a thirteenth-century gateway as its oldest portion. But the same place was the site of an earlier Norman stronghold, and apparently of a Celtic one long before that. An Irish book, *Cormac's Glossary*, probably means Dunster when it refers to "Dun Traduc" as the three-fossed fort of an Irish prince. This area may well have been temporarily in Irish hands during a phase of raiding and land-seizing in western Britain before Arthur's time. However, it is as Dindraithov or Dindraethou, a fort of the Britons, that the place figures in a Welsh story of Arthur during his early career. He is said to have held court here as the colleague—apparently the junior colleague—of a local ruler named Cato or Cadwy.

For the story, see **Carhampton**. Cadwy can be traced far back and was a real person. He reappears in Geoffrey of Monmouth's *History* as Cador, the duke or "king" of Cornwall, who accepts Arthur's supremacy when the latter becomes sovereign of Britain, and serves him loyally in his wars. It has been suggested that the name "Cadbury" in Somerset means "Cadwy's Fort". If he was lord of **Cadbury Castle** as well as Dunster, perhaps Arthur took it over from him. See also **Cadon Barrow**.

It is possible that Dindraithov was not on the medieval site, but should be identified with the hill-fort Bat's Castle (SS 988421).

Edinburgh

NT 252736

At the Scottish capital the visible Arthurian feature is the hill to the east, **Arthur's Seat (1)**. Its name may only reflect medieval fancy. However, a sixth-century date for its defences cannot be ruled out. This area was then part of the British kingdom of Manau Guotodin. One of the oldest surviving poems in Welsh is Aneirin's lament for the band of warriors who, some decades after Arthur, rode from here and fought the Angles at **Catterick**. Their base is a "Din Eydin" which seems to be Edinburgh. Another Welsh poem speaks of Arthur's own men fighting "on Eidyn's mountain".

Edinburgh is often said to be later than that, and to have grown round a fort built on Castle Rock by King Edwin of Northumbria, when the Angles had pushed forward and conquered this region. But the story would not conflict with an earlier British presence. Hence **Arthur's Seat** may quite well have got its name from a tradition of British military use in the sixth century, which was taken, rightly or wrongly, to mean use by Arthur.

Whether this hill or Castle Rock itself was the Britons' Din Eydin is another question again. Geoffrey of Monmouth claims that Edinburgh was founded about 1000 BC by the "British" king Ebraucus, who also founded Alclud, i.e. **Dumbarton**. Here he locates the **Castle of Maidens**, the hill on which it stands being Mount **Agned** or the **Dolorous Mountain**, and he is probably thinking of Castle Rock and whatever fortifications were on it in his own day. By calling it Agned he implies that Edinburgh was the scene of Arthur's eleventh battle, though his own account of Arthur's wars never mentions it.

The French romancers sometimes call Edinburgh "Daneborc".

Eildon Hills
—see **Melrose**

Eliseg, Pillar of
—see **Llangollen**

Ercing or Erging

In early Welsh geography this is the cantref (district) later called Archenfield. Here Nennius locates the grave of Arthur's ill-fated son Amr. "Ercing" is derived from Ariconium, the name of a Roman settlement 2½ miles east of Ross-on-Wye, but the cantref extended far across Herefordshire.

Nennius lists the grave among a number of "marvels", for a reason which appears at the end.

> There is another marvel in the district which is called Ercing. Here is a burial mound near a spring which is known as Licat Amr, and the name of the man who is buried in the mound is Amr. He was the son of Arthur the soldier, and Arthur himself killed him there and buried him. And men come to measure the length of the mound, and find it sometimes six feet, sometimes nine, sometimes twelve, and sometimes fifteen. Whatever length you find it at one time, you will find it different at another, and I myself have proved this to be true.

"Licat" means "eye" in Old Welsh, and also the source of a river. This is one of the earliest written stories of Arthur. No one knows the background of his grim deed. The

grave-mound of Amr (or Anir; the spelling is uncertain) is supposed to have been near the spring of **Gamber Head**, identified with Licat Amr. Its changing in size is another riddle.

Ercing reappears, spelled Erging, in Geoffrey of Monmouth's *History* as the cantref where Vortigern had a stronghold which was his last refuge from the avenging Ambrosius. See **Ganarew**.

Nennius has another marvel in **Buelt**.

Escalot

—see **Astolat**

Ffon y Cawr

Gwynedd (Caernarvonshire)   *SH 738717*

The "Giant's Staff" in the hills south of Penmaenmawr, a thin standing stone also called Picell Arthur, Arthur's Spear. The giant is said to have thrown it at a dog who was

Ffon y Cawr:
Arthur's Spear.

not minding his sheep properly. It is possible that the stone was actually set up about Arthur's time.

Fowey

Cornwall   *SX 112522*

Shortly before the A3082 enters Fowey, a weather-worn monolith stands beside the road on a pedestal. It was moved here in 1971 from the nearby Four Turnings crossroads opposite the lodge gates of Menabilly. Before being planted at the crossroads it was in at least two other places, and lay for years in a field 200 yards to the north. At some stage a piece may have broken off the top.

The stone is about seven feet high. Down one face of it is a two-line inscription, which, slightly corrected, reads:

DRUSTANUS HIC IACIT CUNOMORI FILIUS

The lettering is in a style suggesting the early or middle sixth century. The words mean "Drustanus lies here, the son of Cunomorus." "Cunomorus" is a Latin version of "Cynvawr". A Cynvawr ruled this corner of Britain, and, it seems, some of Brittany too, early in the sixth century. The stone probably stood over the grave of a son of his.

Since the name "Drustanus" is found in other forms proving it to be the same as "Tristan", the stone is called the Tristan Stone, and has often been claimed as the monument of the Tristan of romance. Certainly this is the only inscription of the right period which gives us the name of an Arthurian knight. Furthermore, a ninth-century author says that Cynvawr was otherwise known as Mark—the name of Iseult's husband. It has been maintained that **Castle Dore**, only a couple of miles away, was a residence of his. Other clues also point to this area as the main locale of the Tristan story (see **Golant**, **Lantyan**).

So it is natural to conclude that here, at any rate, we have hard fact at the root of an Arthurian legend. To judge from the inscription Tristan was a son of Mark, not a nephew as he is in the story; and Iseult, presumably, was a young second wife taken by his father. Poets might have changed the relationship to put the lovers in a less unattractive light. The real trouble is that the tales of Tristan and Mark have other antecedents besides Cornish ones. "Drust" in various forms was a Pictish name (though Britons were being called so as early as the sixth century), and one or two of Tristan's early adventures recall tales that were told of an eighth-century Drust in Scotland, where there is a **Trusty's Hill**. The great medieval love-

Fowey: the Tristan Stone.

romance itself has Welsh and Irish ingredients. King Mark appears in other places—conspicuously, in Wales.

It has even been maintained that the legend is not Cornish at all, and was only planted in the Fowey neighbourhood because of the monument. Somebody jumped to the conclusion that Drustanus was the Tristan in question, and everything else followed. That conclusion is assumed to have been mistaken. However, so little is known of the way stories were spread and elaborated, in the two or three centuries after Arthur, that the assumption cannot be proved and the conclusion, even if jumped to, may have been right. The Tristan Stone could indeed be the memorial of the man himself.

Gamber Head
Hereford and Worcester (Herefordshire)   *SO 495296*

The source of the Gamber, by the A466 five miles south of Hereford, is a spring asserted to be the Licat Amr of Nennius (see **Ercing**). It is at the edge of a farm. The water that wells up through sandy soil is believed to come from a long way off, perhaps from the Black Hills to the west, perhaps from the Malverns. Nothing is here to account for Nennius's bizarre statement about a grave-mound that varied in size. It has been claimed that he means Wormelow Tump (SO 492303), a little nearer Hereford. But this mound, which may or may not have been a barrow, no longer exists.

Ganarew
Hereford and Worcester (Herefordshire)   *SO 530161*

In Geoffrey of Monmouth's *History*, when Merlin confronts the wicked King Vortigern, he prophesies his imminent doom. Aurelius Ambrosius, Britain's rightful sovereign, is about to return from overseas. Vortigern takes refuge in "the castle of Genoreu", on a hill called Cloartius. Ambrosius arrives and besieges him. The castle catches fire and the usurper dies in the flames.

Genoreu is Ganarew, a couple of miles from Geoffrey's native Monmouth along the road to Ross-on-Wye, the A40. Cloartius is the nearby hill of Little Doward, which has an Iron Age fort. Fifth-century timber buildings (easier to set alight than a medieval castle) may once have stood on it.

The name "Cloartius" is due to a mistaken copying of "Doartius", the Latin form of "Doward".

These events take place before Arthur's birth, but they prepare the way for his reign. The area has other associations with him. In a hillside near Little Doward itself is **Arthur's Cave**. Geoffrey speaks of Genoreu as being in the district of **Ercing**, and in the same district Nennius places the burial-mound of Amr, the son whom Arthur mysteriously slew.

Gawain's Tomb
—see **Dover**, **St Govan's Head**

Genoreu
—see **Ganarew**

Gerrans
Cornwall *SW 873352*

This village, on the promontory over the water east of Falmouth, is supposed to have been named after the West Country ruler Geraint—an Arthurian character (husband, in some stories, of the Lady Enid) who almost certainly existed. "Geraint" is the Roman name Gerontius, which may itself have a Celtic ancestry. According to legend, when he died, his body was rowed across Gerrans Bay in a golden boat with silver oars, and buried with a huge mound heaped over it. The mound was identified with Veryan Beacon (SX 913387). In 1855 this round barrow, now overgrown with gorse, was excavated and a stone container with ashes in it was brought to light.

Several Geraints are on record in the West Country, and it is hard to tell which is which. One of them, maybe the Arthurian one, figures in a poem about a battle at **Llongborth**. Another, probably senior, is said to have been the father of Cadwy, Arthur's co-prince at **Dunster**.

To judge from a "Life" of a British saint, Teilo, and allusions to a church, the Geraint buried at Gerrans—if hardly in the barrow—may have been younger than the Arthurian one, and the village was named after him in the belief that he was a saint himself. Much later again, a Geraint is mentioned as fighting at **Catterick**, in the battle commemorated by Aneirin.

Glastonbury
Somerset   *ST 501388*

Beside the main roads entering this little town, signboards
welcome the visitor to "the ancient Avalon". Glastonbury's
identity with that fabled island, the **Avalon** of legend, is one
of several hard questions. Others arise out of its claims to the
Holy Grail and the grave of Arthur. But certainly it is unlike
anywhere else. It nestles in a strange cluster of hills, all
differently shaped. The highest, Glastonbury Tor, is a wildly
distorted cone with a tower on its summit. Wirral or
Wearyall Hill is a ridge stretching out towards the Bristol
Channel. Chalice Hill is a smooth natural dome. Windmill
Hill, more outspread, masks the others as you approach
from Wells.

Around is flat country. At the beginning of the Christian
era, much of it was submerged or swampy. Glastonbury's
hill-cluster was not far from being an island. In the middle
distance were Celtic lake-villages at Godney and Meare,
on ground artificially banked up. These were centres of the
"La Tène" culture, and objects from them are on view in
the town museum, which is housed in a medieval building
called the Tribunal. They witness to a high degree of
craftsmanship and sophistication. In Roman times, to judge

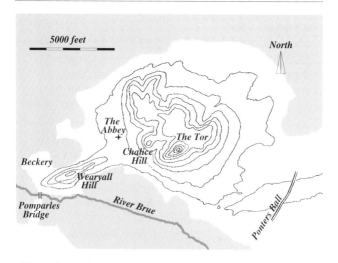

*Glastonbury island: contours at 50-foot intervals. The shaded
area was flooded until recent times.*

from traces of a wharf by Wearyall Hill, Glastonbury was a port. The water was still there in Arthur's day—very probably more of it, and closer in. The reclamation and draining of the levels came later, and even in fairly recent years, floods have been known to surge over the whole green expanse between town and sea.

People of Celtic stock formerly spoke of Glastonbury as Ynys-witrin, the Glass Island. Whether this was its name before the Saxons gave it its present one, or whether it was a mis-rendering of the Saxon name which sounded as if it had "glass" in it, is another hard question. Glass would have evoked Celtic fairy-lore and otherworld mythology, Avalonian or not (as at **Bardsey**). But whatever else was happening here before the Saxons' arrival, the "island" or near-island was the home of a community of British monks living in wattle cells.

Their monastery had a high reputation. Many saints of the Celtic Church are said to have come to it, and a Welsh triad makes it one of the handful with the distinction of a perpetual choir (see **Amesbury**). It was far enough west to escape the horrors of the early waves of Saxon invasion. Checked by the counter-attacks of Ambrosius and Arthur, the conquerors paused a long way short of Glastonbury and did not reach it till 658. By then they had become Christians themselves. The kings of Wessex took charge of the monastery, endowed and enlarged it, with no break in continuity. It became a temple of reconciliation between the races, where they worked together instead of killing each other. Here in a sense the United Kingdom was born. The monastery grew into a vast Benedictine abbey, a national shrine, so rich in its history, traditions, and multitude of great names that Glastonbury was spoken of as a second Rome.

Something of the abbey is still there, a huge, cryptic, haunting memento of an amazing past. The entrance is through an arch beside the Town Hall and up an approach path. It can also be reached directly from the adjoining carpark. A bookshop by the entrance offers illustrated guides, books and souvenirs.

Glastonbury Abbey at its height was the largest and wealthiest in the kingdom after **Westminster**. As a popular saying put it, "If the abbot of Glastonbury could marry the abbess of Shaftesbury they would have more land than the king of England." In 1539 the Abbey was dissolved by

Henry VIII with exceptional ruthlessness, and its last abbot, Richard Whiting, was hanged. A few years afterwards it came into private hands. Its successive owners tore most of it down to sell as material for walls and roads. In 1908 the Church of England acquired the site and took steps to preserve what little was left. The scanty ruins standing today are fragments of buildings dating from the late twelfth century onward, replacing much older ones destroyed by a fire in 1184.

The Arthurian and related stories centre on the western end of the ruins. Here is the shell of the Lady Chapel, with a crypt below. The chapel was built on the site of the "Old Church", a deeply revered structure which the fire of 1184 wiped out. Dedicated to the Virgin Mary, it was a plain building, basically of wattle-work, though reinforced with timber and lead. According to a legend which story-tellers and poets have elaborated over the past seven or eight centuries, its builder was Joseph of Arimathea, the rich man who obtained the body of Christ after the crucifixion and had it buried in his own tomb. Joseph and several companions came to Britain bringing the Holy Grail, and made Glastonbury their home.

This famous and beloved story grew round the simple fact of the Old Church. At the earliest times we can document, it had already been standing there for many years, and no one really knew who had built it. In the tenth century, some said it had been miraculously planted by God himself and dedicated to his earthly Mother. In the early twelfth century its foundation was ascribed, by some, to disciples of Christ. But the leader of those disciples was not named as Joseph, the Grail-bringer, in any known writing till 100 years or so later again. It remains a puzzle why he should have begun to figure in chronicle and romance when he did. There may have been a far older tradition of his coming, preserved orally in Wales, and rediscovered with other Celtic matter in the Arthurian upsurge of the twelfth century. Nothing can be proved. What is very likely indeed, however, is that behind the legend—behind the mystery of the Old Church itself—is a solid and remarkable fact: that Glastonbury truly was the first British Christian community, or at any rate the first that survived, with an origin possibly in Roman times and almost certainly not long after, whoever the founder may have been.

Glastonbury: artist's impression of the original wattle church, known as the Old Church in the Abbey's earliest records and finally destroyed in the great fire of 1184.

Once Joseph was established in that role, the Abbey grew to value him more and more. Towards the end of its existence the crypt under the Lady Chapel was a separate chapel for him. Here the pilgrims came with offerings. It has been repaved and is now in use again as a place of worship, weather permitting, since it is open to the sky.

A late growth is the legend of the Holy Thorn, said to have sprung from Joseph's staff when he planted it in the ground after disembarking from a boat at Wearyall Hill. The original Glastonbury Thorn grew on that hill; a stone marks the spot where the tree is popularly supposed to have stood. Today, descendants of it are flourishing in the Abbey and in front of St John's Church in the High Street, and on Wearyall Hill beside the stone. The Thorn's peculiarity is that it blossoms at Christmas or thereabouts. A sprig of the white blossom is cut off and sent to the reigning sovereign. It is not a native English tree, and the closest parallels to it are found in Syria—which, to be fair, does adjoin the Holy Land where Joseph came from! The truth may be that the first specimen was brought back by a pilgrim in the Middle Ages.

Another late growth is the belief that Joseph was Jesus's uncle or great-uncle, and that he brought the boy with him on an earlier visit to Glastonbury. It is not known when or how this story originated, but it can hardly have been current at Glastonbury in the Middle Ages, since the

Glastonbury: William Camden's drawing of the cross found in Arthur's grave. The style of lettering may be earlier than the 1190s when the discovery was announced, but there is no agreement as to what date it does indicate.

Abbey's chroniclers would certainly have made much of it, and they never mention it.

About 50 feet from the south door of the Lady Chapel is the site of Arthur's grave. This can be located roughly by standing on the far side of a path that runs parallel to the chapel wall. It was found—so the report goes—because when Henry II was in Wales, a bard divulged a long-kept secret. Arthur was buried at Glastonbury in the monks' graveyard between two pillars, probably the shafts of old crosses. Henry passed this on to the abbot. Nothing was done at the time, but in 1190 or 1191, during reconstruction after the fire, the monks decided to dig. Seven feet below ground level they unearthed a stone slab and a leaden cross, with the inscription

HIC IACET SEPULTUS INCLITUS REX ARTURIUS
IN INSULA AVALONIA

—Here lies buried the renowned King Arthur in the Isle of Avalon. Considerably farther down was a coffin hollowed out of a log like a dugout canoe. Inside were the bones of a tall man, with damage to the skull suggesting death by a blow on the head. Some smaller bones, and a scrap of yellow hair which crumbled when touched, were explained as Guinevere's.

We have an account of this exhumation by Giraldus
Cambrensis, an observant Welshman who was there soon
afterwards and discussed it with witnesses. Nevertheless,
until a few years ago, historians were apt to argue that the
monks invented the whole business for publicity because
they needed money to rebuild after the fire. But then critics
began to point out that this was unlikely. The description
suggests an actual ancient burial, and medieval monks
lacked the knowledge to get it right. In 1962 Dr Ralegh

*Glastonbury: the north door of St Mary's Chapel in the Abbey
ruins, about 1910. The chapel was built to replace the wattle
church, and this view just about frames the site on the south side
where the monks dug to find Arthur's grave in 1190.*

Radford excavated the site and showed that they had told the truth, at least to the extent that they did dig where they said, and did find an early grave. Its stone lining was still there, and it was in a part of the graveyard which would have been regarded as a place of honour.

So the question narrows down to this: Was it Arthur? (And, of course, Guinevere.) Most historians would still insist that it was not, that the claim was only a fund-raising stunt, though in fact no evidence exists that it was ever exploited for that purpose. The answer must depend at least partly on whether or not the inscribed cross was a fake. It has been lost, but perhaps not for ever, since it can be traced to a Mr Hughes in Wells in the eighteenth century. Meanwhile we have a drawing of one side of it, published by William Camden in 1607. This is the "Here lies Arthur" side. The other may have had writing about Guinevere. Again there are riddles. The style of lettering on the cross is crude, and curious. If the monks forged it they did a more interesting job than most medieval forgers. But scholarly opinion differs as to the date which the style does indicate. Guesses range from the twelfth century back to the sixth, the latter view implying that the cross could have been authentic and the grave genuine.

It is sometimes urged that the find was too sudden and opportune to be credible. If Arthur's grave had been there all along, the community would have known, and said so before. However, that is far from certain. Once again we must remember that because of the Anglo-Saxon conquest, many traditions handed down on the Celtic fringe were quite unknown in England till the rush of rediscovery in the twelfth century. With Arthur's grave, the story of the bard and Henry II seems to imply just such a rediscovery, rather than an invention out of nothing. And in view of the grave's prestige value, it is worth noting that Glastonbury's claim was never seriously contested. Once the secret was out, apparently, even Welshmen were aware of some reason why they could not challenge it.

Having found the bones, the monks enshrined them in their church. When this was enlarged, they made a black marble tomb in front of the high altar, and there the remains of Arthur and Guinevere were reinterred in 1278 during a state visit by Edward I. The place is marked today by a notice-board, whereas the original grave is not, a fact which can confuse visitors.

Coupled with the belief that Glastonbury was Arthur's last resting-place is a belief about the casting-away of Excalibur. Bedivere threw the sword into the mere at Pomparles Bridge—*pont périlleux*, the dangerous bridge—which spans the River Brue near the far end of Wearyall Hill on the way to Street, though the present structure, of course, is only a modern successor of the one intended. That area was then probably under water, and a mere would have been available. However, Pomparles has rivals (see **Bosherston**, **Dozmary Pool**, **Llyn Llydaw**, **Llyn Ogwen**, **Loe Pool**). Apart from this romantic motif, Arthur's death in or near Glastonbury would have a serious bearing on the problem of **Camlann** where he fought his last battle.

Glastonbury's other Arthurian focus is the Tor, which is the highest hill in the cluster, and National Trust property. It is reached from the town by heading out as for Shepton Mallet on the A361. Still within the built-up area, a minor road called Well House Lane turns off to the left. This leads to both the public paths up the Tor. One of them starts a few yards from the intersection, the other on higher ground some distance along, near where the lane swings right to circle the hill.

The Tor is a strange formation, with its whaleback shape and its ruined tower on top. It can be seen a long way off—the distant view from the Mendips, as you approach from Bristol or **Bath**, is especially striking—but in the centre of Glastonbury itself it vanishes, because the lower and rounder Chalice Hill is in the way. Ridges or terraces along the sides give an odd stepped effect. They are best seen in profile from the higher part of Well House Lane. Whatever the reason for them, the Tor itself is not (as many suppose) artificial. Of the two ways up it, the one that begins near the Shepton Mallet road is a long but mostly gradual climb; the other, at the far end, is shorter and steeper.

At the summit by the tower is a small plateau. It is 518 feet above sea-level. The impressive view includes the Mendips, and **Brent Knoll** near the Bristol Channel. In clear weather it extends to Wales. On the other side of the Tor **Cadbury Castle** is visible, whence in part the "beacon" theory, for which see **Brent Knoll**. But it is hard to pick out becase it blends with a line of hills behind it.

The Tor is the probable locale of the oldest story connecting Arthur with Glastonbury, one that was current long before any claims were made about his grave. It is told by Caradoc, a monk of **Llancarfan** in his "Life" of Gildas. Melwas, king of the Summer Land (Somerset), carried off Guinevere and kept her at Glastonbury. Arthur arrived to rescue her with Cornish and Devonian levies, though his operations were hampered by the watery country round about. Before the fighting could grow too serious, Gildas and the abbot arranged a treaty. Arthur and Melwas made up their quarrel in the church of St Mary—that is, the Old Church—and Guinevere was restored.

This is the first known version of a tale which appears in several medieval romances, changing as it goes along. Melwas becomes "Meleagant" and later "Meliagaunt" or "Mellyagraunce", a sinister knight. His castle is moved to Lambeth and the rescuer becomes Lancelot. But the Glastonbury tale is the original, and the Tor would have been an obvious place for a local chief to make a strong-point. In 1964–65 Philip Rahtz excavated the summit area and found, on the south and east sides, traces of buildings of more or less Arthurian date. The complex may have been part of Melwas's establishment. However, it may also have been monastic. The question is not settled.

The Tor's stepped appearance, though usually ascribed to agricultural work, has prompted theories about its use in pre-Christian ritual. Certainly it once had an otherworldly aura and was held to be an abode of strange beings—as indeed it still is, by some. The "Life" of the sixth-century St Collen preserves a tradition of this type. He is said to have spent some time as a hermit on the Tor's lower slope. One day Gwyn ap Nudd, king of the fairy-folk and lord of the Otherworld realm of **Annwn**, sent a messenger inviting Collen to visit him at the top of the hill. The saint demurred, but the invitation was repeated and at last he went. Taking some holy water, he climbed up and passed through a secret entrance into a palace. Gwyn, seated on a golden chair, offered him food, but he knew that this was a trap. After a brief conversation he tossed his holy water around him. The palace vanished and Collen found himself alone on the Tor.

Gwyn is a figure from Celtic paganism. His father Nudd is the British god Nodons, who had a temple at Lydney in Gloucestershire. Gwyn and his hidden realm of **Annwn** both appear in early Welsh legends of Arthur, who, in spectral form, rides with him on the Wild Hunt through the sky.

It was doubtless because the monks felt the Tor to be uncanny that they built a small church on top, and dedicated it to St Michael the Archangel, conqueror of the powers of hell. The powers of hell were perhaps incompletely conquered, because it fell down in an earthquake. The present tower is the last fragment of another church of St Michael, built to replace it. Local legend speaks of a hidden chamber under the tower. People who find their way into it go mad. The notion may be a last echo of ancient Celtic belief about the entrance to **Annwn**.

Glastonbury: the Tor much as Arthur would have seen it, except that there was no tower on top and the flat land was flooded.

If the terraces around the Tor's sides were made for any ritual purpose, they must date from an earlier period than St Collen. They are much worn and weathered. However, attempts have been made to reconstruct a pattern in the shape of a spiral path winding in and out and in again, circling the hill several times, and ending near the top. The strength of the argument is that the same septenary maze-spiral occurs in other places—though, admittedly, not carved in hillsides—and was clearly strong magic thousands of years ago.

Hence, there is a case for the spiral maze theory which archaeologists are willing to entertain. More speculative is the zodiac theory. This asserts that the landscape overlooked by the Tor is covered with immense figures which represent zodiacal signs. They are marked out by streams, hills, old trackways, and other features, and form a circle ten miles across. Even believers are divided about them, disagreeing as to how they were made and what exactly the outlines are. They are only visible (if at all) from the air and it is useless to climb the Tor in the hope of seeing them. The Tor itself is said to be part of Aquarius. The Sagittarius figure is a mounted warrior, claimed as a divine or symbolic "Arthur" of great antiquity, whose mythology shaped the legends about the human one.

At the Tor's foot on the side towards Chalice Hill is a garden containing Chalice Well. This is owned and looked after by the Chalice Well Trust, a religious body, which sponsored Rahtz's excavations. The intending visitor should check in advance whether the garden will be open. Chalice Well itself, up a long slope, is enclosed by medieval stonework. The spring that feeds it, nine feet down, flows copiously even in drought. Owing to an iron impregnation the water has a slight "spa" quality, and gives a reddish-orange tinge to the stone of the channels which carry it away.

Chalice Well used to be called "Chalk" Well, or, because of its tinted water, the Blood Spring. The significantly altered name, and fancies about the "blood" being the blood of Christ in the Grail somewhere underground, are fairly recent. In the days of Arthur, however, when the spring was probably at ground level without superstructure, it does seem to be mentioned and thus described in one of the Grail romances, *Perlesvaus*, known in English translation as *The High History of the Holy Grail*. Clues here and elsewhere hint that it may have supplied water for a small early Christian community, in and around the little valley between Chalice Hill and the Tor, distinct from the one on the Abbey site. This perhaps is the retreat between hills—near Glastonbury, but not, at that time, in it—to which Lancelot and other survivors retire at the end of Malory's story.

The neighbourhood has one further Arthurian spot, Beckery on the west of the town near a defunct factory. In a chapel here, Arthur is said to have seen a vision of the Virgin Mary, which was the reason for his putting her image on his shield (see **Guinnion**). Excavation has shown that an early chapel existed, but its date is unknown. Nothing can be seen today.

When all these beliefs are taken together, they show how the name "Avalon" could have settled on Glastonbury as an expression of several of them at once. First came its eerie non-Christian aspects as an enchanted Glass Island and as a point of contact with **Annwn**. One Celtic Other-world could easily be equated with another; **Annwn** and **Avalon** did tend to merge or overlap; and at some stage, no one knows when, the idea took hold that Glastonbury might be the true **Avalon**.

Then, in the twelfth century, the monks learned the Welsh tradition of Arthur's burial and supposedly con-firmed it by digging him up. His last earthly destination was agreed to have been **Avalon**—Geoffrey of Monmouth said it. That clinched the identification. If the inscribed leaden cross was genuine it proved it anyway, because it said "here in the Isle of Avalon". But even if it was faked, it was faked with the identification in mind. Glastonbury was now **Avalon** indeed, and the low-lying area round about became the Vale, or Vales, of Avalon.

Soon afterwards Robert de Boron wrote the first romance about the bringing of the Grail to Britain. It had been brought, he declared, by the first Christians to come there, who had been disciples of Christ himself. Glaston-bury Abbey already claimed a foundation as early as that, and by such disciples. Robert took the obvious step of sending his early Christians to the "Vales of Avalon". Thereby Glastonbury-as-Avalon was explicitly built into the Christian legend as well as the Arthurian. Not that the equation was accepted by all, then or afterwards, but it was there to accept if one so chose. It appears again in the

Abbey's chronicles and in the Grail romance *Perlesvaus*, which is based, so the author truly or falsely assures us, on a document "in a holy house of religion in the Isle of Avalon, where King Arthur and Queen Guinevere lie".

Glein

According to Nennius, Arthur's first battle was "at the mouth of the river which is called Glein". This could mean either the place where it flowed into a larger body of water —lake or sea-- or its confluence with another river. The name is derived from a British word meaning "pure" or "clear". Many rivers might have been so called, and been renamed after the Anglo-Saxon Conquest. However, there are two which keep the same epithet today, altered only to "Glen", and these are the favoured candidates. One is in Lincolnshire; the other is in Northumberland.

The Lincolnshire Glen joins the Welland near Spalding, and the combined stream empties into the Wash a short distance farther on. The Northumberland Glen, formed by the junction of Bowmont Water and College Burn, flows eastwards past Kirknewton to meet the Till near Doddington.

At Yeavering by Kirknewton the Northumbrian kings had a royal summer residence which is mentioned by Bede. The missionary Paulinus instructed Anglian converts here and took them to the Glen for baptism. Excavation suggests the presence of an earlier British centre of some kind, and attempts have been made to connect Arthur's battle with the hill-fort above, Yeavering Bell (NT 929293). But Yeavering Bell is by no means "at" the Glen–Till confluence. On the whole the Lincolnshire Glen seems more likely, in view of known early settlements of the Angles in that area. It also fits in better with the most plausible location of **Linnuis**, the scene of Arthur's next four battles.

"Glen" meaning a valley is a different word. Hence, geographical names containing "glen" in that sense are ruled out. These two rivers stand alone today as identifiable candidates for the "Glein" where Arthur fought.

Glyn Arthur
—see **Moel Arthur**

Golant
Cornwall   *SX 120551*

A village lying a mile down the side road that runs east
from **Castle Dore**, the reputed home of King Mark in the
Tristan romance. It is in the parish of St Sampson or
Samson. The parish church, on a hillside overlooking the
estuary of the Fowey, is dedicated to him. The fact is of
some interest because, in an early version of the story,
Mark's courtiers ride along a paved road to "the monastery
of St Samson". Iseult presents the monks with an embroid-
ered silk robe, which they make into a chasuble and use
only once a year, on their anniversary feast. The poet, whose
name is Beroul, says the chasuble "is still kept in the church
of St Samson as those who have seen it bear witness".

Beroul wrote in the twelfth century, but used source
material dating from before the Norman Conquest. St
Sampson, named here as the founder of the monastery, was
a real person and is better documented than most Celtic
saints; we even have his signature. Born about 486, he was
educated at **Llantwit Major** and joined the Caldey community. When its abbot died through falling down a well
while drunk, Sampson became abbot. Later he travelled
widely about south-western Britain and may even have
visited the Isles of **Scilly**—one of them is called after him.
He died in Brittany in the early 560s. His biography was
composed about 600 on the basis of written reminiscences
by an old man named Enoch, who was a cousin of
Sampson, and had lived most of a long life in a Cornish
monastery founded by him. The description makes it clear
that this monastery was at Golant. In his poem, therefore,
Beroul is talking about a community which actually
existed near **Castle Dore**, though it may not have existed
quite early enough for the Tristan characters to visit it.

The passage is one of several proofs that Beroul (or an
unknown author on whom he drew) had this part of the
country in mind, and that some of the traditions woven into
his poem were local ones. Other proofs are the nearness
not only of **Castle Dore** itself, but also of **Lantyan**, and
the Tristan Stone outside **Fowey**.

Great Arthur
—see **Scilly, Isles of**

Guinevere's Grave

—see **Glastonbury**, **Meigle**

Guinevere's Monument

Mid-Glamorgan

Said to be in the parish of Llanilterne. Capel Llanilterne is four miles outside Cardiff on the westbound A4119. One or two writers mention a monumental stone supposed to be Guinevere's, and speak of an "almost undecipherable *Hic jacet*" inscribed on it, but its identity is doubtful. There is a prehistoric burial-chamber up a side road to the right, a little farther on (ST 079821). We might suspect a link with the Arthurian cave-legend of Llantrisant, but this is hazy itself. See **Cave-legend, sites of**.

Guinnion

Scene of Arthur's eighth battle according to Nennius, who says:

> The eighth battle was in Fort Guinnion in which Arthur carried the image of St Mary, ever virgin, on his shoulders and the pagans were turned to flight on that day and a great slaughter was upon them through the virtue of our Lord Jesus Christ and through the virtue of St Mary the Virgin, his mother.

This fort remains unknown. It may have been Roman. An attempt to identify it with a fort near Stow, on Gala Water above Galashiels in Selkirkshire, has not carried conviction. At Stow itself, however, the church of St Mary of Wedale once possessed what were said to be fragments of the image which Arthur carried into battle. The claim can be traced back to a thirteenth-century commentator on Nennius, whose statement about this image certainly raises points of interest.

The curious phrase "on his shoulders" is probably due to a mistake by an early scribe. He thought the word in Old Welsh text was *scuid*, "shoulder", and because of him it came through to Nennius translated into Latin thus, whereas it was really *scuit*, "shield". A religious image on a shield would not have been odd at all. When Geoffrey of Monmouth takes up the topic, he says that the Virgin was painted on Arthur's shield ... and also says that Arthur slung it across his shoulders. It looks as if he noticed the same ambiguity, and tried to cover both readings.

The second point is the query whether a Briton of Arthur's day would have viewed Mary with that kind of veneration. Her cult was already popular in Italy and the Christian East. But sceptics have claimed that there are no early traces of it in Britain, so that Nennius's account is suspect.

Actually, however, a few traces do exist. Gildas, writing perhaps in the 530s, refers to someone swearing an oath in church "in the presence of the Mother". He means the Virgin, and his word for "mother", *genetrix*, is the same that Nennius uses. He seems to locate this event in the West Country. The church may have been the ancient one at **Glastonbury**, which was dedicated to Mary long before any other in Britain. Gildas's own biographer Caradoc speaks of it as St Mary's in Gildas's time and Arthur's. It need not have been wildly anachronistic to associate Arthur with a religious practice taught there, even if it was unknown to his people otherwise.

Gwal y Filiast
Dyfed (Carmarthenshire) *SN 170257*

A prehistoric burial-chamber in a quiet place near the River Taf. Owing to the flat surface of the capstone it is known also as Bwrdd Arthur, Arthur's Table—hardly with any claim to being the Round one, however. In the bed of the Taf below is a hollow called Crochan Arthur, Arthur's Pot or Cauldron. This is a natural formation, but legend says Merlin shaped it for cooking.

Gwal y Filiast means "the greyhound bitch's lair". Wales has several burial-chambers named after the greyhound bitch. Whoever she was, she seems to have had some Arthurian connection—at least in the Carmarthen area. Gwal y Filiast in the Mynydd Llangyndeyrn (SN 487130) is likewise called Bwrdd Arthur. Near Twlc y Filiast at Llangynog (SN 336161) is yet another Bwrdd Arthur, a natural boulder in a field to the north.

Gwely Arthur
—see Appendix

Gwynedd

The modern Welsh name corresponds to a kingdom which took shape during the fifth and sixth centuries, though it extended farther east. Its chief royal residence was at **Aberffraw**. Another was at **Deganwy**. Many stories about the post-Arthur period introduce a king of Gwynedd named Maelgwn. Gildas calls him "the Dragon of the Isle", presumably **Anglesey**, and he was the last British ruler with any claim to paramount status: a tall, brave, generous man, well educated but frighteningly erratic, putting relatives to death and repenting, making war on his neighbours and endowing monasteries. He died in the "Yellow Plague" of the 540s, leaving a strong kingdom and a tremendous name. Nearly 100 years later Gwynedd was still powerful. Another of its kings, Cadwallon, led the last major counter-attack against the Anglo-Saxons, briefly reconquering northern England in 633.

Under Maelgwn, Gwynedd may have played a key part in the assembling of traditions about the days of Arthur, and their transmission in early Welsh verse. Inscribed memorial stones in this part of Wales suggest a higher-than-average culture. While the first bards whose names are on record flourished in **Cumbria**, Gildas mentions a previous group at Maelgwn's court (Welsh legend, in fact, credits him with holding the first Eisteddfod). The famous Taliesin is said to have begun his career at the same court, as a young challenger to the bards' pretensions. He moved northwards later, carrying whatever he had learnt from them. Poetic tradition rooted in Gwynedd probably explains the profusion of Arthurian sites and stories through northern Wales, several of the legends being surprisingly detailed, as in **Snowdonia**.

Hadrian's Wall
Cumbria (Cumberland) and Northumberland

While the Roman wall is mentioned by Gildas, and by the Byzantine author Procopius soon after Arthur's time, neither knows much about it and it hardly figures at all in British tradition.

It runs across northern England for over 70 miles. Parts are well preserved, especially the stretch near Housesteads. Another of the forts, **Camboglanna**, has been proposed as

Hadrian's Wall: a stretch on Walltown Crags, Northumberland. The wall as such does not figure in Arthurian stories, but several are located in its neighbourhood.

Camlann where Arthur fought his last battle. Some Arthurian folklore, including a version of the cave-legend, hovers around **Sewingshields**. See also **Arthur's Well (1)**.

Heltor
—see **Blackingstone Rock**

High Rochester
Northumberland   *NY 833986*

In hilly country south-east of the Cheviots, above the A68 and the River Rede, is the Roman fort of High Rochester or Bremenium. It was founded soon after this part of Britain was conquered, but most of the remains date from the third century. This was then the most northerly fort garrisoned by the Roman army, part of the forward defensive system beyond **Hadrian's Wall**. From such forts, long-range mounted patrols went out on reconnaissance expeditions.

Like many Roman place-names in Britain "Bremenium" is a Latin form of a British word. In Welsh poetry it becomes "Brewyn". For that reason the fort has been suggested as the **Breguoin** where, according to some copies of Nennius, Arthur fought his eleventh battle. It is strategically placed by one of the few routes across the Cheviots. Roman stone-throwing machines based here commanded the river valley and road below. Nearby in 1388 the invading Scots won the battle of Otterburn. Arthur might have been attempting to halt an early advance of Angles, who were marching along Redesdale in the other direction.

Bremenium is set back behind the village of Rochester and the modern army camp alongside it, and is reached by a lane which turns off the main road at the Otterburn end. Historically it has a special point of interest. Roman forts do not seem to have figured often in post-Roman warfare, but this is one that did—not provably in Arthur's time, but during the sixth century. In a poem in praise of Urbgen, the king of **Cumbria** who drove back the Angles in the 570s, the bard mentions "the battle of the cells of Brewyn". The phrase refers to the derelict walls and rooms of this fort.

As to its history for the previous 200 years, no one can be sure. Most such forward posts were abandoned by the Roman army during the later fourth century. But the northern lands were not written off. The Roman Empire tried to exert some sort of political control as far as the Clyde and Forth, working with settlements of friendly Britons, and thus laying the basis for successor states such as **Strathclyde**. High Rochester could have been a British stronghold in Arthur's time as it very likely was in Urbgen's. The lack of any traces of a relevant garrison does not rule out occasional military use.

Ilchester

Somerset   *ST 521226*

During the Roman period, the Britons in this part of Somerset were called the Lindinienses, and Ilchester was Lindinis. It was a junction of Roman roads and therefore had some importance, though no large population. It can be argued that we ought to look in this area for Arthur's campaign on the River **Dubglas** in the region **Linnuis**. Early copies of Nennius's list of his battles disagree on the spelling of the second name. It may be that an *i* has been dropped and it is really "Lininuis", in which case it would be derived from "Lindinienses" and would refer to their territory.

How much ground did they cover? They were a section of the British tribe of the Durotriges, who occupied all Dorset and large parts of the neighbouring counties. If their own share of the land extended as far as 20 miles south-eastward from Ilchester—that is, half-way across Dorset—it contained not merely one but two rivers which would qualify as **Dubglas**. One is the Divelish. It rises in the cluster of hills around Bulbarrow and joins the Stour just above Sturminster Newton. The other is the Devil's Brook, flowing southward from the same hills into the Piddle or Trent. "Devil", here, is an extreme corruption of the same British word, which survives in a form closer to the original at the village of Dewlish.

The theory has attractive points. Ilchester is the only Roman town where imported **Tintagel** pottery has been found, proving occupation about Arthur's time. A few miles towards Wincanton the A303 passes **Cadbury Castle**, which may be the real **Camelot** so far as anything is. Beyond the two "Dubglas" rivers, more Roman roads converge at **Badbury Rings**, which is at least a possible candidate for **Badon**, scene of Arthur's most famous victory.

But the counter-arguments are strong too. In the first place, we have to make a guess about a scribe's spelling mistake to arrive at this at all. No manuscript of Nennius actually says "Lininuis". Secondly, it cannot be proved that the land of the Lindinienses stretched far enough into Dorset to include either of the rivers. Finally, the area seems too far west for a major campaign involving four battles, as Nennius says this one did. The only Saxon settlements anywhere close were small ones in the direction of Southampton Water. Raiding parties might have probed into "Lininuis", but there is no reason to suspect armies there till many years later.

Joyous Gard

Sir Lancelot's castle. Formerly called Dolorous Gard, it was spellbound by an evil enchantment. Lancelot captured it and broke the spell. Inside he found a coffin with his own name on it, showing that this was to be his home and final resting-place. Having established his household in the castle, he received Arthur and Guinevere and renamed it Joyous Gard. Later he was host to Tristan and Iseult also, giving the lovers a spell of peace under his protection.

When he rescued Guinevere from the stake at **Carlisle**, he brought her here. Arthur besieged him. The Pope intervened to stop the civil war. Lancelot returned the queen, but Gawain's enmity prevented a reconciliation, and Lancelot left for France where he set up a rival court. Because of these tragic happenings the castle reverted to its old name of Dolorous Gard. After the downfall of the Round Table and the passing of Arthur, Lancelot spent his last years as a hermit near **Glastonbury**, but his dying wish was that his body should be taken to his own castle for burial, and so it was.

Joyous Gard is portrayed as in the north of what is now England. A French romance puts it on the Humber, but English romance prefers Northumberland. Malory offers **Alnwick** and **Bamburgh** without deciding between them. At the latter place we do perhaps find a morsel of historical fact behind Lancelot's castle, Joyous Gard.

Kelliwic (Celliwig)

Cornwall

In Welsh tradition Kelliwic or Celliwig is a Cornish stronghold where Arthur lived and held court. A triad says it housed one of the "Three Tribal Thrones of the Island of Britain". The others were at **Pen Rhionydd** and **St David's**. However, while Arthur could sit as chief prince in all three, only Kelliwic was a home for him. That belief about it is far older than the triad—older, indeed, than any debatable belief about his having a capital at **Caerleon** or **Camelot**.

The name "Kelliwic" means "woodland", a fact which is unhelpful in locating the place. However, it is probably Castle Killibury or Kelly Rounds (SX 018737), a hill-fort up a side road which leaves the A39 two miles east of Wadebridge. A letter written by St Dunstan in the tenth century mentions a Cornish estate which he spells "Caellwic", and it is likely to have been in this area. The road enters the fort by the old gateway, and goes right through it and out the other side. The southern half is almost obliterated. However, the plan is clear. Killibury was circular with two earth ramparts like **Castle Dore**, the inner one being 15 feet high. It dominated the little valley of the Allen between it and St Mabyn. Also, it was within easy distance of the ancient trade route from sea to sea, represented today by the A389 out of Wadebridge. In that too it resembled **Castle Dore**, though it was not nearly so close.

As might be expected, Killibury is not without rivals in its claim to be Kelliwic. It is simply the favourite which has emerged from many years of sporadic debate. Would-be identifiers have also suggested Callington, on the other side of Bodmin Moor; Gweek Wood, near Helston; Cally-with, east of **Bodmin**; Barras Nose, the headland across the cove from the castle promontory at **Tintagel**; and Willa-park, the next headland along the coast after that. None of these has any strong recommendation. Only Callywith (SX 087679) can challenge the favourite with a right-sounding name, and whilst it has a "woodland" nearby, it lacks fortifications.

The most interesting thing about the Welsh references to a home of Arthur is that they do make it Cornish. We would expect patriotism to place him in Wales. Kelliwic is proof of a deep-rooted tradition placing him outside. The same might be said of Geoffrey of Monmouth's story of his birth at **Tintagel**. Moreover, both traditions connect him with the same region. It could be that Arthur lived at Kelliwic as a young local lord and never relinquished it, though he made use of other citadels such as **Cadbury Castle** as his military and political status rose.

A Welsh story which is preserved in summary by the triads told how Modred and his men raided Kelliwic and "consumed all", leaving not so much as would feed a fly. Modred dragged Guinevere from her chair and struck her. Soon afterwards Arthur retaliated against the household of Modred. This clash was a chapter in the saga of enmity leading up to **Camlann**. It has an air of antiquity, showing Arthur as a chieftain embroiled in private warfare, rather than a monarch with a troublesome subject.

In another Welsh tale, *Culhwch and Olwen*, a list of Arthur's followers includes Drem, who, from Kelliwic, coud see a gnat in Scotland if the sun was on it, and Medyr, who, from Kelliwic, could shoot an arrow through the legs of a wren in Ireland. One supporter of Killibury pointed out that it is opposite the Irish coast and would therefore have been a more logical place for Medyr to shoot from than, say, Callington. While this may be so, it is not the best of arguments for the Killibury case.

Killibury
—see **Kelliwic**

Kilmarth
—see **Castle Dore**

King Arthur's Bed
—see **Arthur's Bed**

Likewise with all names in the form "King Arthur's So-and-So": see under "Arthur's". This is a matter of consistency. In some cases the prefix "King" is commonly used, in some it is not, and in some the practice varies.

King's Crags
—see **Sewingshields**

King's Oven
Devon   *SX 663803*

A stone structure near the Warren House Inn, on the highest stretch of the B3212 as it crosses Dartmoor near Merripit (the country of *The Hound of the Baskervilles*). It has been claimed as the **Arthur's Oven** shown to a party of French priests in 1113; see **Bodmin**. This is open to question becuase of the extreme rarity of Arthurian sites in Devon. Even here, if Arthur's name was ever applied, it has dropped out. The county does not accept him as its neighbours do.

Knucklas
Powys (Radnorshire)   *SO 250745*

North-west of Knighton. A tradition traceable as far back as the fifteenth century asserts that Guinevere's father, the giant Gogyrfan, was lord of a castle here and she was married to Arthur in it. The site is known, but the castle is gone. Her gigantic father is mentioned in early Welsh texts, his name variously spelled.

Lancien

A place in the story of Tristan and Iseult, identified with
Lantyan.

Langport
Somerset   *ST 422267*

Above the altar of Langport's parish church are two rows
of stained-glass windows. The last in the lower row
portrays Joseph of Arimathea. A Victorian reredos hides
part of this window, so that Joseph's name can be read only
by peering round the end of it. He is carrying two golden
"cruets" containing the blood and sweat of Christ. The
window was made in the late fifteenth century, by which
time the clergy at **Glastonbury** had decided that they
preferred the blood and sweat of Christ—which were safe
and orthodox holy relics—to the suspect Grail.

   Langport is sometimes said to be the battle site of
Llongborth where Geraint led the western Britons, and
"Arthur's heroes" fought beside them. If, as it appears,
this is a Geraint not very remote in time from Arthur (see
Gerrans), the geographical position of Langport presents
difficulties. It lies between Taunton and Somerton, and this
area was at peace till the Saxons overran it about 710.
Advocates of Langport as the site of the battle have made
guesses about early sea-raiders, Saxon or Irish, and also
about a hypothetical war-band which was led by a different
Geraint and was still called "Arthur's Men" in the eighth
century. It is likely, however, that **Llongborth** was **Portchester**, and Geraint was fighting outside his own territory.

Lantyan
Cornwall   *SX 105572*

In the early version of the Tristan romance by the Anglo-
Norman poet Beroul, King Mark's palace is said to have
been in "Lancien". This is a form of the name of Lantyan

or Lantyne, now a farm a mile or two south of Lostwithiel,
near the end of a valley running from Pelyn to the estuary
of the Fowey. In the Middle Ages the manor of Lantyan-in-
Golant was an administrative unit which included **Castle
Dore**, long reputed to be Mark's home and conjecturally
inhabited in his time. Whether or not Beroul imagined the

"palace" precisely there, its nearness is one of several proofs that he was using local traditions. See also **Fowey**, **Golant**.

Leintwardine
Hereford and Worcester (Herefordshire)   *SO 405740*

A village in the north of the county, on the A4113 between Knighton and Ludlow, in the valley of the Clun. Remains of walls mark the boundary of a small Roman town. Its name was Bravonium. That fact makes it a candidate for **Breguoin**, the scene of Arthur's eleventh battle in some versions of Nennius's list. To get from one name to the other we would have to suppose that a Welsh copyist made a slip, and the right spelling was "Breguein". Granted that, a previous change from "Bravonium" to "Breguein" would have been in keeping with known rules of language. But "Breguoin" (or whatever the right word may have been) is given by Nennius as the name of a hill or mountain, and while Leintwardine has hills reasonably close to it, "Bravonium" certainly meant the town.

Licat Amr
—see **Ercing**

Liddington Castle
Wiltshire   *SU 208796*

A hill-fort which is a candidate for **Badon**, because of the presence nearby of one of the villages with the name **Badbury**. The fort, indeed, was once called Badbury Castle itself. There was never a castle here in the medieval sense. This is an Iron Age stronghold with earthwork banks and ditches, very impressive ones.

It overlooks a gap in the hills through which the A345, here incorporating a stretch of Roman road, runs from Swindon to **Marlborough**. Access to this is easy from the M4. A mile or so south of the exit, a small road—part of the ancient Ridgeway—leads off towards Liddington Castle. It passes a gate at the bottom of the hill, which can be climbed here by a steep direct approach, or circuitously by a lane that winds round it. The summit enclosure, 900 feet above sea-level, is open and featureless with a wide view over Swindon and the Vale of the White Horse.

Historically, the main argument for Liddington as the scene of Arthur's great victory is that a Saxon army marching up the Thames valley would have turned southwards through the gap in the hills, along the Roman road, to strike at the British heartland in and around Somerset. Arthur could have foreseen such a move and awaited the enemy on the hill. The novelist Rosemary Sutcliff, advised by a professional soldier, reconstructed the sort of battle that might have followed in *Sword at Sunset*.

A trial excavation in 1976 uncovered traces of work on the top rampart in the fifth or sixth century, suggesting re-use, but nothing like the vast **Cadbury** refortification.

Lindsey
Lincolnshire

From several points of view Lindsey is the obvious choice for **Linnuis**, where Arthur is said by Nennius to have fought four battles by the River **Dubglas**. It is the part of the county extending north and east from the city of Lincoln, for which the Roman name was Lindum. In Arthur's time this was an area where the Angles were strong, and might have forced him to fight a series of battles. The previous battle site in Nennius's list is "the river which is called Glein". If this was the Lincolnshire Glen, we could imagine Arthur seizing Lincoln and using it as a base to strike in several directions.

Even Geoffrey of Monmouth locates an early Arthurian campaign in Lindsey. The obstacle to accepting it as **Linnuis** is that it has no river which is now suitably named. "Dubglas" could be the lost British name of a river since re-named in English. But the claims of two rival territories, discussed under **Ilchester** and Loch **Lomond**, cannot be dismissed although they seem less likely historically.

Linnuis

Four of Arthur's battles in the list given by Nennius are stated to have been fought by a river "which is called Dubglas and is in the region Linnuis". Nennius may have added the "region" so as to single out the correct **Dubglas** from a number of rivers with the same name.

Linnuis appears to come from a Latin word *Lindenses*, meaning "dwellers in (or around) Lindum"—hence, their territory. Essentially the same word survives on the map as **Lindsey**. If we consider Linnuis by itself, that part of Lincolnshire is the best choice for it. However, the "river called Dubglas" still has to be accounted for, and as no river in **Lindsey** now has a name like that, the identification is not certain and other options must be left open. Besides **Dubglas** itself, see **Ilchester** and Loch **Lomond**.

Llanbadarn Fawr
Dyfed (Cardiganshire)   *SN 599810*

Site of an early and important monastic community, on the outskirts of **Aberystwyth**. It was called after St Padarn (the name is Roman, Paternus), who built a church here. The "Life" of this saint is one of several mentioning Arthur, composed at **Llancarfan**. Like others of the group it makes him clash with its hero and come off second best.

The author tells how "a certain tyrant named Arthur", not known in those parts, entered Padarn's cell and coveted a fine tunic. Padarn refused to surrender it. Arthur went away angrily, then came back cursing and stamping his foot, and tried to take the tunic by force. Padarn said: "Let the earth swallow him." It did. Arthur sank to his chin and had to beg the saint's forgiveness, after which the earth spewed him up and he escaped.

The word "tyrant", *tyrannus*, is meant to be rude but need not imply oppression or despotism. It suggests, rather, that whatever power Arthur had was of dubious origin. In the author's eyes he was probably not a legitimate ruler anywhere, and certainly not in western Wales.

There is still a church of St Padarn, and some very ancient crosses may be seen in the churchyard.

Llancarfan
South Glamorgan   *ST 052702*

A village four miles north-west of Barry. This was the site of a monastery founded by St Cadoc, during the British Church's flowering after the temporary repulse of the Saxons. It preserved Arthurian traditions which are drawn upon in several "Lives" of Welsh saints written by members of the community. There may be echoes in the neighbouring place-names **Coed Arthur** and **Penmark**.

Arthur figures twice in the legendary career of Cadoc
himself. The first story is prior to the saint's birth. Cadoc's
mother Gwladys, it is said, was a princess of Brecon. She
eloped with Gwynnlyw, the king of Glamorgan. Her father
Brychan pursued the couple. As they rode over a hill,
perhaps near Merthyr Tydfil, they found Arthur playing
dice with his followers Cai and Bedwyr—the Kay and
Bedivere of romance. Arthur looked at Gwladys and lusted
after her. His knights, however, reminded him of their duty
to help those in distress (the earliest hint of an Arthurian
knightly code). So when Brychan arrived, Arthur supported
the claim that as the couple were now on Gwynnlyw's own
ground, he could not take Gwladys back. They married
promptly, no doubt as a safety measure, and Cadoc was
their firstborn.

Many years later, when Cadoc was abbot of Llancarfan,
he gave sanctuary to a certain Ligessauc, who was "a very
brave leader of the Britons" but had killed three of Arthur's
warriors. Ligessauc hid in the monastery for seven years.
At last someone betrayed his whereabouts. Arthur pro-
tested that sanctuary could not be extended so long. He
came to the River Usk with a band of armed men for the
case to be adjudicated. Cadoc and a party of monks also
came to the Usk, though they kept on the other side of it.
The judges dismissed the claim that Cadoc had exceeded
his rights, but ruled that Arthur must be given 100 cows as
compensation. Arthur demanded that all the cows should
be red in front and white behind. Cadoc, with supernatural
aid, produced such a herd, and the monks drove them half-
way across the stream. Arthur's men waded in to collect
them, but found themselves grasping only bundles of fern.
Abashed at the miracle, Arthur acknowledged Cadoc's
right to give sanctuary for seven years, seven months and
seven days.

These tales are unlikely to be true, even in substance.
But they reveal an attitude to Arthur which reappears in
other Llancarfan "Lives", such as those of Carannog (see
Carhampton) and of Padarn (see **Llanbadarn Fawr**).
These agree with the "Life" of Cadoc in being unfriendly
to Arthur. The authors think of him as a grasping military
upstart, and are far from clear as to the extent and legality
of his power. By the time they wrote he had become a
Welsh national hero, so anything adverse may well have

genuine tradition behind it. Llancarfan, therefore, is an interesting place, even though it has little that is relevant to show today. If we knew more about its past we might know more about Arthur.

Perhaps he did estrange the monks, even though his victories defended them. That is one possible reason (if a reason is needed) why Gildas, a monk himself, does not name him when writing of those victories. The second Cadoc story hints that Arthur may have requisitioned monastic herds to feed his men. Llancarfan was a rich community by the standards of the age, where there might have been a special sensitivity about acts of this type. However, to detect history in these stories would involve extending Arthur's lifetime a very long way. We must recognize also, running through them, a wish to exalt the saints by blackening Arthur so that they can score off him and make him repent.

Llangollen
Clwyd (Denbighshire)   *SJ 215420*

On the south bank of the Dee where it flows between mountains towards the plain of Cheshire, Llangollen is a natural entry point to North Wales. It takes its name from a

Llangollen: Castell Dinas Bran.

monastery founded in the sixth century by St Collen, and still has a church dedicated to him. That fact gives it a curious link with **Glastonbury**.

Within a short distance are three very different items of Arthurian interest.

Dinas Bran   *SJ 222431*

Above the Vale of Llangollen on the north side, this is a mountain with Iron Age ramparts and the ruins of a medieval castle inside them—now scanty, but conspicuous against the sky. Bran is the legendary hero, once a god, whose buried head Arthur most unwisely dug up (see **London**, **Marazion**). A golden harp is said to be hidden in the mountain. It can be found only by a boy who has a white dog with a silver eye. Dinas Bran may have supplied a hint for the castle where, in romance, the Grail was kept.

The Pillar of Eliseg   *SJ 202445*

Across the river from Llangollen, the road running west (A542) turns away from the Dee and up Valle Crucis, the Valley of the Cross. Here are the ruins of a thirteenth-century Cistercian abbey. A little way beyond, on a grassy bank, is the Pillar of Eliseg. Enclosed by a railing, it stands on a square stone base. The top is decorated and formerly had a cross above.

This pillar is more than 1,100 years old. After the Reformation it was knocked down. In 1696, when it was still lying on the ground, an antiquary deciphered some lettering inscribed on it. In 1779 the shaft was set up again. Traces of the Latin inscription, very worn, are still visible. It concerns the pedigree of Eliseg, who ruled over the Welsh kingdom of Powys—east-central and north-east Wales plus part of Shropshire—early in the ninth century. Though it reaches back to ancestors before Arthur, it sheds no light on him personally. But it helps to fill in his background, because it names Vortigern, who brought the Saxons over and (according to Geoffrey of Monmouth) was slain by Arthur's uncle Ambrosius.

The inscription traces the royal line of Powys back to a son of Vortigern called Britu "whom Germanus blessed". St Germanus was a Gallic bishop who visited Britain in 429 and (perhaps) 447. Nennius tells of his visits and

Llangollen: the Pillar of Eliseg. The visible inscription is later than the original.

portrays Vortigern as hostile to him, but confirms that one of Vortigern's sons took the saint's side and had his blessing. More interesting perhaps is another statement on the pillar—that Vortigern's wife who bore Britu was Sevira, a daughter of Maximus. This Maximus was a popular and able soldier who was proclaimed emperor by the legions in Britain in 383. He conquered the western part of the Empire and held it for five years. Strongly supported by the Britons, he presently became a hero of Welsh romance. Vortigern's marriage to Maximus's daughter doubtless had a political motive, the more so as she was almost certainly older. He was able to claim authority as heir-by-marriage to the last Roman emperor whom the Britons respected. As long as he was successful, he made that claim good.

Everyone agreed that Britain was still at least affiliated to the Empire. Vortigern himself, who sometimes has the air of a Celtic nationalist, saw Rome as the fountain-head of power. That belief persisted throughout most of the fifth century.

Craig Arthur   *SJ 224470*

"Arthur's Rock." Behind Dinas Bran a colossal ridge of exposed strata runs north, looking almost artificial. After weaving in and out for three miles it ends in a mass of rock which is Craig Arthur.

Llantrisant
—see **Cave-legend, sites of**

Llantwit Major
South Glamorgan   *SS 965687*

Today this is a small town on the B4265 between Bridgend and Barry. The original Llantwit Major was a monastic community, founded late in the fifth century by St Illtud or Illtyd. He was one of the most remarkable Britons of his time, the chief architect of the renewal of the Church (and much else with it) that followed British recovery from the first Saxon onslaught.

Illtud is said to have been a cousin of Arthur and, for a time, a warrior himself. In a church dedicated to him on Caldey Island, there is a stained-glass window which depicts him as an Arthurian knight. Possibly he was younger than Arthur, and gave up military life for the priesthood after his cousin's phase of command. But whatever the precise dating, his early career was not forgotten. Welsh tradition calls him Illtud Farchog, Illtud the Knight. The soldier-saint combination has led some to claim him as the original of Galahad. From an Arthurian point of view, it is also intriguing that one of the benefactors who gave him land for a monastic foundation was a certain Meirchiaun or Marcianus who may have been the father of Mark (see **Castle Dore**).

His community at Llantwit stressed public service—land reclamation, improvement of farming methods, education. While the first and second activities may not have begun till later than the time of Illtud himself, the third was peculiarly his. An author writing not immensely long afterwards testifies to the range of his knowledge: "This Illtud was the most learned of all the Britons both in the Old Testament and the New, and in all kinds of philosophy—poetry and rhetoric, grammar and arithmetic.

Llantwit Major, inside the church. The cross of St Illtud is at left.

... Were I to begin to relate all his wondrous works I should be led to excess." Besides this knowledge he had the gift of sharing it and inspiring others. Several graduates of his school appear in Arthurian contexts—Gildas (see Introduction, and **Glastonbury**); Samson (see **Golant**); Maelgwn (see **Gwynedd**).

The Llantwit community was sometimes known by the founder's name, Llan Illtud Fawr. It is one of the few which are spoken of as having perpetual choirs, a link with **Glastonbury** and **Amesbury**. The modern town has a church dedicated to the saint, with an old stone cross and the broken shafts of others.

Llanuwchllyn
Gwynedd (Merionethshire)   *SH 873304*

A village on the A494 from Dolgellau to Bala, just before
the road comes up level with Llyn Tegid (Bala Lake). The
district has a tale of its own about the giant Rhita who is
more usually assigned to **Snowdonia**. In this less dignified
version he is said to have lived as a robber, lurking among
the mountains. He waylaid travellers, took their goods and
shaved them, making a fur cloak out of their beards. After
many such victims had perished at his hands, Arthur came
and slew him. The giant was buried under a large stone on
Tyn-y-bwlch farm, up the valley of the Lliw to the north-west.

Nearby is another Arthurian site, **Caer Gai**.

Llongborth

Scene of a battle in a Welsh elegy praising the warrior-
prince Geraint and mentioning Arthur. Two of its eighteen
stanzas run as follows:

> In Llongborth I saw the clash of swords,
> Men in terror, bloody heads,
> Before Geraint the Great, his father's son ...

> In Llongborth I saw Arthur's
> Heroes who cut with steel,
> The Emperor, ruler of our labour.

The second of these stanzas is sometimes translated as
saying he was present in person—"I saw Arthur"—but this
is incorrect. The word "emperor" which is applied to him
could mean that he adopted the Roman title. Or it may be
used in its primary Latin sense of "commander-in-chief".

While the poem as it stands is not very early, its style
and manner hint at an older version behind it, close to the
events. For Geraint, see **Gerrans**. A version that is sometimes quoted says he was killed, but it is not the most
authentic. He led the men of Dyfneint, which was Dumnonia, the West Country. "Devon" is derived from this

name, but the old British kingdom stretched from the
Scillies and Land's End through Somerset and Dorset,
perhaps even farther. Llongborth is often asserted to be
Langport in Somerset. But the name probably means
"warship port". For this and other reasons, **Portchester** in
Hampshire is more likely.

Wherever it was, Llongborth does not figure in the list of Arthur's battles. To judge from the poem as a whole it was indecisive at best, so the author of the list might have been glad of the excuse for leaving it out and not counting it as one of his. Or it may have happened after his death. It is quite possible that a British force continued to use his name, as "Arthur's Men".

Llyn Barfog
—see **Carn March Arthur**

Llyn Llydaw
Gwynedd (Caernarvonshire)   *SH 625540*

A lake—now a reservoir—below Snowdon on the east, where the mountainside descends very steeply. Welsh legend locates the casting-away of Excalibur here. This is part of the clustering of Arthurian themes round **Snowdonia**.

Other places where Arthur's sword was thrown in the water are **Bosherston**, **Dozmary Pool**, **Glastonbury** (Pomparles Bridge), **Llyn Ogwen**, and **Loe Pool**.

Llyn Llydaw, the larger lake, below the steep east face of Snowdon.

Llyn Ogwen
Gwynedd (Caernarvonshire)   *SH 660605*

A shallow lake beside the A5 south of Bethesda. Another
of the places where Excalibur is said to have been cast
away. Reputedly Sir Bedivere's grave is on Tryfan, a
neighbouring mountain. According to a local tradition a
landslide from Tryfan which once fell into the lake buried
a cave where treasure was hidden. Presumably the treasure
is still there.

As to Excalibur, see also **Bosherston**, **Dozmary Pool**,
Glastonbury (Pomparles Bridge), **Llyn Llydaw**, and **Loe
Pool**.

Loch Arthur
Dumfries and Galloway (Kirkcudbrightshire) NX 905690

A small loch near Beeswing, south-west of Dumfries on
the A711.

Loe or Looe Pool
Cornwall   *SW 643242*

Geographically a long, narrow inlet of **Mount's Bay**, Loe
Pool is cut off from open water by Loe Bar, a ridge of sand
and pebbles which is a southward extension of the famous
beach of Porthleven. The lagoon thus enclosed is the
biggest lake in **Cornwall**. At its inland end, the Loe valley
runs up to Helston.

Here as in various other places Sir Bedivere is said to
have cast away Excalibur. Tennyson may have had it in
mind when he wrote his *Morte d'Arthur*.

> So all day long the noise of battle roll'd
> Among the mountains by the winter sea;
> Until King Arthur's table, man by man,
> Had fall'n in Lyonnesse about their lord,
> King Arthur; then, because his wound was deep,
> The bold Sir Bedivere uplifted him,
> Sir Bedivere, the last of all his knights,
> And bore him to a chapel nigh the field,
> A broken chancel with a broken cross,
> That stood on a dark strait of barren land.
> On one side lay the Ocean, and on one
> Lay a great water, and the moon was full ...

Since at least a part of the lost land of **Lyonesse** is presumably under **Mount's Bay**, Tennyson (who spells it with two *n*s) may have counted all this area as being included in it. The unanswered question is whether he was using an already-existing story told him by some Cornish informant, or whether the popularity of the poem itself turned his fiction into established "legend".

At Loe Pool as at Dozmary Pool, this Excalibur motif has attached itself to a place which has genuine folklore associations, but with the villainous Jan Tregeagle, not Arthur. Tregeagle, or his ghost, was condemned to carry out various impossible tasks. One of them was to carry sacks of sand from Berepper across what was then an open inlet and dump them at Porthleven, till Berepper beach was reduced to bare rock. He toiled for a long time without making much progress, because the tide kept sweeping the sand south again. Finally, a demon tripped him. The sack he was carrying fell and spilt, and the sand completed Loe Bar.

If Tennyson did have the pool in mind, he had not heard or did not approve this tale, because Tregeagle lived in the seventeenth century and Tennyson depicts the bar (the "dark strait of barren land") as already there in Arthur's time. As a matter of fact it is later than Arthur but earlier than Tregeagle, having been built up in the thirteenth century.

See also **Bosherston**, **Dozmary Pool**, **Glastonbury** (Pomparles Bridge), **Llun Llydaw**, **Llyn Ogwen**.

Lomond, Loch
between Strathclyde and Central
(Dunbartonshire and Stirlingshire)   *NS 380900*

The largest inland body of water in Scotland, just north of the Clyde estuary at **Dumbarton**. Nearby is the mountain **Ben Arthur**. Geoffrey of Monmouth says that when Arthur had defeated the Saxons, he marched north against an army of Picts and Scots, who fled to Loch Lomond and took refuge on its islands. Arthur gathered a fleet of boats and cut off their supplies, so that they were soon powerless to hold out.

Describing the loch, Geoffrey goes into curious detail. He asserts that it has sixty streams flowing into it, and sixty islands, and sixty crags on the islands, and sixty eagles' nests on those. Arthur, it seems, knew the neighbourhood quite well, and told a companion of another strange sight not far away, a perfectly square pool with a different kind of fish frequenting each corner.

Somewhere near Loch Lomond, according to the classical geographer Ptolemy, there used to be a place called Lindum. Its name could have a bearing on the problem of the "region Linnuis" where Arthur is said to have fought four battles beside the River **Dubglas**. Attention is usually focused on a more famous Lindum, the Roman city of Lincoln, and its adjoining district **Lindsey**. But whereas Lindsey has no river now with a name like "Dubglas", a river called Douglas Water runs down along Glen Douglas into Loch Lomond, on its western shore near Inverbeg (NS 345980). Hence "Dubglas in the region Linnuis" might be fitted in here.

It looks an unlikely spot for the real Arthur to have fought even one battle, let alone four. Geoffrey himself distinguishes Arthur's war on the Picts and Scots from the campaign associated with **Dubglas** and **Linnuis**, putting it later in his career. Still, the passage may hint at a tradition of his having been active hereabouts.

London

Though London, as Londinium, was the chief city of Roman Britain, it is not conspicuous in stories of Arthur. When mentioned at all it is in British hands, but never as a capital, only as a place where people of note occasionally gather.

This picture may have some slight relation to the facts of Arthur's time. London may have fallen to the Saxons, but it may not. The walls of the Roman town, which nearly covered the square mile of the City, would still have been standing. However, if the Britons did hold it, they held it as a forward strongpoint with no more than a remnant of civil population.

Early tradition, as it comes down dimly through the Welsh triads, speaks of only a single act performed by Arthur in London, and it is counted against him. He is guilty of one of the "Three Wicked Uncoverings" or "Unfortunate Disclosures". On the White Hill—that is, Tower Hill—the head of the legendary hero Bran had been buried long before with its face turned towards the Conti-

nent. It possessed magical powers, preventing the triumph
of the Saxons. Arthur dug it up and removed it. He said
Britain should not rely on such things, but on the military
effort he led himself. And so the protection was dispelled.
However, something of it is said to linger in the Tower
ravens ("Bran" means The Raven). The kingdom will
survive as long as the ravens do. See also **Marazion**.

In Geoffrey of Monmouth's *History* the Britons lose
London to the Saxon onslaught and then recapture it.
Arthur goes there to hold the first council of his reign, but
although it remains one of his major cities, nothing is ever
said about another visit.

Malory makes London the scene of the test which
proves Arthur to be heir to the kingdom. On Merlin's
advice, the archbishop of Canterbury summons the nobles
to a conclave at Christmas. In the yard of the city's greatest
church—presumably St Paul's—is a large stone with an
anvil on top, embedded in it. A sword passes down through
the anvil into the stone. Whoever can extract the sword is
the rightful king. None of the nobles can manage this. The
young Arthur, who has come with his foster-brother Kay,
does not know about the test. But when Kay is going to a
tournament and has left his sword behind, Arthur draws out
the one in the stone and takes it to him. The discovery that
Arthur can do this, and no one else can, establishes his
claim to the throne.

Malory has a few further incidents in London, and in the
nearby city of **Westminster**, but he does not make it the
centre of Arthur's rule. It appears for the last time in the
story of Modred's revolt. While the king is absent in
France, Modred gives out a false report of his death, has
himself crowned, and seeks to marry Guinevere. She
escapes to London and shuts herself in the Tower with a
loyal garrison. (Malory assumes that the Tower existed, in
keeping with the legend, known also to Shakespeare, that it
was founded by Julius Caesar.) Modred arrives with an
army and besieges her, but is forced to break off the siege
to contest the landing of the returning Arthur at **Dover**.

London Bridge is the starting-point of the Welsh story of
Craig-y-Ddinas. Today, the British Library possesses
many Arthurian manuscripts. In the royal Robing Room at
the House of Lords there is a Victorian oak carving of the
wedding of Arthur and Guinevere.

London: Victorian oak carving at the House of Lords portrays Arthur's wedding.

Looe Pool
—see **Loe Pool**

Lundy
Devon   *SS 135450*

Eleven miles off Hartland Point, in the mouth of the Bristol Channel, Lundy Island is three miles long and half a mile wide. It has a ruined castle, two lighthouses, and traces of prehistoric inhabitants. Today it is a bird sanctuary. In Welsh lore it has an uncanny character and is supposed to be **Annwn**, or rather, a place where that mysterious realm can be entered.

Lyonesse

Several Arthurian tales mention a land called Lyonesse. Tristan is the son of its king, and Galahalt (not to be confused with Galahad) is one of its chief lords, ruling over the district of Surluse. Romancers are vague about it. Occasionally it seems to be Leonais in Brittany, or Lothian in Scotland, known in Old French as Loonois. However, it is best known as a south-western British promontory which, after Arthur's time, vanished under the sea. As such, Lyonesse is the same as the country called Lethowstow in Cornish tradition.

Once, it is said, the Isles of **Scilly** were joined to each other and to the mainland. This expanse of country ran on towards the Lizard so that **Mount's Bay** did not exist in anything like its present shape. Most of it was low-lying. It had several towns, and 140 churches. The ocean swallowed it up quite suddenly. A man named Trevilian jumped on a white horse and outran the advancing flood. He reached Perranuthnoe near **Marazion**, where he took refuge in a cave and watched the disaster. The coat of arms of the Trevelyans portrays a horse coming out of water.

In the sixteenth century, William Camden and other antiquaries collected stories of the same kind. Fishermen declared that the reef of the Seven Stones off Land's End marked the site of a town, the City of Lions, and that their nets drew up fragments of masonry and windows. To this day church bells are reported to be heard tolling under the waves.

Lyonesse, or Lethowstow, is one of several legendary submerged lands. Atlantis is the most famous. Closer to home are the Lost Cantref (district) of Wales which is alleged to be under Cardigan Bay, and Ker-Is, a drowned city off Brittany. Sometimes a belief of this type has a fairly clear basis in historical fact, sometimes its origin is doubtful. The Cornish legend belongs to the first class. It is a composite of folk-memories, improved by fancy. Spectacular elements like the Trevilian tale are probably medieval, and recall massive flooding which is known to have happened in the eleventh and twelfth centuries. But the memories reach back to a far earlier time when the Scillies were more or less united, and probably to an even earlier time when a large tract of **Mount's Bay** was above water, forested and inhabited.

With the Scillies we have a clue from written history. In 387, when the emperor or pretender, Maximus, banished a heretic, the victim's place of exile was the "Sylina Insula" —the *isle* of Scilly. As late as the fourth century, then, enough of the islands were joined together to give the impression of one main piece of land rather than a cluster. Archaeology confirms a loss of ground to the sea. At low tide, in the Samson Flats between Samson and Tresco, rows of stones appear which are plainly ancient field walls. On St Martin's there are foundations of huts with floors now below high-water mark. One of them dates from the

early Iron Age. Another, of the Roman period, was excavated in 1948 and yielded pottery of the third and fourth centuries AD. The island of Old Man was broken into two by the sea in quite recent times, and here a stone grave below high-water mark was found to contain Roman brooches of the first century.

Mount's Bay has been much as it is now for longer than the Scillies have. However, parts of its bed were still above the surface when this area was already well settled. Stone axes were being made on what is now the sea-bottom between 1800 and 1500 BC. Off **Marazion** are fossil remains of a submerged forest. Beech trees have been identified with nuts still on the branches. The Cornish name for St Michael's Mount is "Carrick luz en cuz", "the ancient rock in the wood". Since the Mount was an island at high tide as early as 300 BC, the name seems to refer back to a period before that, and the remotely recalled wood was undoubtedly a factor in the making of Lyonesse.

Maen Arthur
—see **Arthur's Stone (3)**, **(4)**, **(5)**

Maidens' Castle
—see **Castle of Maidens**

Manchester

Said to have been the setting of a fight between Sir Lancelot and the sinister Sir Tarquin or Turquin. Malory describes this combat, which is the theme of a ballad quoted by Shakespeare—Falstaff sings a couple of lines of it in *Henry IV* Part Two, Act II, scene 4 ("When Arthur first in court ...") Tarquin was hostile to Arthur and imprisoned several loyal subjects in his own castle. He defied the Round Table by hanging a metal basin on a tree nearby. Any knight could challenge him by striking the basin, but every time this happened, Tarquin rode out to fight and invariably won. At last Lancelot struck the basin, killed Tarquin, and set the prisoners free.

Before the Industrial Revolution, Manchester was a market town of moderate size, which had grown round the site of a Roman fort on the road from **Chester** to **Carlisle**. The Mancunian locale of Sir Tarquin can be traced back only as far as a local historian in the seventeenth century,

who seems to think Tarquin lived in the Roman fort and
hung up his basin near a ford. Any scenes of legend here
have of course been swallowed up by Manchester's
growth.

Marazion
Cornwall   *SW 518308*

Cervantes, in *Don Quixote* (Part I, Chapter 13), speaks of a
belief among people in Britain that King Arthur was turned
into a raven. The statement is odd. It adds yet another
version to the accounts of his fate. The grave at **Glastonbury**, the cavern of millennial sleep, the retreat in **Avalon**
—all these themes are familiar. Transformation into a
raven is not. Nevertheless, Cervantes finds some support in
a few recorded scraps of folklore.

Marazion is on **Mount's Bay** three miles east of Penzance. From it a causeway runs out to St Michael's Mount.
Arthur is overshadowed here by the giant Cormoran, who
built the Mount as his stronghold. On Marazion Green,
however, when an eighteenth-century sportsman took a
shot at a raven, an old gentleman of the village rebuked
him because the bird might be King Arthur.

Whatever the background of this idea, it would have
been in keeping with other folklore. The raven has an
impressive aura. In parts of England it used to be ill-
omened, a bird of the Devil. But in the West Country and
Wales, ravens were esteemed as royal. Somerset men
tipped their hats to them. That gesture may have been
vestigial homage to the hero Bran, a sometime god of the
Celts who became, in Welsh legend, "Bran the Blessed"
and king of Britain: his name means The Raven. His
legend has links with Arthur's, and the traditions of Tower
Hill in **London** bring them—after a fashion—together.

It could even be that all three versions of Arthur's
immortality are derivatives from Bran. Arthur's sleep in
the cave, and his enchanted life in the Isle of **Avalon**, were
both inspired (at least partly) by the Celtic British myth of
a god asleep in a cave in a western island. Plutarch, the
classical author who has preserved this myth, does not give
the Britons' name for the god. But there are grounds for
suspecting that he was no other than Bran, the Raven-hero
himself in his ancient divine quality.

Modern Cornish fancy sometimes gives Arthur a

different bird form. He has become a red-legged Cornish chough, or even a puffin. Choughs are occasionally seen perching on the cliffs at **Tintagel**.

Marchlyn Mawr
Gwynedd (Caernarvonshire)   **SH 617620**

"Great Horse Lake." A Marchlyn Bach, "Little Horse Lake", is nearby. The larger one lies in a hollow among the mountains east of Llanberis, in the parish of Llandegai. It is the scene of a version of Arthur's cave-legend in which there are no sleepers at all.

One evening a farmer's son was helping a sheep that had got caught among the rocks by the lake. He stumbled on the entrance to a huge cavern, full of treasures and weapons. As it was growing dark, he went home for the night and returned at dawn. Entering the cave he found that the whole interior was lit up. In the centre was a golden table with a golden crown on it, encrusted with pearls. He knew that he was in the presence of the crown and treasures of Arthur. As he reached out to touch the crown there was a thunderous crash and the cave was plunged in darkness. He groped his way back to daylight and saw that the lake was heaving up like a sea, dashing spray against the rocks. Out in the middle was a coracle with three beautiful women in it, and an oarsman of terrifying appearance. It glided uncannily through the white-crested waves towards the cave-mouth. The youth fled and made for home. He was never in good health again, and if anyone mentioned Marchlyn Mawr in his hearing, he fell into a fit of madness.

A rocky hillock beside the lake is Bryn Cwrwgl, the Hill of the Coracle. In the nineteenth century a cave is said to have been found and explored, but without yielding any treasure. (Compare the story of Merlin's lost hoard at **Dinas Emrys**.)

To the south-east in the direction of Ogwen is a stream known as the River of Arthur's Kitchen (Afon Cegin Arthur).

Like Llyn Cwm Llwch in the **Brecon Beacons**, Marchlyn Mawr has its fairy-folk. Once, according to a report, a man was fishing in a boat when clouds descended from the mountains and covered the lake. A gust of wind cleared an open space and he saw a haystack with a ladder propped against it, and a figure up the ladder at work on the stack, all resting on the water as if it were solid ground.

Marlborough

Wiltshire   *SU 183686*

In the Middle Ages Marlborough's name was sometimes Latinized as "Merleburgia" and said to be derived from Merlin. To explain why it should have been, a conspicuous mound was pointed out has his grave. Today this is in the grounds of Marlborough College, and called Merlin's Mount. The notion can be found as far back as 1215 or thereabouts, in a poem by Alexander Neckham, a schoolmaster who became abbot of Cirencester and was the first European to describe the use of the magnetic compass at sea. He states bluntly: "Merlin's tumulus gave you your name, Merleburgia."

The Mount is a terraced mound rather like a small Silbury. Its present shape owes something to "improvements" carried out in the mid-seventeenth century. A Norman castle once stood on it, but it is probably prehistoric, with a purpose as elusive as Silbury's. The seventeenth-century workers unearthed Roman coins.

Despite Neckham's undoubted learning, the derivation of the town's name from the wizard's seems to have been due to a misunderstanding. "Merlin" spelled with an *L* is unknown before the 1130s, being Geoffrey of Monmouth's adaptation of the original "Myrddin". But coins of William the Conqueror bear the name of the town in the forms "Maerlebi" and "Maerliber", decades before Geoffrey. It has been pointed out that Merlin in legend is the builder of

Marlborough: Merlin's Mount, an eighteenth-century picture.

Stonehenge, and the sarsen stones of the largest circle came from the Marlborough Downs. However, there can hardly be anything in this but coincidence.

See also **Carmarthen** (for more about Merlin and place-names), and **Drumelzier** (for another grave).

Meigle
Tayside (Perthshire)   *NO 287447*

In the churchyard here, down the A94 from Glamis, they used to exhibit the grave of Guinevere. The more familiar story of her last resting-place is that she was buried at **Glastonbury** with her husband. The Perthshire legend challenges that account with a different and distressing one. She is called "Ganore" (or "Vanora" or "Wander") and is accused of having gone willingly with Modred when he carried her off to **Barry Hill** near Alyth. After Arthur recaptured her he put her to death for adultery, which, in the circumstances, counted as treason.

The poet Gray writes of a visit to Ganore's grave in Meigle churchyard. He was told by a local woman that the queen was "riven to death by stoned horses for nae gude that she did". (A stoned horse is a stallion, not a horse under the influence of cannabis.) A still more ruthless version declared that she did not, strictly speaking, have a grave at all, because after the horses had dismembered her, the pieces were buried in four places.

Her supposed grave was formerly marked by several worn carved slabs which were explained as fragments of a monument. Some interpreted the carvings as showing a person being dragged behind wheels and torn apart by animals, though dogs were preferred to horses. Others discerned a goddess in a chariot. Today the visitor must go to Meigle Museum behind the church, where the principal stone is housed, with many more dating from the seventh to the tenth centuries. On one side of it is a ring-cross of Celtic type surmounting a shaft, with human and animal figures. The cross with its ring could have been imagined to look like a wheel dragging someone. On the back, there actually is a design which includes a number of beasts threatening to tear a victim apart, but this is now said to portray Daniel in the Lions' Den.

As an old man of the neighbourhood remarked to a Victorian traveller: "Thae auld histories are maistly lees, I'm thinking."

Melrose

Borders (Roxburghshire)   *NT 548339*

A small town on the Tweed with the ruins of a Cistercian abbey. Scott's house, Abbotsford, is three miles to the west, and in his writings he has much to say of the country round about. The most famous of several Arthurian traditions is concerned with the Eildon Hills, a compact triad of peaks on the south side of the town. They have a version of the cave-legend which combines themes found at **Alderley Edge**, **Richmond** and **Sewingshields**.

One night a horse-dealer called Canonbie Dick was riding home with a pair of horses he had been unable to sell. On Bowden Moor south-west of Melrose he was stopped by a stranger dressed in the robes of a bygone age, who offered to buy the horses. After some bargaining they agreed on a price, and the man paid in gold coins which were also antique specimens. Dick, however, accepted them. The meeting was repeated on several further nights with the same outcome. At last Dick expressed curiosity as to the stranger's dwelling, and suggested that they should go there for a drink. The stranger consented, but told him that if he showed any fear he would suffer for it.

Not put off by this warning, Dick followed him to a hillock in the Eildon cluster, known as the Lucken Hare. A hidden door opened and they passed through into a vast torchlit cave under the main peak, the Eildon Tree. All along it Arthur's knights lay asleep, fully armed beside their horses. At the far end was a table with a sword and a horn on it. Dick's companion told him that he must choose whether to draw the sword or blow the horn first. If he chose right he would be "king of all Britain", presumably as Arthur's forerunner or deputy.

Dick considered. He thought that to draw the sword might seem an aggressive gesture and cause trouble. Fatally preferring discretion, he blew the horn. With a noise like thunder the knights began to stir. Not unnaturally he did show fear, and a voice told him he had chosen wrong. His action had not been that of a warrior but that of a man summoning help.

> Woe to the coward, that ever he was born,
> Who did not draw the sword before he blew the horn!

Melrose: the Eildon Hills.

A terrific wind arose, lifted Dick off his feet, and swept him out of the door, which closed behind him. In the morning he told his tale to some shepherds and dropped dead. No one, of course, ever found the cave.

The Eildon Hills can be traversed on foot via the Eildon Walk, which leaves the B6359 through a space between two rows of houses, on the hill going up to Dingleton. The Walk ascends a steep bank by ninety-five arduous steps, after which the climber must get over a stile and continue uphill through fields. A complication of gates and fences may give the impression that the way is blocked, but it is not. The path emerges beyond the fields on the heather and gorse of the upper slopes. It swings to the right over trodden red soil, climbs between the northern and central peaks, and descends on the other side near the scene of Dick's adventure.

However, there is an easier way to see that spot. Bowden Moor, where Dick met the stranger, can be reached by carrying on along the B6359 instead of turning off for the Walk. Opposite the moor are the central and southern peaks, and low down in the space between them is the Lucken Hare. It is a miniature hill with much bare rock, and looks so odd in its setting that it is easy to see how it might have inspired notions of the uncanny. Witches, in fact, often used to meet here.

The presence of Arthur's knights in their slumbering aspect may have been suggested by older beliefs about underground passages and chambers, and beings living in them. Thomas of Ercildoune or Earlstone near Melrose,

"Thomas the Rhymer", who (it is said) vanished into Elfland for seven years, also has links with the Eildon range. In fact, Scott's version of the Arthurian tale makes him out to have been the stranger who ushered Dick into the underworld. So likewise with the **Alderley Edge** cave-legend, where actual caves and vague memories of Roman mines may have played a part, while **Richmond** has a separate ghost story about a secret tunnel.

It is in the Melrose neighbourhood, rather than at **Edinburgh**, that the twelfth-century romancer Chrétien de Troyes locates the "Mont Dolerous" or **Dolorous Mountain**. His reason is probably that Wedale, the nearby valley running from Galashiels to Stow, was sometimes called Wodale and the name was taken to mean just that, Woe-dale. See also **Guinnion**.

Menabilly
—see **Fowey**

Merlindale
—see **Drumelzier**

Merlin's Bridge and Merlin's Brook
Dyfed (Pembrokeshire)   *SM 946145*

Merlin's Brook is a tributary of the western Cleddau which joins it just below Haverfordwest. Merlin's Bridge takes the A4076 over it, outside the town on the way to Milford Haven.

Merlin's Cave
—see **Carmarthen**, **Tintagel**; and compare **Bardsey**

Merlin's Grave

Strictly speaking the Merlin of romance could not be said to have ever had a grave, since he was immured alive by Vivien (or Nimuë) in a cavern or tree. Two places, however, have claimed a grave in apparent defiance of this account.

See **Drumelzier** and **Marlborough**. Also **Bardsey** has a hazy tradition on the subject.

Merlin's Grove
—see **Carmarthen**

Merlin's Hill
—see **Carmarthen**

Merlin's Mount
—see **Marlborough**

Merlin's Rock
—see **Mousehole**

Merlin's Tree
—see **Carmarthen**

Moel Arthur
Clwyd (Flintshire)   *SJ 145660*

"Arthur's Hill." A hill-fort with two deep ditches, about midway betwen Denbigh and Mold in the Clwyd range. A minor road that runs south-west from the A541 passes close to it, and continues down by Glyn Arthur in the

Moel Arthur, Clwyd.

direction of Llandyrnog. The hill rises to a height of 1,494 feet above sea-level.

See also **Brecon Beacons**.

Mote of Mark

Dumfries and Galloway (Kirkcudbrightshire) NX 845539

As third figure in the Tristan–Iseult triangle, the Mark of romance is king of **Cornwall**. So he may have been (see **Castle Dore**). But the full-blown legend has elements from the north, and the name Mote of Mark seems to echo it somehow—the more so as **Trusty's Hill** in the same part of Scotland recalls the name "Tristan".

Mote of Mark is on a rise beside Rockcliffe, overlooking Rough Firth. This falls away steeply to the sea, but the landward slope is more gradual. The top is fairly level, 200 feet by 130. On the inland side there was once a defensive rampart. Excavation has revealed two phases of work. The first fortification was a drystone wall in a frame of timber. At some unknown period the wood caught fire and the structure crumbled. Later—perhaps centuries later— someone carried out crude repairs by shoring up the wreckage with packed rubble.

Within the protected area, fragments of metal and jewellery have been found, giving glimpses of craftsmen working under patronage. These, together with imported pottery of the kind found at **Tintagel**, prove occupation in the sixth century. All this area may then have belonged to the British kingdom of Rheged (see **Cumbria**). It is unlikely that anyone who ever lived in the Mote was Mark in person. But long afterwards, some northern form of his legend may have suggested the name.

Mount's Bay

Cornwall

The body of water lying east of Penzance, in which the tidal island St Michael's Mount (SW 515298) is a prominent feature. Geologically the bay in its present shape is recent. Traditions of inhabited ground in it, afterwards lost to the encroaching sea, contributed to the legend of **Lyonesse**.

Arthur kills a giant on a hill called St Michael's Mount, but this is the similar Mont-Saint-Michel in France. Some

Mount's Bay, Cornwall: St Michael's Mount. In times still traditionally recalled, this was a hill rising above an expanse of low-lying forest. Everything except the Mount vanished under the sea. Hence, in part, the legend of Lyonesse.

other stores about him, and Merlin, do belong in this area. See **Loe Pool**, **Marazion**, **Mousehole**.

Mousehole

Cornwall   *SW 470259*

The name of this fishing village is pronounced "Mouzel". At the southern end of it near the quay, Merlin's Rock rises from the water. The wizard is supposed to have prophesied:

> There shall land on the Rock of Merlin
> Those who shall burn Paul, Penzance and Newlyn.

Just beyond is Point Spaniard. It was a Spanish flotilla that fulfilled the prophecy. In July 1595 four galleys with accompanying small craft anchored in Mount's Bay. Two hundred men disembarked and burned Mousehole down, leaving nothing standing except the Keigwin Arms, now a private house. Detachments went on to Paul and Newlyn destroying further buildings. The Spaniards then returned to their ships and rowed to Penzance. Here 400 landed and started more fires, still without meeting much resistance. Having celebrated Mass on a nearby hill they sailed away. Their exploit provoked a famous reprisal, the English attack on Cadiz in 1596.

While we find Merlin's prophecy quoted in writing soon after the raid, it cannot be proved to have been current before. In any case he would hardly have spoken English. There is, however, a Cornish version, which would be a shade more plausible. This is not the only prophecy ascribed to him with a Cornish theme. Another says:

> When the Rame Head and Dodman meet
> Man and woman will have cause to greet.

"Greet" means to weep. As the two headlands are 40 miles apart, any cataclysm that brought them together would doubtless be a source of woe. See also **St Levan**.

Myrddin's (i.e. **Merlin's**) **Quoit**
—see **Carmarthen**

Nanteos
Dyfed (Cardiganshire)   *SN 620787*

An eighteenth-century mansion near Capel Seion, three miles inland from **Aberystwyth**. This house is the focal point of a Holy Grail legend, which began as a family tradition, and has had wider publicity in modern times.

It is said that when the Abbey of **Glastonbury** was dissolved, seven of the monks fled to Strata Florida Abbey

The Nanteos Cup.

in Wales. They brought with them a cup or rather bowl made of olive wood, very old, cracked and blackened. Strata Florida could not survive as a community either, in the face of the policies of Henry VIII. A number of its inmates, including the party from Glastonbury, found haven with the Powells who lived at Nanteos in a house on the present site. The last of the seven handed on the cup to the head of the family for safe keeping, telling him the sick could be healed by drinking from it.

Whatever its origin, the Nanteos cup is real. From the sixteenth-century Powells it has come down to the later owners. Water which has been poured from it has often been sent to sufferers from various ailments. About 1900 people began suggesting that it was the vessel used by Christ at the Last Supper. For a while the owners admitted visitors, but they finally decided against further access. The cup was put in a bank vault in **Aberystwyth**, where the National Library of Wales has a photograph of it. Nothing is now to be seen at Nanteos itself, and travellers should not intrude.

The "Grail" theory is based on a misunderstanding. In Arthurian romances the Grail is not pictured as a holy relic comparable, say, to the Holy Shroud of Turin. The stories are mystical and symbolic, with a background of pre-Christian myth. Also, while they diverge widely, they agree that the Grail (so far as it has a physical being at all) is no longer in Britain.

Even if we set the romances aside, and consider the Grail simply as a relic, Nanteos's account of its wooden cup is open to a grave objection. The fourteenth-century chronicler John of Glastonbury gives a long list of the relics which were then at his Abbey. Some are most far-fetched. The list even includes a splinter from the table of the Last Supper. But it does not include the cup, and if the monks had possessed that, it would surely have been publicized as their proudest treasure.

Nant Gwrtheyrn

Gwynedd (Caernarvonshire)   *SH 350450*

"Vortigern's hollow" or "water-course". "Gwrtheyrn" is the Welsh form of the name Vortigern, the ever-execrated king who brought the Saxons into Britain. His grave is said to be near a short stream that rises among the hills and old quarries north of Llithfaen, and flows down a ravine into Caernarvon Bay. This claim conflicts with Geoffrey of Monmouth's description of his end by burning alive in the fort of **Ganarew**.

Nant Gwrtheyrn is a secluded spot. It once had a village, now deserted, which has passed through phases of dereliction, squatting, and attempted revival as a Welsh cultural centre. When people lived here in past times, the whole district was rich in fairy lore, because of a lively tradition of oral story-telling. Nant Gwrtheyrn has its own version of the Mistletoe Bough. It was the custom on a wedding morning for the bride to play a brief game of hide-and-seek before consenting to be led to the church. Once a bride vanished completely and was not found at all. Long afterwards a hollow tree was struck by lightning and her skeleton tumbled out.

Ogof Arthur
Gwynedd (Anglesey)   *SH 328707*

At the seashore west of Llangwyfan (reached by leaving the A4080 between **Aberffraw** and Llanfaelog) is Ogof Arthur, Arthur's Cave. High tide closes the entrance, but when the sea is low there is a way in, and the cave is said to run a mile underground. Its name has nothing to do with Arthur's widespread and familiar cave-legend. He is not lying asleep in it, and it does not appear that he was ever supposed to be. Traditionally he sheltered in the cave during a war with the Gwyddelod or Goidels, turbulent descendants of Irish settlers. Tales of hidden treasure used to be told also, as at **Marchlyn Mawr**—not only of the cave itself but of the ground neighbouring a megalithic tomb on the hill above, Barclodiad y Gawres.

Another **Arthur's Cave** near Monmouth is likewise exceptional. The name "Ogof Arthur" is also given to a probably fictitious cavern in Merioneth where the "sleeping king" motif does occur: see **Cave-legend, sites of**.

Ogo'r Dinas
Dyfed (Carmarthenshire)   *SN 613165*

"Cave of the fortress." A locale of Arthur's cave-legend, on a limestone hill about a mile from Llandybie, to the left of the A483 going north. Quarrying has altered the scene. Local people, however, used to speak of an actual cave in the highest part of the hill. The entrance was small, but the passage broadened and heightened, with further caves branching out and leading a long way—perhaps even to other outlets. Seemingly, however, the cave-mouth was blocked more than a century ago to prevent sheep and cows from straying in.

The Ogo'r Dinas form of the cave-legend, as recorded some years later by a clergyman born in Llandybie, was simpler than most. It asserted that Arthur and his warriors were asleep somewhere underground, with their right hands grasping their sword hilts, ready to drive out anyone who disturbed them.

Pen-Arthur
Dyfed (Carmarthenshire) *SN 717237*

A hill south-west of Pontarllechau, three miles up the River Sawdde from Llangadog on the A4069. It is on the fringe of the Black Mountain, the high ground between Carmarthenshire and Brecknockshire. This is one of the places where Arthur and his men fought the boar Twrch Trwyth, in the hunt described in *Culhwch and Olwen*. There is a river called the Twrch, which flows from the Black Mountain to join the Tawe below Ystradgynlais. See further **Arthur's Quoit (9)**, and the Appendix.

Pencraig Arthur
Gwynedd (Denbighshire) *SH 815649*

A hill near Llanddoget, east of the road running northward from Llanrwst.

Pendeen
Cornwall *SW 375345*

A village north of St Just. Here a visitor was told, some decades ago, that the neighbourhood "swarmed with giants, until Arthur, the good king, vanished them all with his cross-sword". This is another version of an exploit of Arthur which figures in the **Zennor** legend, though in that, his enemies are red-headed Danes.

Pendragon Castle
Cumbria (Westmorland)   *SD 782026*

Geoffrey of Monmouth applies the title "Pendragon" (head dragon, i.e. foremost leader) to Arthur's father King Uther, not to Arthur himself. Uther is shadowy, but by no means a pure invention of Geoffrey's, since his name occurs—with the title—in earlier Welsh poetry.

Pendragon Castle is four miles south of Kirkby Stephen, among the hills of Mallerstang Common. The River Eden runs deep down in a valley. At a point where the B6259 comes close to it, the castle ruins stand on an artificial mound between the road and the river. A few trees grow around them.

The castle is small. It was built in the twelfth century by one of the assassins of Thomas à Becket, Hugh de Morville, whose lands were in this part of England. Those who take its name seriously contend for a previous fortification

Pendragon Castle.

on the same site, belonging to Uther. It is not certain that this was even hinted at before Tudor times. However, while visible signs of Uther are lacking, the place has a legend about him—that he tried to divert the Eden to make a moat. The plan fell through, and his failure is recalled in a local rhyme:

> Let Uther Pendragon do what he can,
> Eden will run where Eden ran.

Some entrenchments and earthworks could be viewed as relics of an attempt to cut a channel around the base of the mound. If the excavation was meant to achieve that aim, letting the water in, it would have had to go far deeper and the effect would have been to undermine the whole structure. Hence, the story of a project that had to be given up fits in with appearances, but no more can be said than that.

Penmark
South Glamorgan   *ST 059689*

A village west of Barry, near Rhoose Airport. It has the remains of a castle. **Llancarfan**, where St Cadoc's monastery preserved memories of Arthur, is a mile to the north. "Penmark" may be derived from the name of Iseult's husband. If that is so, it is one of several hints at traditions of Mark a long way from the scene of the romance and from **Castle Dore**, his reputed home.

A skull formerly enshrined here as a holy relic was alleged to be the skull of *Saint* Mark. Another story interprets the name as "Pen March", "horse's head". A horse belonging to a Welsh prince, carrying a message to Arthur in Somerset, was decapitated in an accident.

Pen Rhionydd

A place mentioned in the Welsh triads as housing one of the "Three Tribal Thrones of the Island of Britain". Here Arthur sat as chief prince in the north. The name is spelled in various ways. "Pen" can mean a headland, and Pen Rhionydd may have been in the Galloway peninsula beyond Stranraer, but this is quite uncertain.

The other tribal thrones were at **Kelliwic** and **St David's**.

Penrith

Cumbria (Cumberland)   *NY 516302*

In St Andrew's churchyard, to the left as you approach it
from the town centre, is the Giant's Grave. This was once
thought to be the resting-place of Owein, the late sixth-
century British prince who plays an anachronistic part in
Arthurian romance (see **Cumbria**). Actually the grave is a
composite, formed by putting six monuments together. At
its ends are two tapering stone pillars, formerly crosses.
They stand 15 feet apart. Between them are four carved
semicircular tombstones of a type known as "hog-back",
resting on their straight edges. The six components are not

Penrith churchyard: the Giant's Grave.

all of the same date, but all belong, in reality, to the period AD 950–1000. They may have been rearranged when the church was rebuilt in 1722.

The belief that the whole assemblage marked the grave of one immense man—the hero Owein—can be traced several centuries back. It is even alleged that in the reign of Elizabeth I it was opened, and the bones of the immense man were discovered. Owein's name comes down in various forms ("Yvain", for instance, in French Arthurian romance) and here he is called Ewan Caesarius, and said to have been a mighty boar-hunter.

The Penrith neighbourhood has other Arthurian echoes. See **Brougham Castle** and **Round Table (4)**.

Portchester
Hampshire   *SU 625046*

Site of a Roman fort at the head of what is now Portsmouth Harbour. Portchester's status as a naval base makes it a good candidate for **Llongborth**, supposedly the "warship port", where the West Country warrior Geraint fought in a battle in which "Arthur's heroes" took part. The *Anglo-Saxon Chronicle* records a Saxon landing near here in 501 and the killing of a young Briton of very high rank.

The fort suffered little damage. Excavation has shown that Saxons moved into it and stayed. The Normans made it into a castle, but without destroying the Roman part, which is one of the finest surviving Roman structures in Britain.

Portchester Castle.

Pumsaint
—see **Cave-legend, sites of**

Queen Camel
Somerset   *ST 598250*

A village on the A359 running north from Yeovil, just
before it joins the A303. To the west are the hamlet Wales
(its name implying British inhabitants whom the Saxons
called "Welsh") and West Camel. The **Cam** flows through
all three.

Queen Camel was formerly plain Camel. The "Queen"
comes from a medieval royal connection. **Cadbury Castle**
is not far off, and the repeated name "Camel" has encouraged the belief that Cadbury was—in some sense—
Camelot. Sceptics have maintained that when John Leland
called the hill-fort "Camelot" in Henry VIII's time, he was
merely making a guess inspired by the villages. But
archaeology has proved that he did in fact hit on the only
known hill which qualifies as a citadel for Arthur. Hence,
one may suspect that the alleged guess was a shade too
good to be true, and there was more to this than accident.

Queen's Crags
—see **Sewingshields**

Rheged
—see **Cumbria**

Richmond
North Yorkshire   *NZ 172006*

A market town on a hill west of the A1 near Scotch Corner.
Its ruined castle is Norman. Below the castle, wooded
ground drops away steeply to the Swale. A potter named
Thompson is said to have found a tunnel here running into
the hillside. He made his way along it, and came to a
cavern where Arthur and a number of knights were sitting
at a round table, asleep. On the table lay a sword and a horn.
Thompson picked up the horn (or in another version, laid
his hand on the sword) and the sleepers began to wake. As
he fled, panic-stricken, he heard a voice calling after him:

Potter Thompson, Potter Thompson!
If thou hadst drawn the sword or blown the horn,
Thou hadst been the luckiest man e'er born.

Compare the cave-legends of **Melrose** and **Sewingshields**.

The best place to see where the tunnel entrance is supposed to have been is not the castle itself, but the Castle Walk which runs along the hillside below the walls. It may be that the king and his knights are an afterthought, and the original legend concerned the tunnel rather than Arthur. It figures in another story without him. Here, it is said to run from Richmond Castle to Easby Abbey, a mile away. Once some soldiers found the way in and sent a drummer boy to explore it. As he walked along it he beat his drum, and the soldiers followed above ground. Half-way to the abbey the drumbeat stopped. The boy never returned, but a ghostly drumming is still sometimes heard.

River of Arthur's Kitchen

—see **Marchlyn Mawr**

Round Table

Only one extant piece of furniture bears this name, the painted wooden disc, now legless, at **Winchester**. But there are "round tables" of other kinds at five places.

Round Table (2): a hill-fort in Anglesey.

(1)   Caerleon
Gwent (Monmouthshire)   *ST 339906*

In this Roman town, where Geoffrey of Monmouth portrays Arthur holding court, the name "Round Table" used to be applied to the amphitheatre—or rather to the bank of earth which had grown up over it. The idea seems to have been that a large number of people could have sat round it facing inwards, as indeed they did when the benches were exposed and the theatre was in use. See main **Caerleon** article.

(2)   Bwrdd Arthur
Gwynedd (Anglesey)   *SH 588816*

"Arthur's Table." A hill-fort near the coast north of Beaumaris, to the east of Red Wharf Bay. As with **Caerleon**'s amphitheatre, the shape seems to have conjured up a picture of men sitting round it facing inwards. Why this particular fort, is not clear.

(3)   Bwrdd Arthur
Clwyd (Denbighshire)   *SH 961672*

Another "Arthur's Table". The nearest place of any size is Llansannan. Bwrdd Arthur is north-east of it, along the B5382 and up a side road. It is a rough circle of indenta-

Round Table (3): Bwrdd Arthur, near Llansannan.

tions in a rocky hillside. In the words of John Leland, writing in the time of Henry VIII, "There be 24 holes or places in a roundel for men to sit in, but some less, and some bigger, cut out of the main rock by man's hand; and there children and young men coming to seek their cattle use to sit and play." He speaks of kids (presumably goats, not children) "skipping from seat to seat".

(4)   Mayburgh
Cumbria (Westmorland)   *NY 523284*

"Arthur's Round Table" is south of **Penrith** across the Eamont, at the intersection of the A6 with the B5320 going off towards Ullswater. It is an earthwork consisting of a round central platform encircled by a ditch, with a bank outside the ditch, breaking at two opposite points to provide entrances. The south entrance is better preserved. From it a causeway crosses the ditch to the central mound. This mound, with its level surface, forms the "table". Its diameter is 50 or 60 yards. Hence, it is about the size the Round Table would have had to be to seat the full complement of 150 knights in any comfort.

The monument is thought to date from the early Bronze Age, towards 4,000 years ago, and to have been built for unknown religious purposes.

(5)   Stirling
Central (Stirlingshire)   *NS 789936*

William of Worcester, in 1478, says "King Arthur kept the Round Table at Stirling Castle". Courtly entertainments of the kind known as "Round Tables" were held here in the Middle Ages, and there seems to have been a permanent structure given that name, since the sixteenth-century Scottish poet Sir David Lindsay writes of Stirling's "Chapell-royall, park, and *Tabyll Round*". It may have been a raised platform of earth afterwards incorporated into the royal garden known as the King's Knot. This, at any rate, is still there, with what is sometimes called the Round Table as its principal feature.

The King's Knot lies below the castle on the south-west. In Stuart times a considerable area round about was enclosed as the King's Park. Within it, in 1627, a knot-garden was constructed, with a formal design of paths and

Round Table (5): below Stirling Castle.

embankments. It is no longer a garden, but the layout survives and can be seen by looking down from the castle ramparts. The King's Knot is open to the public at all times, and is reached from the town by the A811.

The most elaborate part of it is a two-tiered earthwork. On top of a raised base is a smaller octagonal "rampart". Inside this is a hollow space, and at the centre of the space is a flat-topped mound about 6 feet high and 40 or 50 feet across. Writers recalling William of Worcester, and under the impression that the King's Knot is of immemorial age, have dubbed the central mound the "Round Table". In its present form the whole system is far too neat to look ancient, and an any case we know it is not. However, the royal garden planner may have had the table in mind as a motif, whether or not he built an earlier mound into the new one.

Finally, to revert to Wales—specifically Brecknock-shire, now part of Powys. It has no other Round Table comparable to any of these, but it has a related story, for which see **Brecon Beacons**.

Ruthin
Clwyd (Denbighshire)   *SJ 123583*

A rough block of limestone in the market-place by Exmew Hall is called Maen Hueil, Hueil's Stone. This warrior appears in Welsh stories as a dashing and resolute opponent of Arthur (see **Strathclyde**). Their first clashes were in the north. Raiding southward, perhaps as far as Wales, Hueil continued to make trouble. According to one chronicler it was not confined to matters of war. When Arthur was at Caerwys, about nine miles to the north of Ruthin, Hueil arrived in the neighbourhood and paid court (presumably during a truce) to one of Arthur's mistresses. A duel resulted, and Arthur was wounded in the knee. He promised that there should be peace between them so long as Hueil kept silent about the knee. However, he remained slightly lame.

Some time later Arthur went to Ruthin in female disguise to visit another lady. He took part in a dance. Hueil,

Ruthin: Maen Hueil in the market-place.

who was watching, noticed the limp and realized who it was. "You would be a good dancer," he said, "if it weren't for that knee of yours." It was a fatal blunder: he had mentioned the wound and released his enemy from all obligations towards him. Arthur ordered his arrest, and ended their long conflict by beheading him on the stone in the market-place.

While the story of Hueil's end is doubtless pure romance, he or some other dissident Briton may have had a war base in this area. Two miles east of the town, a small road climbs towards Moel Fenli, one of the highest points in the Clwydian range. This was a hill-fort, and a hoard of late Roman coins discovered there suggests that in the fourth or fifth century it was the stronghold of a local chieftain. Others may have succeeded him in possession.

St Columb Major
Cornwall   *SW 913637*

A stone here is supposed to bear four hoofprints of Arthur's horse. The notion is connected with the legend of **Castle-an-Dinas** as his "hunting lodge."

St David's
Dyfed (Pembrokeshire)   *SM 752254*

Welsh "Mynyw", i.e. Menevia. Named in a triad as housing one of the "Three Tribal Thrones of the Island of Britain", where Arthur sat as chief prince in Wales. It is likely that St David's was substituted by a twelfth-century copyist for **Aberffraw**, which was a centre of authority much earlier. However, the cathedral has crosses and memorial stones of great antiquity.

The other tribal thrones were at **Kelliwic** and **Pen Rhionydd**.

St Dennis
Cornwall   *SW 951583*

Though more than 20 miles from **Tintagel**, this is probably the place Geoffrey of Monmouth intends when he tells the story of Uther's siege of **Dimilioc** and the death of Duke Gorlois. It lies south of Goss Moor in the narrowing part of the county between Newquay and St Austell. The Domesday Survey—which was compiled before Geoffrey wrote, and therefore gives names he could have known—mentions two manors in the St Dennis parish, and calls one of them "Dimelihoc".

Dimelihoc included the steep conical hill on the north side of the town. This rises to 640 feet above sea-level, and today has a church on top. The churchyard wall is circular, marking the outline of an old fortification. In fact, the "St Dennis" to whom the church is dedicated may be a figment: "Dennis" could be a corruption of *dinas*, meaning a stronghold.

A hazy tradition that Geoffrey had this district in mind seems to have lingered for several centuries. William of Worcester, writing in 1478, locates the death of the duke hereabouts, though he prefers the more dramatic hill-fort of **Castle-an-Dinas** across Goss Moor.

St Govan's Head and Chapel
Dyfed (Pembrokeshire)   *SR 967930*

St Govan's Head is the most southerly point on the stretch of coast near Pembroke. It has been claimed that the tomb of Gawain is just west of it.

In some form the Gawain story goes back a long way— at least to William of Malmesbury writing c. 1125. This

St Govan's Chapel.

historian says that Gawain's tomb was found during the reign of William the Conqueror. It was by the seashore in Pembrokeshire, and was 14 feet long. Some said that the knight had been mortally wounded by enemies on a ship, and thrown overboard; others, that they murdered him at a banquet.

William of Malmesbury is believed to have been thinking of a place on the north side of Milford Haven, between the islands of Skomer and Skokholm, not very close to St Govan's Head. But "Govan" is rather like "Gawain", and hence the claim has been made that the grave is under St Govan's Chapel near the headland, the saint being a purely imaginary figure conjured up by misunderstanding of the name. It must be confessed that although many miracles are credited to St Govan, he remains phantasmal. Rival stories speak of a disciple of St David, or a converted robber, or even a woman named Cofen.

The chapel is in a narrow break in the cliffs. A flight of steps cut in the rock leads down to it from above, and a further flight continues down to the cliff foot. According to local lore you cannot count the steps, because you will get a different number going down from the one you get going up. The chapel itself is 18 feet by 12. Most of it probably dates from the thirteenth century, but the altar, and a seat cut in the rock, may be parts of a hermitage 700–800 years older. Govan's tomb—or Gawain's, if that theory is right—is supposed to be underneath the altar.

A cleft in the wall opened miraculously for him to slip into when pursued by enemies. The rock closed round him and parted again when they had gone. If you stand in the cleft and make a wish while facing the wall, it will be granted so long as you do not change your mind before turning round. Near the chapel there used to be a holy well, but it has been filled in. The red clay of the cliffs has a reputation for curing sore eyes.

Those who accept the Gawain version say that he retired here after Arthur's passing and finished his days as a hermit. The separate St Govan was invented later when his name had been corrupted and his identity forgotten. Conversely, if Govan was the real hermit, the warrior's presence is due to a confusion. Someone knew vaguely that the tomb was on the Pembrokeshire coast, and thought Govan and Gawain were the same. Of course, if we wish to combine the stories, we can: Gawain lived here as a hermit, but died somewhere else, and was buried in the coastal tomb William of Malmesbury heard about.

For a completely different account, see **Dover**.

St Levan

Cornwall *SW 380222*

A church approached through Porthcurno by a small road running south from the B3315, near Land's End. In its churchyard is a cleft stone called Levan's, said to have been revered in Arthur's time as sacred or magical. After a Cornish journey he made with Merlin, the wizard uttered a prophecy about it:

> When, with panniers astride,
> A packhorse can ride
> Through St Levan's stone,
> The world will be done.

The feat would be on the same lines as a camel passing through the eye of a needle. Merlin's meaning seems to be that in some unforeseeable way the thing will happen, and that this marvel will be a portent of the end of the world. The tale is open to the same objection as the one told of Merlin's Rock at **Mousehole**, that he would not have spoken English.

St Levan, Cornwall: the cleft stone in the churchyard.

Salisbury Plain
Wiltshire

An expanse of chalk upland north-west of Salisbury, covering about 200 square miles. In prehistoric Britain it was the chief centre of population, notably during the heyday of the Wessex culture, about 2000–1500 BC. It is rolling grassy country, mostly 400–500 feet above sea-level, with few trees. Ancient grave-mounds, earthworks, and other remains are numerous. The most famous is **Stonehenge**. Geoffrey of Monmouth associates this with the arts of Merlin, and with events at **Amesbury**.

In Arthurian romance, Salisbury Plain becomes the scene of the fatal battle—the **Camlann** of earlier tradition —in which the knighthood of the Round Table perishes. It has this role in the thirteenth-century French *Death of King Arthur*, from which Malory's version is adapted, though he pictures the battlefield as much nearer to water than the Plain actually is.

Malory heightens the tragedy by making the battle unnecessary and accidental. Modred, he says, having failed to prevent Arthur's advance from Dover, collected more troops and awaited the king on Salisbury Plain. After a warning dream, Arthur tried to arrange a truce. His negotiators offered a treaty making Modred overlord of parts of the kingdom, and acknowledging him as heir to the whole of it. Next day Arthur and Modred met between the armies to sign the treaty.

But both suspected trickery, and with good reason. Modred was already a proven traitor, in revolt against his sovereign, while the covert aim of Arthur himself was to buy time till Lancelot came from France with reinforcements. In this nervous atmosphere the officers on both sides were under orders to attack instantly if anyone drew a sword. The treaty was signed, and the opponents were drinking together in seeming amity, when a knight was bitten in the foot by an adder. Without thinking he drew his sword to kill it. The blade flashed in the sunlight, the armies surged forward, and fighting continued stubbornly till most of the knights were dead. Arthur killed Modred, but sustained a mortal wound himself.

Scilly, Isles of
Cornwall

The Scillies are small, low-lying granitic islands 28 miles west-south-west of Land's End. There are about 140 of them. Most are tiny, and only five have appreciable populations. However, they are rich in prehistoric remains, and traditions about them probably had a share in forming the legend of **Lyonesse**. One of the islands in the eastern part of the group is called Great Arthur (SV 942135), and there is an islet Little Arthur. A larger island (SV 878125) is named Samson after a saint whose career has a bearing on the Tristan legend: see **Golant**.

Sewingshields
Northumberland   *NY 800700*

From Housesteads, one of the finest forts on **Hadrian's Wall**, a well-preserved stretch of wall runs north-east. It climbs the height of Sewingshields Crags, overlooking a sweep of open country with small lakes called loughs, once the wild borderland of the Roman Empire. In a dip farther along, and a little to the north of the wall, Sewingshields Castle formerly stood. Scott calls it the Castle of the Seven Shields. In the nineteenth century its ruins were levelled. Before then, a form of Arthur's cave-legend had attached itself to them.

   Deep below (the story ran) there was a cave or perhaps a castle vault where Arthur lay sleeping, together with Guinevere and their courtiers, and a pack of hounds. On a table were a horn, a sheathed sword made of stone, and a garter. To restore Arthur to waking life, the correct procedure was to draw the sword, cut the garter, and then blow the horn. Once a farmer was knitting among the castle ruins when his wool fell down a crevice. Following it, he found the underground chamber. He cut the garter and Arthur woke. Unfortunately the farmer put the sword back in its sheath and neglected to blow the horn, whereupon Arthur said:

> O woe betide that evil day
>   On which this witless wight was born,
> Who drew the sword, the garter cut,
>   But never blew the bugle-horn ...

... and fell asleep again. The farmer's error was the opposite of Canonbie Dick's in the **Melrose** legend. But both of them got further than Potter Thompson at **Richmond**.

In another version Arthur wakes as the intruder enters, and promises to confer knighthood on him if he draws the sword and blows the horn. However, the man is afraid, runs off to look for a friend, and can never find the entrance again.

The neighbourhood has other stories of Arthur, rather barbaric ones. He is said to have stayed at the castle during his reign. When a northern chief visited him, and was sent home with gifts, Arthur's sons (rare figures in tradition) thought their value excessive, waylaid the chief at "Cumming's Cross", killed him, and took the gifts back. Cumming's or Comyn's Cross is a standing stone about two miles to the north, on the far edge of Haughton Common.

North-west of Sewingshields are King's Crags and Queen's Crags, two outcrops of sandstone half a mile apart. On King's Crags is a rock formation called Arthur's Chair. Here he took his seat during a quarrel with Guinevere, and heaved a boulder at her where she sat on Queen's Crags. It bounced off her comb and fell between the two outcrops, where it lies to this day with the toothmarks of the comb still on it. The image of Arthur and Guinevere as giants is an unusual touch, but not unparalleled. Compare the legends of **Arthur's Quoit (9)**, **Arthur's Stone (1)**.

Slaughter Bridge

Cornwall   *SX 110855*

Sometimes spelled as one word. Slaughter Bridge crosses the River Camel about a mile above **Camelford**. The river is at the bottom of a small valley, and overhung with trees. This is where local legend places the battle of **Camlann**. The belief can be traced back to Geoffrey of Monmouth. Whether it is prior to him there is no telling. He does not say where along the river the battle was fought, but legend has fastened on a meadow near the bridge. Dead and dying men, it is said, fell in the water till it ran red with blood. John Leland (the same Tudor traveller who wrote the first account of **Cadbury Castle**) came to Slaughter Bridge and was told that "pieces of armour, rings, and brass furniture

for horses are sometimes digged up here by countrymen".
According to the story he heard, and perhaps improved
upon, Arthur and Modred met on the bridge in hand-to-
hand combat. Arthur killed Modred, but not before the
rebel had wounded him ... and Modred's sword was
poisoned. Arthur managed to walk away upstream, but
then sank down and died.

The word "slaughter" seems to favour the story.
However, both this and any remnants of warriors' gear can

*Slaughter Bridge: Arthur's Tomb, so-called, a memorial slab
beside the river.*

be explained by a battle which was fought in 823, when the Saxons under King Egbert of Wessex were campaigning against the still-unconquered Cornish.

At the place upstream indicated by Leland for Arthur's death is his "tomb". A path through the meadow leads to a bluff beside the river, overgrown with hazel bushes. Below, near a spot where a tree has fallen, and not easy to reach, lies a flat stone slab 9½ feet long by 2 feet wide. It has a Latin inscription running along it, in fairly good capital letters 6 inches high. Leland saw this, and so did a late Elizabethan traveller, Richard Carew, who reported on it in a book published in 1602: "The old folk hereabouts will show you a stone, bearing Arthur's name, though now depraved to Atry."

The stone was not always here. It was dumped on its present site in the eighteenth century, having been, before that, a footbridge over a stream on the estate of Lord Falmouth. Before that again, it was somewhere in the fields, and it actually was a monument, but not to Arthur. The lettering runs:

LATINIICIACIT FILIUSMAGARI

This presents no problem if we accept that the man who carved it left a word meaning "monument" to be under-stood, and also dropped the *h* which would have begun the word *hic*, "here". Both omissions would have been quite in keeping with post-Roman casualness. The inscription says: "(The monument of) Latinus: here he lies, son of Magarus."

Carew's error—or the error of somebody before him—seems to have been due to a simple accident. The last five worn letters, AGARI, are formed in a way which could have suggested ATRY in the different Gothic script of the sixteenth century. Arthur's Tomb is a misunderstanding.

Sneep
—see **Cave-legend, sites of**

Snowdonia
Gwynedd (Caernarvonshire)   *SH 610545*

In Welsh, Eryri, the place of eagles. The behaviour of these birds as they flew among its crags used to be taken as an omen. When they flew high, it meant that the Welsh would win their battles. When they flew low, it meant defeat. When they screamed incessantly, it was a sign of disasters of other kinds. Since 1951 Snowdonia has been a National Park centred on Snowdon, the highest mountain in Wales, with five peaks of which the topmost rises to 3,560 feet above sea-level. A rack-and-pinion railway runs up to Snowdon from Llanberis. It is the only mountain railway in Britain. The lake of Glaslyn near the summit is greenish owing to copper ore, and alleged to be bottomless and the home of an *afanc* or water monster, like Llyn Barfog near **Carn March Arthur**.

A cairn formerly at the top (removed to make way for a hotel) was known as Carnedd y Cawr, the Giant's Cairn. The giant in question was Rhita, said to have been slain by Arthur. Geoffrey of Monmouth tells the story, spelling the name Retho, and it appears in Malory too. The giant ruled over northern Wales. Having subdued some chiefs who rose against him, he shaved off their beards and made them into a fur cloak. He next demanded Arthur's beard, promising, as a token of respect, to sew it higher up on the cloak than the rest. Should Arthur demur, Rhita challenged him to a duel, with the cloak as prize plus the beard of the loser. Arthur accepted the challenge, came to Snowdon, and killed the tyrant. In a more grandiose account the "cairn" is the entire peak, formed by each of Rhita's warriors placing one stone on his grave. See also **Llanuwchlyn**.

Snowdonia has a very circumstantial legend of Arthur's passing. It may have been inspired by the fancy that Cwm-y-llan or Cwmllan, a valley among the mountains, was **Camlann**. According to this tale, Arthur set out with his army from **Dinas Emrys** near Beddgelert and marched northwards up the height of Hafod-y-porth, then over the shoulder of Yr Aran to Cwm Tregalan above the upper portion of Cwm-y-llan. Measured in a straight line the distance is about three miles. At Cwm Tregalan he met his enemies, Modred's men. They withdrew towards the top of Snowdon and came round into a pass running back south-east. Arthur's army pressed after them. At a high point in the pass they let loose a shower of arrows and Arthur fell.

His body was buried in the pass, which was known thereafter as Bwlch y Saethau, the Pass of the Arrows—as it still is. A heap of stones piled over him was Carnedd Arthur, Arthur's Cairn. So long as he lay there, no enemy could go that way (compare the legend of Bran's head in **London**). The spot is a mile or so from the summit.

After this catastrophe, Arthur's surviving soldiers continued along the pass to the Lliwedd ridge and went down the steep side of it into a cave, since called Ogof Llanciau Eryri, the Cave of the Young Men of Snowdonia. They are still sleeping there. In this version of the cave-legend Arthur himself is not with them, yet despite his burial it is assumed that he will somehow return.

Snowdonia: a typical scene.

As usual we get a story of someone finding the cave. In this case it was a shepherd. He was collecting his sheep on top of the Lliwedd when one of them tumbled down to a ledge. The shepherd followed and saw the entrance. The cave was lit within and many men were lying asleep, with weapons beside them. He tried to squeeze in through the narrow aperture, but struck his head against a bell which was hanging above. The bell rang, the warriors woke with a shout, and seized their weapons. The shepherd fled in terror and never enjoyed a day's health afterwards. No one else has ever been able to find the entrance.

This form of the cave-legend is like several others—thus, the touch about the bell occurs also at **Caerleon** and **Craig-y-Ddinas**—but it has the special difficulty that nobody but a mountaineer could have got down to where the cave is supposed to be. Arthur's men could hardly have managed it, neither could the shepherd. And in one account the warriors' weapons are said to have been guns!—as also at **Caerleon**.

The Snowdonian tale of Arthur's passing prompted one of the notions about the casting away of Excalibur: that Bedivere tossed it into **Llyn Llydaw** on the east side of the mountain. He would have had to climb all the way down the Lliwedd to do it, carrying the sword, so this claimant to the location of the act seems the least promising of the six: its rivals being **Bosherston**, **Dozmary Pool**, **Glastonbury** (Pomparles Bridge), **Llyn Ogwen**, and **Loe Pool**. Another offshoot story places a cairn of Tristan on a spur of Carnedd Llywelyn, which almost equals Snowdon in height (SH 683644).

The poet and novelist Robert Graves records how he was taken as a child to the top of a hill near Snowdon and heard the story of Arthur's fatal wounding. He was told that "when seven church steeples could be seen from there, and when a pair of twins, a boy and a girl, went looking for lost lambs on a Sunday afternoon", they would find Arthur's dented crown among the bracken.

South Cadbury Castle

—full name of the hill-fort **Cadbury Castle**

Stone Arthur
Cumbria (Westmorland)   NY 348092

A stone on top of a mountain north of Grasmere, the
village where William and Dorothy Wordsworth lived. The
brook Greenhead Gill runs below. Wordsworth mentions it
in his poem *Michael*; he spells it "Ghyll".

Stonehenge
Wiltshire   SU 123422

This unique megalithic structure on **Salisbury Plain** owes
its role in legend to Geoffrey of Monmouth. He makes it
out to be a memorial. In his account of the reign of Vortigern, he tells how Hengist's Saxons treacherously slew 460
British nobles during a peace conference. They were
buried in the precinct of a monastery on "Mount Ambrius",
meaning, with some geographical confusion, the high
ground near **Amesbury**. Some years after, when the
Britons had recovered the upper hand for a time, King
Aurelius Ambrosius (that is, Ambrosius Aurelianus) visited
the spot and decided to build a worthy monument.

One of his advisers suggested consulting Merlin, who
told him that the right structure existed ready-made in
Ireland. It was called the Giants' Ring. Long before, a
number of colossal stones had been brought over from
Africa by giants, who set them up in a circle they used for
religious rites. The giants believed that the stones gave
healing properties to water poured over them.

Merlin's advice was accepted. Aurelius's brother Uther,
afterwards the father of Arthur, took him to Ireland with a
large company of Britons. They swept aside an Irish force
that stood in their path, and arrived at the Ring. However,
conventional techniques failed to shift it. Merlin laughed
and dismantled it without trouble by his own mysterious
arts. The stones were loaded on to ships and taken to
Britain. Merlin, again by his arts, put them up round the
burial-place in the same formation. Thus the Giants' Ring
became the Britons' national memorial. Later Aurelius and
Uther were buried in it themselves. "Stonehenge" is its
English name.

A folklore version seeks to improve the story. In this,
Merlin gets the help of the Devil, who steals the stones
from an old Irishwoman (doubtless a witch), binds them

together, and flies with them all the way from Ireland to their new home. Geoffrey has nothing as fantastic as this. But in terms of history, or prehistory, most of what he says is wide of the mark. While he is right in speaking of Stonehenge as having once had a ritual purpose, it was in place long before the fifth century, and is unlikely to have ever been a memorial. It was built as a sanctuary with a plan related to movements of the sun and moon. The process happened in stages, mostly during the third millennium BC, to judge from recent rethinking which has pushed it backwards in time. With the largest stones, which once formed a complete circle of uprights and cross-pieces, the architectural design and implied skill are unparalleled anywhere among the megaliths of northern Europe. Such a marvel could easily have suggested the hand of a super-human wonder-worker.

But the most intriguing part of the Merlin story focuses attention on the smaller bluestones which formed an older ring. These are thought to have come from the Prescelly Mountains in Pembrokeshire. If, as has been suggested,

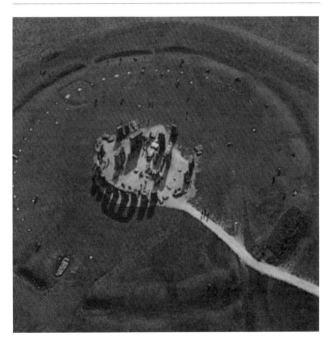

Stonehenge.

they were conveyed by raft to a landing-place up the Bristol Channel, Geoffrey's account of stones transported over sea from the west may echo an authentic tradition thousands of years old. Merlin, as a character, certainly combines two figures (see **Carmarthen**) and may well combine three, the earliest of them being an otherwise forgotten magician or demigod who was the hero of a saga about Stonehenge and its building.

Stone of Arthur
—see **Arthur's Stone (2)** and **(6)**

Stow
—see **Guinnion**

Strathclyde

"Vale of Clyde". The modern regional name recalls a British kingdom occupying what is now south-west Scotland. Its capital was the fort of **Dumbarton**, called by the Britons "Alclud", the "Rock of Clyde". In Arthur's time this name was used also for the whole kingdom, the domain of the Rock of Clyde, Alclud in a broader territorial sense. However, while "Strathclyde" may be a later term, it is more familiar and most historians apply it to this kingdom throughout its existence.

Strathclyde was a product of Roman policy during the imperial twilight. Unable to conquer the ever-troublesome Picts, Rome tried to create a safety zone north of the Solway Firth by favouring settlements of friendly Britons under official tutelage. Also, a Christian mission begun by St Ninian, a Roman-trained British priest, attempted to influence the tribes. Pacification was never total. Hostile Picts continued to wander and raid. But the British families kept their footing even when Roman backing failed, and their leaders contrived a kind of state.

Its first known ruler was Ceredig or Ceretic, who flourished in the middle of the fifth century. To judge from archaeology his people already held the **Dumbarton** strongpoint, and his kingdom was "the domain of Alclud". He lived on good terms with at least some of the Picts, perhaps even enlisting them in his armed forces. He had

Pictish subjects of his own and may have had Scottish ones as well. Most of the Scottish nation was still in Ireland, its original home. A few, however, had settled in the peninsula of Kintyre, perhaps under British auspices.

Partly because of his barbarian friends, Ceredig was immortalized by a clash with St Patrick. Some time during the 450s he sent a raiding force across the North Channel. His soldiers pounced on a gathering of Christian Irish, some of them just baptized. They killed several and carried off others to sell as slaves. For Patrick's converts it was a depressing introduction to Christian ways. A copy of his letter of protest has been preserved—his second letter, since the first went unanswered. He Latinizes Ceredig's name as Coroticus. The king, he complains, purports to be heir to Roman citizenship and Roman Christianity. Yet he has sanctioned this crime against fellow-Christians, innocent neophytes at that. He has actually offered his Christian slaves to Pictish apostates: that is, defectors (already) from the faith taught by Ninian's mission. The soldiers of Ceredig, says Patrick, are outside the pale of civilized humankind. He should punish them and release the prisoners.

There is no evidence that he did. One implication of Patrick's protest is that these northern Britons were using their forces in attacks on their neighbours at a time when the southern Britons were struggling with the Saxon invasion, and needing any help they could get. Britain had crumbled. It is an open question how far Ambrosius or Arthur restored cooperation in the decades that followed. Arthur's battle of **Celidon** implies at least a movement towards Strathclyde, and the hints at a campaign near Loch **Lomond** imply a march right across the area. He might have been acting in concert with the Strathclyde Britons, to repel Pictish marauders. But he might have been at war with the Britons themselves. A tradition of enmity among them survives in the story of Hueil.

This is an offshoot of the biography of Gildas, the sixth-century monk who wrote about the Britons' misfortunes. Gildas, it is said, was one of the many sons of Caw, a nobleman holding lands near the Clyde. Hueil was the oldest. Except for Gildas himself they were a turbulent family, and when Arthur was in this part of the country he had much trouble with them. In the end most of them gave up or migrated to north Wales, where Gildas presently

embraced his monastic career. Hueil, however, remained in
the north with a war-band of his own, and raided southward by land and sea. The author of one of the "Lives" of
Gildas declares that Arthur held a council of war in the
Isle of Man, and caught Hueil and put him to death—it is
not stated where. (If the Welsh tale *Culhwch and Olwen* is
anything to go by, this final hunting-down must have
followed the breaking of a truce during which Hueil and
his brothers were enrolled among Arthur's men; and a
romantic chronicler tells how he came to Wales, how the
truce was breached, and how his execution by Arthur took
place at **Ruthin**.)

Whatever the amount of history in this, it offers a clue to
the battle of **Celidon**, and perhaps **Tribruit** also. It even
suggests how **Chester** might be the **City of the Legion**
where Arthur fought his ninth battle. Sea-borne Britons
from Strathclyde, such as the story of Hueil recalls, could
have raided the town. The actual Hueil story is unlikely,
and it presents chronological difficulties. But a general
motif of northerners causing trouble could have played a
part.

Threlkeld
—see **Cave-legend, sites of**

Tintagel
Cornwall   *SX 049891*

Visitors to Arthur's birthplace on the north Cornish coast
should not allow themselves to be put off by the village,
where his fame has had unpleasing commercial results. To
get to the scenes that matter, you leave the street where it
turns at the seaward end, and go down through a ravine
which passes out of sight of the village. The lane is rough,
and at first very steep. In the tourist season public transport
is provided by a Land-Rover service. Alongside the lane is
a rapid stream.

The ravine ends at the top of a small cliff. Nearby, there
is a visitor centre. The stream tumbles over the cliff as a
waterfall, dropping into a cove between two dramatic
headlands. At low tide the sea draws back exposing a
sandy beach. Above, paths go off to the right and left. The
path on the left divides into two stairways. The lower one

descends to the cove (but visitors are advised against using it, for safety reasons). The upper one climbs to the promontory on that side of it.

This towering mass is very nearly an island. Its link with the mainland is a ridge of rock which has crumbled forming a chasm. The chasm used to be spanned by a drawbridge. It is now wider and has a permanent bridge. Crossing this, you climb a further flight of steps to a gate, leading into the ruins of a castle. Another part of the castle is on the mainland and is reached by a path from the

Tintagel: Arthur's Footprint.

ravine, farther back. However, it is the promontory that has the "Arthurian" part.

The visible remains do not go back anywhere near Arthurian times. There has been some re-thinking as to how far they do go back. It used to be supposed that the castle was started about 1141 by Reginald, Earl of Cornwall, and that Geoffrey of Monmouth, who tells the tale of Arthur's begetting, very possibly located it here because a relative of Reginald's was his literary patron. Geoffrey's *History* was composed a little before 1141, but advocates of this theory could argue that the version we have is a second edition and the Tintagel episode was added in revision. However, it is now thought that the castle dates from much later—about 1230—and that the earl who founded it chose the site because of the Arthurian glamour which, by then, it had acquired. If anyone influenced anyone, it was Geoffrey who influenced the castle-builder, not the other way about.

The tale itself is none too creditable to Arthur's father, the British king Uther. His passionate desire for Ygerna, the wife of Duke Gorlois of Cornwall, led to a local war with the duke. Gorlois put Ygerna in his stronghold on the Tintagel headland, knowing that a few guards could hold the narrow approach against any attackers. But while he was away fighting at **Dimilioc**, Merlin used magic to make Uther look exactly like him. By means of that effective disguise Uther passed the guards, entered, deceived Ygerna, and begot Arthur. Shortly before, the real Gorlois had been killed, so the parentage of the child was not in doubt. Mary Stewart gives a modern version of Merlin's stratagem in her novel *The Crystal Cave*.

However fictitious the tale may be, a walk beyond the castle ruins dispels any supposition that Geoffrey contrived it out of nothing. Paths along the face of the headland above the cove bring you to a series of low stone enclosures. They are tidied-up restorations of the remains of buildings discovered in the 1930s by C. A. Ralegh Radford. Above on the plateau there are more. In and around them, Radford found objects of momentous importance: pieces of what is now sometimes called Tintagel pottery.

These were fragments of high-quality vessels, some of them of a type used for expensive goods such as wine and oil, and the vessels were not of British make. They had been imported from the east Mediterranean region and could be dated to the late fifth century or the sixth. The significance of this pottery in its various types is that its presence on a site proves that people were living thereabouts in more or less Arthurian times. It also points to a wealthy household, able to import goods from far-off countries. Some years passed before these facts were realized, but when they were, similar pottery in other places gave the first reliable clues to occupation by "Arthurian" Britons. Chance findings of it at **Cadbury**

Tintagel: Merlin's Cave.

Castle, the reputed Somerset **Camelot**, supplied the
evidence needed to justify large-scale archaeological study.

At Tintagel itself, Radford concluded that the vessels
had been imported by a monastery built in the fifth or early
sixth century, and that the buildings were a chapel, a guest-
house, a library, a refectory, and so forth. If so, Geoffrey of
Monmouth may have known of a community existing on
the headland at the right date, but he was wrong in thinking
it was the kind of community where a lady might have
lived and become a mother. However, more recent studies
have shown that the pottery unearthed by Radford probably
came from a fifth-century chieftain's stronghold, and that

*Tintagel: Doré's engraving for Tennyson's tale of Merlin finding
the baby Arthur washed up on the beach.*

Tintagel is best interpreted as a regional centre of government in the early aftermath of Rome. In that case the story of Arthur's begetting could—in substance—be true, and Geoffrey could be drawing on authentic tradition. In favour of that view is the fact that he places the event here at all, when we would have expected him to prefer Wales.

The top of the promontory is an open, windswept plateau more than 250 feet above the sea which almost surrounds it. Below are rocks on all sides, and formations have been given fanciful names—Arthur's Chair, Arthur's Cups and Saucers. In the chasm between the promontory and mainland, the locals used to point out a gigantic "footprint" of Arthur.

Tintagel Castle reappears in the romances of Tristan and Iseult, where it is said to have belonged to King Mark. There is no reason to look for anything factual behind this, or behind assertions that it was built by giants, that it was chequered in green and blue paint, and that it regularly vanished on two days of the year. But the senior legend lingers in another place. Back at the point where the path divides, the lower stair descends to the beach near a cave at the rocky base of the headland. This is Merlin's Cave, and it is a natural tunnel running right through to an opening at the other end. Merlin's ghost is said to haunt it. Since it can only be reached at low tide, an intending visitor should find out about the tides in advance, and arrange to get there when the cave is accessible, descending by an alternative route if use of the stair is discouraged. The opening of the cave at the far end is lower than the one in the cove. When the tide is coming in, the rising sea boiling and swirling over the rocks at that end, and gradually surging into the cave, is a deeply impressive sight.

The headland on the opposite side of the beach, Barras Nose, also has a cave that goes through like Merlin's. The rocks make it harder to explore, and it has no role in the legends. Around the neighbourhood, however, are one or two outcrops from them, such as Arthur's Quoit, which is the capstone of a cromlech, and a pond from which the Round Table rises if you watch for it on the right night.

Tennyson, who was unhappy about the Uther–Ygerna affair, gave Arthur an alternative origin. The scene is still Tintagel, and the witnesses are Merlin and a companion, who ...

... from the castle gateway by the chasm
Descending thro' the dismal night—a night
In which the bounds of heaven and earth were lost—
Beheld, so high upon the dreary deeps
It seem'd in heaven, a ship, the shape thereof
A dragon wing'd, and all from stem to stern
Bright with a shining people on the decks,
And gone as soon as seen. And then the two
Dropt to the cove, and watch'd the great sea fall,
Wave after wave, each mightier than the last,
Till last, a ninth one, gathering half the deep
And full of voices, slowly rose and plunged
Roaring, and all the wave was in a flame:
And down the wave and in the flame was borne
A naked babe, and rode to Merlin's feet,
Who stoopt and caught the babe, and cried "The King!
Here is an heir for Uther!" And the fringe
Of that great breaker, sweeping up the strand,
Lash'd at the wizard as he spake the word,
And all at once all round him rose in fire,
So that the child and he were clothed in fire.
And presently thereafter follow'd calm,
Free sky and stars.

Another fantasy, perhaps as recent as Tennyson's, is that when Arthur was mortally wounded at **Slaughter Bridge** he was brought to Tintagel and died there. Strange wind-sighings and sea-moanings were heard around the head-land, and continued while his body was being conveyed to **Glastonbury** for burial, ceasing only when he was laid in the grave.

Tregeare Rounds
Cornwall   *SX 033800*

About five miles south of **Tintagel**, just before the B3314 enters Pendoggett, it passes Tregeare Rounds. This is a late Iron Age earthwork camp, on the slope of a hill and not the top, with three ramparts. It is sometimes called Castle Dameliock, and identified with Geoffrey of Monmouth's **Dimilioc**, where Duke Gorlois was killed. But the name "Dameliock" seems to have been given it in quite recent times, perhaps as late as the nineteenth century, with no genuine basis in tradition. Antiquarian writers tried to guess where **Dimilioc** was, and hit on Tregeare Rounds because it was near **Tintagel**. Their guess was taken up by others, and hardened into a belief. They missed what was probably the real location through not looking far enough away. See **St Dennis**.

Trereen Dinas
Cornwall   *SW 432387*

An Iron Age promontory fort on Gurnard's Head. It is claimed as Arthur's "castle" in the legend associated with this part of the county, for which see **Zennor**.

Trethevy Quoit, once inside a mound.

The nearest road is the B3306. At the right of the Gurnard's Head Hotel, a track leads off seaward. The final approach is by footpath only. Trereen Dinas has three ramparts. The innermost is designed for the launching of slingstones by the defenders. As with many such sites, re-use in the time of Arthur cannot be ruled out, but Trereen Dinas has no known traces of it as some others have.

Trethevy Quoit
Cornwall   *SX 259689*

Sometimes called Arthur's Quoit; a megalithic burial-chamber dating from the second millennium BC. Between St Cleer and Darite, it is reached by a small road forking left from the B3254 a mile north of Liskeard.

The "quoit" proper is the flat capstone which was set up on top of eight uprights. It is 12 feet long, and still in place, though tilted owing to the fall of one of the support stones. The supports still form an enclosed U-shaped chamber divided by a partition. The whole structure was formerly inside a mound.

Tribruit

Arthur's tenth battle in Nennius's list was "waged on the shore of the river which is called Tribruit". The Welsh form is "Tryvrwyd". A battle by the river—doubtless the same battle—is mentioned in an early Welsh poem which includes Bedwyr, the original Sir Bedivere, among the men taking part.

> By the hundred they fell,
> They fell a hundred at a time,
> Before Bedwyr
> On the shores of Tryvrwyd.

No river has a name today which comes anywhere near to fitting. According to one theory Tribruit was in what is now south-west Scotland. If so, the battle was very likely fought against the same enemies who drew Arthur to the forest of **Celidon**. They may have been British. The story of Hueil (see **Strathclyde**) preserves a tradition of hostile Britons in this area. Picts, however, may be more likely.

Tristan's Cairn
—see **Snowdonia**

Tristan Stone
—see **Fowey**

Trusty's Hill
Dumfries and Galloway (Kirkcudbrightshire) NX 589561

A hill-fort across the river from Gatehouse of Fleet, near the A75. It has traces of a second fortification, and may have been reoccupied at the same time as **Mote of Mark**. The name "Trusty" is derived from the Pictish "Drust", and the same is true of "Tristan". So Trusty's Hill is equivalent to Tristan's Hill.

Quite a number of Picts had the name Drust, and so did other Britons besides the hero of romance. A hill could have been called so, independently of the story and its characters. But **Mote of Mark**, less than 20 miles away, gives us the other male character in the love-triangle as well, with evidence of somebody on the spot at about the right time.

The familiar tradition places both men in Cornwall, and is supported by an assortment of facts (see **Castle Dore, Fowey**). Mark has apparent Welsh connections too. But if the names of the two Scottish hills are due to more than coincidence, they are a salutary reminder of the baffling wanderings of legend.

Valle Crucis
—see **Llangollen**

Wansdyke
Avon, Somerset and Wiltshire

A great ditch with a bank of earth alongside, which begins at the hill-fort of Maes Knoll south of Bristol. In varying states of preservation, it passes eastward across the A37 at Hursley Hill, goes over Stantonbury Hill, and skirts **Bath** on the south. After 13 miles it vanishes, or nearly so. Fifteen miles farther east it resumes, and runs on for another 10 miles, traversing high ground near Silbury and Avebury, and stopping just short of Savernake Forest.

Dubious fragments extend to the Bristol Channel at one end and the Inkpen area at the other. One of the best-preserved stretches is in Wiltshire between Easton Down (SU 060657) and Tan Hill.

"Wodensdic", the old form of the name, means "Woden's Dyke". The West Saxon settlers called it after their chief god, the mythical ancestor of their kings. It existed, therefore, before their conversion to Christianity in the 630s. Almost certainly they found it there when they arrived, in the second half of the sixth century, and said Woden had made it because they did not know who really had. On the other hand, archaeology has shown that it cannot be earlier than the last phase of the Roman Empire. Since it does not look Roman, it has often been explained as part of a defensive system for south-west Britain under Ambrosius, or Arthur, or both.

The ditch is on the north side, so, as a fortification, the Wansdyke does face north. Also, this dating for it is credible. Yet its purpose remains a puzzle. In the first

Wansdyke: a stretch of this long bank-and-ditch earthwork north of Devizes.

place, as it breaks in the middle, we have no actual proof
that East and West Wansdyke are parts of the same work;
and the western part might seem to belong to a later
strategic situation, after 577, when the Saxons were in
Gloucestershire. Secondly, if it is a line of defence, how
was it used? With a small population it could not have been
held like the First World War trenches. Its manning would
have been confined to patrols marching back and forth, and
an army massed along a short stretch of it could have
crossed without much trouble. Hence a theory has been put
forward that it was meant as a frontier line rather than a
work of defence, and that it may mark the limit of the
once-mighty British kingdom of Dumnonia (see **Cornwall**),
just before the Saxons overran Wiltshire.

West Arthurlie
—see **Arthur Lee**

Westminster

Now embedded in a hugely expanded **London,** Westminster used to be a separate city. It grew round an abbey
founded by King Sebert of the East Saxons in the seventh
century. From the viewpoint of **London**, the abbey church
was the "West Minster". After it was destroyed the present
Westminster Abbey was begun on the site by Edward the
Confessor.

The city, therefore, did not exist in Arthur's time, and
the principal Arthurian writers seem to have known this,
since they barely speak of it and never make it a centre of
population. Malory, however, brings it in as a locality.
Thus when the barge carries the corpse of Elaine down the
Thames (see **Astolat**), Arthur sights it in the Westminster
neighbourhood. Since Guinevere and many of the knights
come to look, the court cannot be far away, but there is no
suggestion of a town on the river bank. In a later episode
the queen rides out on a May morning through the Westminster fields and woods, where Sir Meliagaunt kidnaps
her and carries her off to his castle (an exploit transferred
from its original scene at **Glastonbury**). Again—correctly
—the story gives no hint of a town.

Winchester

Hampshire   *SU 480295*

Formerly the Roman town of Venta Belgarum, Winchester
became the capital of Wessex under Alfred the Great. It
remained England's chief city till after the Norman Conquest. Geoffrey of Monmouth mentions it a few times—
Arthur fights a battle with Modred here during the final
struggle—but seems to have realized that its primacy in
the kingdom did not begin so early. A hazy awareness of
that primacy, as having existed in a hazy past, is probably
one reason why Malory usually locates Camelot here.
Another may have been Winchester's possession of the
finest of "Arthurian" relics: its Round Table.

   In Malory's time, to judge from the preface written by
Caxton in 1485, the Table was believed to be the original.
Though certainly not that, it is a highly interesting object.
It is housed in Castle Hall near Westgate, the surviving
fragment of a castle founded by William the Conqueror.
Strictly speaking it is a table-top only, without legs. Fixed
to the wall, it looks (one must confess) a little like an
enormous dartboard, because it is painted in segments,
green and white. There are twenty-four of these, allotted to
knights whose names are round the rim. At the top is
Arthur's place, with a picture of a king. The Table is made
of oak. It is 18 feet across and 2¾ inches thick, and has
mortice holes for twelve legs. It weighs 1¼ tons.

   Several guesses have been made as to its true date and
purpose. The first known author to mention it is John
Hardyng, about 1450. Since Hardyng, like Caxton, sup-
poses it to be the real thing, its actual construction was
probably earlier enough to have been forgotten. As to its
purpose, one guess is that it was the centre-piece for a
"Round Table" entertainment such as medieval lords
staged from time to time. Another is that it was made for
Edward III about 1340, when he planned to revive the
Round Table knighthood, though he dropped this idea and
founded the Order of the Garter instead.   In 1976-77
various tests were carried out. Tree-ring patterns in the
wood, and clues from the method of carpentry, seemed at
first to favour the Edward III theory. Carbon-dating,
however, points to a somewhat earlier date, closer to the
period when Arthur began to be popular with kings of
England, and to be claimed by them as an illustrious

predecessor. If it was a king who had the table built, Edward I, who enjoyed Round Table entertainments, might be the best candidate.

Ten reigns after him, Winchester could still play a part in what is sometimes called the Tudor Myth. When Henry VII came to the throne, in the same year as Caxton published Malory, he tried to exploit the prophecy of Arthur's return. A Welsh dynasty—that is, a truly British one—was now in power, and Henry called his first son Arthur in the hope that a reign of Arthur II would be welcomed as fulfilling the prophecy. Accepting that Winchester was **Camelot**, he held his son's baptism there in 1486. At Winchester College a mat beside the warden's bed was recognized in the twentieth century as a tapestry with British legendary motifs, probably woven for the baptismal ceremony.

This royally promoted interest may have had something

Winchester: the oaken Round Table (or rather table-top) in Castle Hall, divided into segments showing places for the king and 24 knights. The design was first painted in the reign of Henry VIII, but the table itself may be as much as three centuries older.

to do with the college's acquisition of a Malory manuscript, which was rediscovered in 1934, with startling
effects on the understanding of his work and Caxton's
editorial role. Unfortunately the intended Arthur II died
young. His brother reigned as Henry VIII. He too, at least
in his earlier years, kept up the family pretension. The
design on the Round Table was painted in 1522 to make it
more impressive for the visiting emperor, Charles V. The
rose in the centre is a Tudor rose, and the figure of the king
is Henry himself, with the beard which he had recently
grown. In 1789 the design was repainted, without
alteration.

Wirral
Cheshire

Sir Gawain's quest for the Green Knight takes him to
"Wirral Forest". Since, to reach it, he rides along the north
coast of Wales with **Anglesey** on his left, the real peninsula
in north-west Cheshire is clearly intended. In the Middle
Ages this actually was a royal forest, but it can hardly have
been the fearsome wilderness described in the poem, full
of wolves, bears, trolls, ogres, and dragons. It has been
suggested that some of the topographical details are taken
from the wild country north of Leek in Staffordshire,
nearer, perhaps, to where the poet lived.

Zennor
Cornwall   *SW 454385*

Between St Ives and Land's End is a stretch of coast and
high moorland with an Arthur legend of its own. Zennor is
the only populated place which has any part in it. According to the tale, **Cornwall** was menaced by a host of red-
headed Danes who landed at Whitesand Bay north of
Land's End. As they made their way slowly round the
coast, Arthur came to Zennor and summoned four Cornish
"kings" to help him fight the invaders. They marched from
the direction of Madron, and dined with him off a flat rock
on the moor, or, as some say, on Zennor Head. Then he led
the combined force to Vellan and fought the Danes, who
eventually sailed away. But they had been ashore long
enough for birds to build nests in the rigging of their ships,
and also long enough to beget a good many children. Their

exploit was supposed to account for certain families in this part of the country with a strong red-haired strain, disliked by the other country folk, who preferred not to marry into them.

Vellan is just west of Pendeen, which has echoes of the same legend, as has **Trereen Dinas**.

Appendix

Much of the basic work on Arthurian sites was done during the late nineteenth and early twentieth centuries. Authors who wrote during that period give details which are still usually sound, at least to the extent that the sites can still be recognized. However, some problem cases remain.

Thus E. K. Chambers, in *Arthur of Britain*, supplies a valuable list which is nearly always trustworthy. But he says there are two Arthur's Halls in Cornwall. I do not think there are. He was misled because John Stuart Glennie, in 1869, described the stone enclosure Arthur's Hall as "not far from Camelford" and erroneously called it "a little entrenchment", while another writer seemed to imply that the enclosure was much farther east, near Callington. Chambers assumed that there were two different halls.

F. J. Snell, in *King Arthur's Country*, raises several Welsh difficulties. He mentions a large cromlech near the park of Mocras Court, Brecknockshire. The source of his information is Glennie again, who says the cromlech is on rising ground and called Arthur's Table. I have not succeeded in finding it. In Brecknockshire likewise, Snell makes a curious mistake, referring to a stone on the edge of "Gossmoor" marked with the hoofprints of Arthur's horse when he went out hunting from "Castle Denis". Through some oversight Snell has transferred this from Cornwall (see **Castle-an-Dinas**, **St Columb Major**, **St Dennis**), even though, at another stage of his researches, he clearly did know where it belonged—as he betrays on page 35 of his book.

Snell also gives several places in Dyfed which no one else mentions. Some can be identified. Others are harder. He says part of the Black Mountain near Pen-Arthur is known as Gwely Arthur, Arthur's Bed. The name seems to have fallen into disuse. He also mentions Blaengwaith Noe ab Arthur, near Lampeter Vale east of Narberth. This also is elusive.

Finally of course, a doubt must sometimes be admitted as to whether the Arthur in a place-name is the right one. On that ground it might be fair to query a few items in the gazetteer, and, more certainly, those which I have not included—such as Arthur's Hill in Newcastle, and, to take an extreme case, the medley of Arthur roads, Arthur streets, and so forth in London and other cities.

Key by characters and themes

This list gives only those places where the character, or theme, is important. Minor references can be traced by way of the Index.

AMBROSIUS (EMRYS), British leader in the fifth century

Amesbury	**Stonehenge**
Dinas Emrys	**Wansdyke**
Ganarew	

ANEIRIN, bard

Catterick	**Edinburgh**
Cumbria	

ARTHUR, British war-leader and legendary king

(a) Birth and youth

Caer Gai	**London**
Cornwall	**Tintagel**

(b) Military operations

Agned	**Caerleon**
Arthur's Cave	**Celidon**
Badbury	**Chester**
Badbury Rings	**City of the Legion**
Badon (Mount)	**Dover**
Barham Down	**Dubglas**
Bassas	**Edinburgh**
Bath	**Glastonbury**
Ben Arthur	**Glein**
Breguoin	**Guinnion**
Cadbury Castle	**High Rochester**

Ilchester
Langport
Leintwardine
Liddington Castle
Lindsey
Linnuis
Llongborth

Lomond (Loch)
Ogof Arthur
Portchester
Strathclyde
Tribruit
Wansdyke
Zennor

(c) Places of residence and holding court

Aberffraw
Cadbury Castle
Caerleon
Caerwent
Camelot
Caverswall
Dunster

Kelliwic
Pen Rhionydd
Queen Camel
St David's
Sewingshields
Winchester

(d) Sons

Cerrig Meibion Arthur
Ercing

Gamber Head
Sewingshields

(e) Dealings with ecclesiastics

Brent Knoll
Carhampton
Glastonbury

Llanbadarn Fawr
Llancarfan

(f) Encounters with giants, monsters, etc.

Arthur's Grave (2)
Arthur's Stone (2)
Blackingstone Rock
Buelt
Carhampton

Carn March Arthur
Corngafallt
Llanuwchllyn
Pendeen

(g) Last battle, death (or "passing"), and burial

Arthur's Grave
Arthur's Stone (2)
Avalon
Cader Idris
Cam (River)
Camboglanna
Camelford
Camelon

Camlann
Glastonbury
Loe Pool
Salisbury Plain
Slaughter Bridge
Snowdonia
Tintagel

(h) Immortality (in various forms) of himself and his
warriors

Alderley Edge	**Craig-y-Ddinas**
Annwn	**Marazion**
Avalon	**Melrose**
Bodmin	**Ogo'r Dinas**
Cadbury Castle	**Richmond**
Caerleon	**Sewingshields**
Cave-legend, sites of	**Snowdonia**

(i) Miscellaneous local associations

Arthurhouse	**Cerrig Arthur**
Arthur Lee	**Coed Arthur**
Arthur's Bed	**Corngafallt**
Arthur's Bridge	**Ercing**
Arthur's Cave	**Ffon y Cawr**
Arthur's Chair	**Gamber Head**
Arthur's Fold	**Gwal y Filiast**
Arthur's Fountain	**King's Oven**
Arthur's Grave	**Llangollen**
Arthur's Hall	**Loch Arthur**
Arthur's Hunting Lodge	**London**
Arthur's O'en	**Moel Arthur**
Arthur's Oven	**Ogof Arthur**
Arthur's Quoit	**Pen-Arthur**
Arthur's Seat	**Pencraig Arthur**
Arthur's Stone	**Ruthin**
Arthur's Well	**St Columb Major**
Ben Arthur	**Scilly, Isles of**
Bodmin	**Stone Arthur**
Brecon Beacons	**Tintagel**
Buelt	**Trethevy Quoit**
Carn March Arthur	

BEDIVERE (BEDWYR), follower of Arthur and knight in
romance
> **Llancarfan**, and places associated with his casting
> away of Excalibur *(q.v.)*

BRAN, legendary British hero and ruler
Llangollen	**London**

CADOC, ST, abbot
Caerwent	**Llancarfan**

CADWY, British chief
- **Cadbury Castle**
- **Cadon Barrow**
- **Carhampton**
- **Dunster**
- **Gerrans**

CARANNOG, ST, monk
- **Carhampton**

COLLEN, ST, monk
- **Glastonbury**
- **Llangollen**

DRAGONS AND SERPENTS
- **Carhampton**
- **Dinas Emrys**

ELAINE, the "lily maid"
- **Astolat**
- **Westminster**

EXCALIBUR or *CALIBURN*, Arthur's sword
- **Avalon**
- **Bosherston**
- **Dozmary Pool**
- **Glastonbury**
- **Llyn Llydaw**
- **Llyn Ogwen**
- **Loe Pool**

GALAHAD, knight in romance
- **Castle of Maidens**

GAWAIN, knight in romance
- **Anglesey**
- **Carlisle**
- **Dover**
- **St Govan's Head**
- **Wirral**

GERAINT, British chief, and knight in romance
- **Gerrans**
- **Langport**
- **Llongborth**
- **Portchester**

GIANTS
- **Arthur's Grave (1)**
- **Arthur's Quoit (9)**
- **Arthur's Stone (1), (2)**
- **Brecon Beacons**
- **Brent Knoll**
- **Brougham Castle**
- **Cader Idris**
- **Ffon y Cawr**
- **Knucklas**
- **Llanuwchllyn**
- **Marazion**
- **Mount's Bay**
- **Pendeen**
- **Penrith**
- **Sewingshields**
- **Snowdonia**
- **Stonehenge**

GILDAS, monk and author

Badon (Mount)	**Strathclyde**
Glastonbury	

GORLOIS, legendary duke of Cornwall

Castle-an-Dinas	**Tintagel**
Dimilioc	**Tregeare Rounds**
St Dennis	

GRAIL, THE HOLY

Annwn	**Langport**
Avalon	**Nanteos**
Glastonbury	

GUINEVERE, Arthur's wife

Amesbury	**Kelliwic**
Barry Hill	**Knucklas**
Carlisle	**London**
Caverswall	**Meigle**
Dover	**Sewingshields**
Glastonbury	**Westminster**
Guinevere's Monument	

GWYN-AP-NUDD, supernatural being

Annwn	**Glastonbury**

HUEIL, brother of Gildas

Ruthin	**Strathclyde**

ILLTUD, ST, abbot

Llantwit Major

ISEULT, wife of Mark

Golant   See also **Mark**, **Tristan**

JOSEPH OF ARIMATHEA, custodian of the Holy Grail

Cadbury Castle	**Langport**
Glastonbury	

KAY (Cai), follower of Arthur, and knight in romance

Anglesey	**Llancarfan**
Caer Gai	

LANCELOT, knight in romance

Alnwick	**Carlisle**
Astolat	**Dover**
Bamburgh	**Joyous Gard**
Brougham Castle	**Manchester**

LIFESTYLES IN ARTHURIAN BRITAIN

Catterick	**Mote of Mark**
Dinas Powys	

MAELGWN, Welsh king

Deganwy	**Gwynedd**

MARK, semi-legendary king of Cornwall

Carn Marth	**Lantyan**
Castellmarch	**Mote of Mark**
Castle Dore	**Penmark**
Fowey	

MAXIMUS, Roman emperor

Dinas Emrys	**Lyonesse**
Llangollen	

MELWAS, semi-legendary king of Somerset

Glastonbury

MERLIN, prophet and wizard

Arthuret	**Marlborough**
Avalon	**Merlin's Bridge**
Bardsey	**Mousehole**
Carmarthen	**St Levan**
Celidon	**Stonehenge**
Dinas Emrys	**Tintagel**
Drumelzier	

MODRED (MEDRAUT), British chief, and knight in romance

Barham Down	**London**
Barry Hill	**Meigle**
Camlann	**Salisbury Plain**
Dover	**Slaughter Bridge**
Dumbarton	**Snowdonia**
Kelliwic	

MORGAN LE FAY, enchantress
    Avalon   **Castle of Maidens**

OTHERWORLDS
    Annwn   **Glastonbury**
    Avalon   **Lundy**

OWEIN (YVAIN), northern British king
    Cumbria   **Penrith**

PADARN, ST, abbot
    Llanbadarn Fawr

PATRICK, ST, British missionary
    Dumbarton   **Strathclyde**

RHITA, giant
    Llanuwchllyn   **Snowdonia**

ROUND TABLE
    Brecon Beacons   **Round Table**
    Gwal y Filiast   **Winchester**

SAMPSON, ST, abbot
    Golant   **Scilly, Isles of**

TALIESIN, bard
    Cumbria   **Gwynedd**

TREASURE
    Arthur's Quoit (5)   **Llyn Ogwen**
    Carmarthen   **Marchlyn Mawr**
    Dinas Emrys   **Ogof Arthur**
    Llangollen

TRISTAN, British noble, and knight in romance
    Fowey   **Snowdonia**
    Lyonesse   **Trusty's Hill**

TWRCH TRWYTH, legendary boar
    Arthur's Grave (2)   **Corngafallt**
    Buelt   **Pen-Arthur**

URBGEN, northern British king

Cumbria	**High Rochester**

UTHER PENDRAGON, legendary king of Britain, father of Arthur

Castle-an-Dinas	**St Dennis**
Dimilioc	**Tintagel**
Pendragon Castle	

VORTIGERN, British ruler in fifth century

Dinas Emrys	**Llangollen**
Ganarew	**Nant Gwrtheyrn**

VOTEPORIX, Welsh king

Carmarthen

YGERNA, wife of Gorlois and mother of Arthur

Dimilioc	**Tintagel**

Maps

These maps locate places which are the subjects of articles. In other words, they contain gazetteer *headings*. Other places are mentioned in the text but not marked here. They appear in the Index. A key map is on the inside front cover.

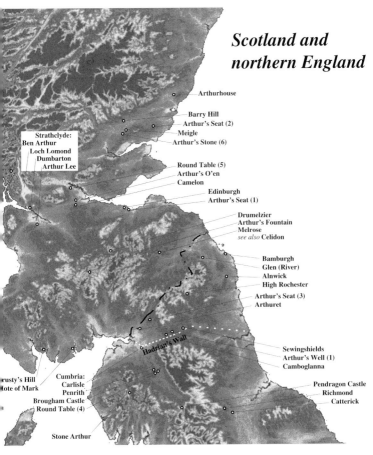

Scotland and northern England

Arthurhouse

Barry Hill
Arthur's Seat (2)
Meigle
Arthur's Stone (6)

Strathclyde:
Ben Arthur
Loch Lomond
Dumbarton
Arthur Lee

Round Table (5)
Arthur's O'en
Camelon

Edinburgh
Arthur's Seat (1)

Drumelzier
Arthur's Fountain
Melrose
see also Celidon

Bamburgh
Glen (River)
Alnwick
High Rochester

Arthur's Seat (3)
Arthuret

Hadrian's Wall

Sewingshields
Arthur's Well (1)
Camboglanna

Trusty's Hill
Mote of Mark

Cumbria:
Carlisle
Penrith
Brougham Castle
Round Table (4)

Pendragon Castle
Richmond
Catterick

Stone Arthur

Wales

Ffon y Cawr
Pencraig Arthur
Deganwy
Llangollen

Anglesey:
Round Table (2)
Arthur's Quoit (2)
Arthur's Quoit (1)
Arthur's Stone (4)
Ogof Arthur
Aberffraw

Arthur's Stone (4)
Moel Arthur
Ruthin
Round Table (3)

Wirr
Ches

Gwynedd:
Marchlyn Mawr
Llyn Ogwen
Snowdonia (peak of Snowdon)
Llyn Llydaw
Dinas Emrys
Nant Gwrtheyrn
Arthur's Quoit (3)
Bardsey
Castellmarch
Arthur's Quoit (4)

Caer Gai
Llanuwchllyn

Arthur's Quoit (5)
Cerrig Arthur
Cader Idris
Carn March Arthur
Aberystwyth
Llanbadarn Fawr
Nanteos

Knucklas

Le

50 miles
50 km

Arthur's Quoit (8)
Arthur's Quoit (7)
Arthur's Grave (2)
Cerrig Meibion Arthur

Arthur's Stone (3)
Corngafallt

Arthur's Quoit (6)
St David's
Merlin's Bridge
Bosherston
St Govan's Head

Brecon Beacons
(Arthur's Chair)

Arth

Craig-y-Ddinas

Guinevere's
Monument

Buarth Arthur
Gwal y Filiast
Carmarthen
Ogo'r Dinas
Arthur's Stone

Pen-Arthur
Arthur's Quoit (9)
Llantwit Major
Coed Arthur
Llancarfan

Cae
Caerleon

Dinas
Powys
Penmark

Hadrian's Wall

Sewingshields
Arthur's Well (1)
Camboglanna

Pendragon Castle
Richmond
Catterick

Southeast
England

Wirral

Manchester

Alderley Edge

Chester

Lindsey

Glen (River)

Caverswall

Leintwardine

Arthur's Stone (2)
Gamber Head
Ganarew
Arthur's Cave

Caerwent
rleon
Bath

Liddington Castle
Marlborough

Wansdyke

Dover

Barham Down

London
(original site of the city)

Portchester
Winchester

Westminster

Amesbury
Stonehenge
Badbury Rings

noll

Arthur's Bridge
Cadbury Castle
Cam (River)
Queen Camel
Glastonbury
Ilchester
Langport

50 miles

50 km

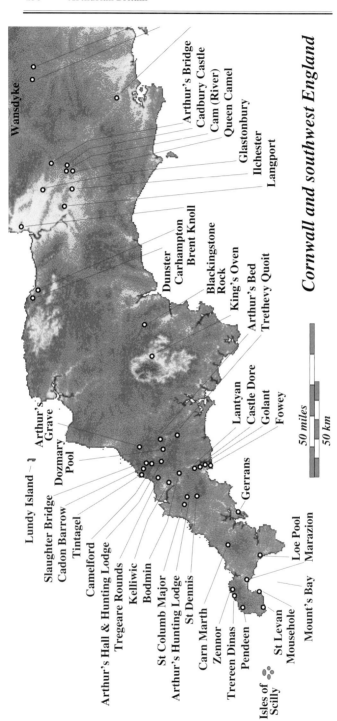

Cornwall and southwest England

Wansdyke

Arthur's Bridge
Cadbury Castle
Cam (River)
Queen Camel
Glastonbury
Ilchester
Langport

Dunster
Carhampton
Brent Knoll

Blackingstone Rock
King's Oven
Arthur's Bed
Trethevy Quoit

Lantyan
Castle Dore
Golant
Fowey

Gerrans

Loe Pool
Marazion

Lundy Island

Arthur's Grave
Dozmary Pool

Slaughter Bridge
Cadon Barrow
Tintagel
Camelford
Arthur's Hall & Hunting Lodge
Tregeare Rounds
Kelliwic
Bodmin
St Columb Major
Arthur's Hunting Lodge
St Dennis
Carn Marth
Zennor
Trereen Dinas
Pendeen

St Levan
Mousehole
Mount's Bay

Isles of Scilly

50 miles
50 km

Bibliography

Alcock, Leslie
>   *Arthur's Britain*. Allen Lane (London), 1971.
>   *"By South Cadbury is that Camelot ..."*. Thames and
>   Hudson (London), 1972.
>   "Cadbury–Camelot: a fifteen-year perspective". In
>   *Proceedings of the British Academy* **68** (London)
>   1982.
Antiquities of the Cornish Countryside. Tor Mark Press
>   (Truro), no date.
Ashe, Geoffrey
>   *Avalonian Quest*. Methuen (London), 1982, and
>   Fontana (London), 1984.
>   "A certain very ancient book". In *Speculum*, April
>   1981, The Medieval Academy of America (Cam-
>   bridge, Massachusetts).
>   *Mythology of the British Isles*. Methuen (London),
>   1990, paperback, 1992.
Ashe, Geoffrey, and Simon McBride
>   *The Landscape of King Arthur*. Webb and Bower
>   (Exeter), 1987.
Ashe, Geoffrey, ed.
>   *The Quest for Arthur's Britain*. Pall Mall Press (Lon-
>   don), 1968, and Paladin (London), 1971
Ashton, Graham
>   *The Realm of King Arthur*. J. Arthur Dixon (Newport,
>   Isle of Wight), 1974.
Beare, Beryl
>   *Wales: Myths and Legends*. Parragon (Avonmouth),
>   1996.
Bord, Janet and Colin
>   *Mysterious Britain*. Garnstone (London), 1972.

Brewer's Dictionary of Phrase and Fable. Cassell (London), 1959.

Bromwich, Rachel
  Trioedd Ynys Prydein (the Welsh Triads with translation and notes). University of Wales Press (Cardiff), second edition, 1978.

Bromwich, Rachel, and others, eds.
  The Arthur of the Welsh. University of Wales Press (Cardiff), 1991.

Cavendish, Richard
  King Arthur and the Grail. Weidenfeld and Nicolson (London), 1978.

Chadwick, H. M. and N. K.
  The Growth of Literature, vol. 1. Cambridge University Press, 1932.

Chadwick, N. K., ed.
  Studies in Early British History. Cambridge University Press, 1954.

Chambers, E. K.
  Arthur of Britain. Sidgwick and Jackson re-issue (London), 1966.

Dickinson, W. Howship
  King Arthur in Cornwall. Longmans Green (London), 1900.

Ditmas, E. M. R.
  "A reappraisal of Geoffrey of Monmouth's allusions to Cornwall". In *Speculum*, July 1973, The Medieval Academy of America (Cambridge, Massachusetts).
  Tristan and Iseult in Cornwall. Forrester Roberts (Gloucester), 1969.

Folklore, Myths and Legends of Britain. Reader's Digest Association (London), 1973.

Forrester Roberts, Ian
  Land of Arthur (illustrated map). Privately published (Gloucester), 1967.

Geoffrey of Monmouth
  The History of the Kings of Britain, trans. with introduction by Lewis Thorpe. Penguin (Harmondsworth), 1966.
  The Life of Merlin, ed. and trans. J.J. Parry. University of Illinois Press (Urbana, Illinois), 1925.

Glennie, John S. Stuart
  Arthurian Localities. Edmonston and Douglas (Edinburgh), 1869.

Graves, Robert
    Introduction to modern English version of Malory by
        Keith Baines. New American Library (New York),
        1962.

Grinsell, Leslie V.
    Folklore of Prehistoric Sites in Britain. David and
        Charles (Newton Abbot), 1976.

Hawkes, Jacquetta
    *A Guide to the Prehistoric Monuments in England and
        Wales*. Cardinal (London), 1973.

Lacy, Norris J., ed.
    The New Arthurian Encyclopedia. Garland (New
        York), 1991.

Land of Legend, The. West Country Tourist Board (Exeter),
    1978.

Miller, Helen Hill
    The Realms of Arthur. Charles Scribner's Sons (New
        York), 1969.

Moore, W.G.
    The Penguin Encyclopedia of Places. Penguin (Har-
        mondsworth), 1971.

Moorman, Charles and Ruth
    An Arthurian Dictionary. University Press of Missis-
        sippi, 1978.

Morris, John
    The Age of Arthur. Weidenfeld and Nicolson (London),
        1973.

Radford, C. A. Ralegh, and Michael J. Swanton
    Arthurian Sites in the West. University of Exeter, 1975.

Rhys, John
    Celtic Folklore, 2 vols. Clarendon Press (Oxford), 1901.

Ross, Anne
    Pagan Celtic Britain. Cardinal (London), 1974.

Snell, F. J.
    King Arthur's Country. Dent (London), 1926.

Sutton, Harry T.
    Knights and Knaves. Batsford-Heritage (London),
        1978.

Tolstoi, Nikolai
    The Quest for Merlin. Hamish Hamilton (London),
        1985.

Westwood, Jennifer
    Albion: a Guide to Legendary Britain. Granada
        (London), 1985.

Geoffrey Ashe: publications

King Arthur's Avalon
    Collins 1957
    E. P. Dutton 1958
    Fontana paperback 1973
    Book Club Associates 1974
    Barnes and Noble (U.S. re-issue) 1992.
From Caesar to Arthur
    Collins 1960.
Land to the West
    Collins 1962
    Viking 1962.
The Land and the Book
    Collins 1965.
Gandhi
    Heinemann 1968
    Stein and Day 1968
    Stein and Day paperback 1969
The Quest for Arthur's Britain (as editor and part author)
    Pall Mall 1968
    Frederick Praeger 1968
    Granada paperback 1971
    Book Club Associates 1972
    Academy Chicago (U.S. re-issue) 1987
All About King Arthur
    Commissioned by W. H. Allen for junior educational series, "Allabout Books", and published in 1969.
    Published in U.S. by Thomas Nelson as *King Arthur in Fact and Legend*, 1971.

Camelot and the Vision of Albion
    Heinemann 1971
    St Martin's Press 1971
    Granada paperback 1975.
The Art of Writing Made Simple
    Commissioned by W. H. Allen for "Made Simple
      Books" and published in 1972.
    Published in Canada by Coles as *Good Writing*, 1977.
The Finger and the Moon (novel)
    Heinemann 1973
    John Day 1974
    Granada paperback 1975.
    Radio serialization, Boston, U.S.
Do What You Will
    W. H. Allen 1974
The Virgin
    Routledge 1976
    Granada paperback 1977
    Arkana paperback 1988
    Penguin (U.S. re-issue) 1991.
The Ancient Wisdom
    Macmillan 1977
    Abacus paperback 1979.
Miracles
    Routledge 1978
    Abacus paperback 1979.
A Guidebook to Arthurian Britain
    Longman 1980
    Aquarian paperback 1983.
Kings and Queens of Early Britain
    Methuen 1982
    Academy Chicago (U.S. re-issue) 1990.
    Ancient History Book Club.
Avalonian Quest
    Methuen 1982
    Fontana paperback 1984. Ancient History Book Club.
The Discovery of King Arthur
    Doubleday 1985
    Henry Holt (Owl paperback) 1987.
    Debrett published a limited edition in England.
    A German edition published by Econ with unauthor-
      ized cuts.
    History Book Club (U.S.)

The Landscape of King Arthur
  Webb and Bower 1987.
  Ancient and Medieval History Book Club.
  There was a re-issue in 1992.
Mythology of the British Isles
  Methuen 1990
  Trafalgar Square 1991
  Methuen paperback 1992.
  Ancient and Medieval History Book Club.
  German edition: Walter 1992.
King Arthur: the Dream of a Golden Age (text for illus-
    trated book)
  Thames and Hudson 1990.
  French edition: Seuil 1992.
  Japanese edition: 1992 or 1993.
Dawn Behind the Dawn
  Henry Holt 1992 (and Library of Science book club).
  Paperback 1993.
Atlantis: Lost Lands, Ancient Wisdom
  Thames and Hudson 1992 (in same series as *King
    Arthur: the Dream of a Golden Age*)
  Spanish edition: 1993.
  Japanese edition: 1994.
Discovering the Goddess (small booklet)
  Crescent Moon 1994.

Associate editor of *The Arthurian Encyclopedia*, Garland
    1986, and *New Arthurian Encyclopedia*, 1991.

Co-author of *The Arthurian Handbook*, Garland 1988.

One contribution to a scholarly journal, "A certain very
    ancient book" in *Speculum*, April 1981. This was the
    starting-point for *The Discovery of King Arthur*,
    above, and discussions in the *Encyclopedia* and
    Handbook.

Index